THE SYMBOLIC STATE

DEMOCRACY, DIVERSITY, AND CITIZEN ENGAGEMENT SERIES

Series editor: Alain-G. Gagnon

With the twenty-first-century world struggling to address various forms of conflict and new types of political and cultural claims, the Democracy, Diversity, and Citizen Engagement Series revitalizes research in the fields of nationalism, federalism, and cosmopolitanism, and examines the interactions between ethnicity, identity, and politics. Works published in this series are concerned with the theme of representation – of citizens and of interests – and how these ideas are defended at local and global levels that are increasingly converging. Further, the series advances and advocates new public policies and social projects with a view to creating change and accommodating diversity in its many expressions. In doing so, the series instills democratic practices in meaningful new ways by studying key subjects such as the mobilization of citizens, groups, communities, and nations, and the advancement of social justice and political stability.

Under the leadership of the Interdisciplinary Research Centre on Diversity and Democracy, this series creates a forum where current research on democracy, diversity, and citizen engagement can be examined within the context of the study of nations as well as of nations divided by state frontiers.

The Symbolic State

Minority Recognition,
Majority Backlash, and Secession
in Multinational Countries

KARLO BASTA

McGill-Queen's University Press
Montreal & Kingston • London • Chicago

© McGill-Queen's University Press 2021

ISBN 978-0-2280-0805-7 (cloth)
ISBN 978-0-2280-0806-4 (paper)
ISBN 978-0-2280-0920-7 (ePDF)
ISBN 978-0-2280-0921-4 (ePUB)

Legal deposit fourth quarter 2021
Bibliothèque nationale du Québec

Printed in Canada on acid-free paper that is 100% ancient forest free
(100% post-consumer recycled), processed chlorine free

This book has been published with the help of a grant from the Canadian
Federation for the Humanities and Social Sciences, through the Awards to
Scholarly Publications Program, using funds provided by the Social Sciences
and Humanities Research Council of Canada.

We acknowledge the support of the Canada Council for the Arts.

Nous remercions le Conseil des arts du Canada de son soutien.

Library and Archives Canada Cataloguing in Publication

Title: The symbolic state: minority recognition, majority backlash, and
secession in multinational countries/Karlo Basta.

Names: Basta, Karlo, 1976- author.

Series: Democracy, diversity, and citizen engagement series; 7.

Description: Series statement: Democracy, diversity, and citizen engagement
series; 7 | Includes bibliographical references and index.

Identifiers: Canadiana (print) 20210249234 | Canadiana (ebook)
20210249307 | ISBN 9780228008064 (paper) | ISBN 9780228008057
(cloth) | ISBN 9780228009207 (ePDF) | ISBN 9780228009214 (ePUB)

Subjects: LCSH: Multinational states. | LCSH: Secession. |
LCSH: Nationalism. | LCSH: Comparative government.

Classification: LCC JC311 .B37 2021 | DDC 320.54—dc23

This book was typeset by Marquis Interscript in 10.5/13 Sabon.

Contents

Tables and Figures

TABLES

FIGURES

Acknowledgments

This book is made of circumstances, personal proclivities, and folly. The circumstances have to do with the implosion of my original homeland – Yugoslavia. The proclivity is the uneven but abiding sociological curiosity that has marked me since I was a boy. And the folly relates to the belief that I could somehow harness that curiosity to explain those circumstances, without in the process burning through my life chances. Without that costly error, this volume would not have been written. But neither would it – nor could it – have been completed without the generosity and involvement of many colleagues, mentors, friends, and kind strangers.

The project started as a doctoral dissertation at the University of Toronto, and as fateful advice by Jeffrey Kopstein, my supervisor at the time, to park the Balkans for a while and learn how to do political science. The upshot was that I dared to look beyond the horizon, and thus came to understand where I came from by knowing other places. I am thankful to Jeff for this and for his guidance over the long years it took me to finish the program. A number of other people in the Department of Political Science provided valuable advice and support, including David Cameron, Phil Triadafilopoulos, Susan Solomon, and Lucan Way.

Two individuals played an outsized role during my time at U of T. Richard Simeon influenced my thinking about institutions in multinational states to an extent I only came to appreciate after his passing. More prosaically, but as importantly, he was my link to scholars (notably via the Ethnicity and Democratic Governance network) who would contribute to this work in ways small and great. This is no coincidence. Richard was both a deep and careful thinker and the kind of person who brought people together as a matter of course. I wish he was here to share in the pride I have in this work, one that has so much of him in it. Edith Klein's office and home were sanctuaries where I felt I could always come for advice to help me navigate academic and non-academic waters. As a total, and clueless, transplant to North America, I very much needed that.

The ideas in this book emerged from the interplay of book knowledge and direct experience and conversations with people during countless field trips over the course of more than ten years. Many of the formal interviews, casual exchanges, and events that provoked and informed the ideas found here have not made it into the book for one reason or another. But they are the hidden and vast reservoir on top of which this work germinated. I am in debt to many who shared their time, knowledge, perspectives, and experiences – stories of their lives – with me.

In the Balkans, Dejan Jović and Tvrtko Jakovina have been a perennial academic lifeline. Companionship, humour, and hospitality were supplied by old friends, Davor Gardijan, Vlado Mirčeta, and Zoran Bojinović. In Spain, which has become a third home over the past decade, I could always count on César Colino in Madrid and Xavier Arbós Marín in Barcelona for good company and to bring me up to speed on developments I had missed out on between visits. I also want to thank Astrid Barrio, Alfons López Tena, Marc Sanjaume, Ferran Requejo, Mireia Grau Creus, Liz Castro, Elisenda Paluzie, and, finally, Adam Holesch, my CaixaForum writing buddy, friend, and an interlocutor on all things related to Catalan and Spanish politics.

Fieldwork required money, of course, and lots of it (for my *lumpen*-intellectual standards at least), as well as administrative support. I received both, with much gratitude, from the University of Toronto, Memorial University of Newfoundland, the Ethnicity and Democratic Governance Project, the Social Sciences and Humanities Research Council of Canada, and the Institute for the Study of Self-Government in Barcelona. I am also thankful for the services of the Croatian State Archive in Zagreb and the Archive of Yugoslavia in Belgrade.

Through the years, many folks read, commented upon, and otherwise improved various bits of writing that made it into this work. I am grateful to my colleagues at Memorial (especially Scott Matthews, who opened my eyes to entirely new areas of inquiry, enriching this book), Alain Gagnon, Jörg Broschek, Michael Hechter, Daniel Ziblatt, Stephen Larin, Marsaili Fraser, and Yoli Terziyska (for countless edits, and for getting my spirits up when the choices I made seemed even more ill-thought-out than they do now). Many thanks also to André Lecours, whose scholarship I admired well before he became a mentor and a friend, and whose encouragement was welcome as I worked to develop my professional identity.

The final push to complete the book benefited from generous and timely assistance by Patricia Greve, Max Bergholz, Hrvoje Klasić, Ana Matan, Núria Franco-Guillén, and Matthias Scantamburlo with the Regional Manifestos Project. I also want to thank Jacqueline Mason at McGill-Queen's University Press for her patience, good spirits, and guidance through various stages of manuscript completion. The two anonymous reviewers she identified pointed to all the right loose ends – their comments helped me put crucial finishing touches on this project.

I assume – perhaps incorrectly – that a typical author of books like this one has a group of like-minded people, an academic family of sorts, to whom they circulate various versions of their manuscripts. For my part, I had an academic doppelgänger with whom, in a case of cosmic coincidence, I had shared a school desk at age eight, and then, after twenty years apart, a destiny as an émigré – in the same country and city, doing a PhD on (sort of) the same theme at the same university. Zoran Oklopčić continues to be the most generous intellectual sparring partner; an inexhaustible library of ideas and concepts; a partner *za zajebanciju* (that eternal spout of creativity) when called for (often); and a friend by chance and by choice. The confidence to make the leap I took in this book I mustered in no small part thanks to him.

I completed this work at about the same age at which my parents' lives came undone by the Yugoslav drama. Both of their stories during those years would, unfortunately, have made great literary or film material. Had I been more self-assured in my youth, I would have told what I had to say here through a different medium. Instead, I took the meandering and much longer road, one that led to the book you are about to read. I dedicate it to Majda and Gojko Basta, and hundreds of thousands of others who were steamrolled by history, somehow put themselves back together, and kept going. And to those who couldn't.

THE SYMBOLIC STATE

1

In Search of Theories
of the Multinational State

This is a book about the functioning and the dysfunctions of an institutional outcast: the multinational state. Our daily political vocabulary has no use for it. We think of the basic unit of politics as the *nation*-state, despite the stubborn historical persistence of the multinational variant. Indeed, journalists, politicians, and most depressingly of all, academics, habitually conflate the terms "nation" and "state."[1] Multinational states normally draw our attention only when they erupt in crises. At such points, we invoke their "artificial" and "temporary" character (think of Iraq, Belgium, or Bosnia), further cementing the perception that they are irritating institutional aberrations instead of a prominent and, above all, *normal* feature of modern politics.

This casual disregard extends into academia as well. There is no explanatory theory of the multinational state.[2] In its place, we find largely isolated islands of knowledge rooted in discrete thematic subfields. The gravitational pull of those disparate fields has stood in the way of coherent, synthetic understanding of the multinational polity. In part, the problem lies in the fundamental premises on which those fields rest – most often the assumption that the modern state is inherently *national*.[3] This has led scholars to either completely ignore the multinational state (as is the case with state formation theories) or treat it as a variant of the nation-state (the trend in comparative federalism and regionalism, and in party politics literature). Where scholars *do* pay attention to multinational political systems, the inquiry has been confined to a narrow sphere of policy-relevant issues, notably institutional conflict management (e.g., work on ethnofederalism and power-sharing). How those institutions come into existence in the first place, and whether their development shapes their ability to contain conflict, are only some of the questions that remain underexamined.

Yet multinational states continue to be a prominent feature of world politics. Their pathologies contribute to regional and global instability,[4] open up spaces for non-state transborder actors such as terrorist groups or illicit trade networks, and produce many other spillovers.[5] Great Power attempts to manage multinational state crises brought about important normative shifts in world politics, from the spread of the principle of national self-determination (Raič 2002, 181), to the repurposing of *uti possidetis* for secessionist struggles (Radan 1997), to the emergence of the Responsibility to Protect doctrine (Evans and Sahnoun 2002). Perhaps as importantly, the multinational state is a supremely useful didactic tool. It allows us to see the central elements of our political reality in an entirely new light. It shows us that the state, democracy, self-determination, and political legitimacy are all far more contingent and fluid than many would like to believe. In this sense, understanding the multinational state can help us imagine alternative political realities beyond, and apart from, the nation-state.

This incongruity between the fragmented scholarship on the multinational state on the one hand, and its theoretical and real-world importance on the other, is the reason for this book. The volume's primary goal is to encourage the formation of a subfield explicitly dedicated to the study of the multinational state as a unique subject, with its own dynamics and concerns. In addition to being an act of *disciplinary creation*, this work is also a *theoretical* contribution, offering an example of how future comparative inquiry into multinational states might proceed. It is an account of two related phenomena in a set of multinational states – Canada, Spain, Yugoslavia, and Czechoslovakia – in the second half of the twentieth, and in the early twenty-first century. First, it explains central government responses to demands for greater territorial autonomy and recognition by minority nations. Second, it demonstrates how responses to these demands – the specific patterns of institutional (non)accommodation – shape the likelihood of secessionist crises. The next section offers a conceptual sketch of the multinational state as a *sui generis* institutional form and serves as an introduction to the summary of the book's arguments.

THE MULTINATIONAL CONDITION

The nation-state is a double sleight of hand. It successfully conceals the artifactual character of both the nation and the state encompassing it. The nation-state's boundaries, demographic content, and symbolic-historical order are naturalized to the point of resembling physical landscape. They are so taken for granted by their citizens that the fact they are human constructs vanishes from view. In the language of social science, the nation-state is institutionalized (Berger and Luckmann 1967, 77), unproblematized (Bourdieu 1994, 15), its symbolic power routinized (Loveman 2005).[6] Its citizens can argue about how to best organize and govern themselves, they may even wage civil wars over such issues, but the territorial-institutional arena within which they do so remains intact. The nation-state's existence is never brought into question due to the tacit understanding that its entire citizenry, whatever its differences, constitutes a single political community.

No such naturalization is possible in the multinational state. Here, at least one segment of the population considers itself to be a political community apart. If multiple political communities coexist in a given state, there are no guarantees that each will be able to govern itself, or receive institutional recognition, as a distinct nation. For minority nations in particular, there is an enduring possibility of being *politically* assimilated. Consequently, the multinational state is characterized by *chronically conditional legitimacy*. For communities whose members consider themselves to be politically distinct, the state is legitimate only insofar as it allows them to govern themselves as they see fit and only as long as it recognizes them as full-fledged nations.[7]

Any possibility that the state might recede from view, or become naturalized, is thus precluded. Indeed, minority elites often make it their business to "problematize" the state and emphasize its conditional legitimacy. If the state was *made* by social actors, it can also be reformed, or in the extreme case, *unmade*. Members of majority communities are far more likely to identify with the state and to be sanguine about the emergence of a state-wide political community (Elkins and Sides 2007; Staerklé et al. 2010). But the efforts of their minority counterparts to denaturalize the institutional order make majorities aware of that order's contingency as well. The differing visions of the state, and the anxieties these produce on all sides, are the key source of conflict in multinational states.

Because of its hegemonic status among the citizenry, the nation-state can withstand even the most catastrophic political earthquakes. Colombia's half-century-long civil war divided the state into government- and rebel-controlled spheres (McDougall 2009), yet, it never occurred to any of the sides to divide the country. If this example appears to be a stretch, consider the fates of nation-states split by geopolitical conflict: Germany, Vietnam, and Korea. In all three cases, both domestic and foreign actors expected the divisions to cease at some point in the future. The idea of a single state unit enveloping a single political community is so powerful that it can survive several generations of separation.

In multinational states, by contrast, even apparently trivial issues can trigger major political crises. A prime example was the confrontation over whether the name of post-communist Czechoslovakia should or should not contain a hyphen (Greenhouse 1990). Another flare-up occurred in 2013 in Bosnia over an otherwise inconsequential issue: whether the administrative areas for citizen registration should respect or ignore the boundary between the country's two entities (Bilefsky 2013). This difference between multinational states and nation-states implies that theories developed to study the political dynamics of the latter may not be appropriate for the analysis of the former. The multinational state requires an analytical apparatus of its own. This book is a step in that direction.

THE ARGUMENT: ECONOMY, INSTITUTIONAL SYMBOLISM, AND FEEDBACK LOOPS

Overview

When central governments first concede territorial autonomy to minority nations, they do so by establishing a territorial unit with formal political institutions, an administrative apparatus, and a degree of policy autonomy.[8] At the same time, they retain extensive fiscal powers to ensure continued political influence over the territorial units. This initial limit on the effective scope of territorial autonomy motivates minority elites to claim greater decision rights in fiscal and economic domains. These *instrumental* demands are nearly always accompanied by calls for the acknowledgment of national specificity, or else, for *symbolic recognition* (Swenden 2013). This book explains how central governments respond to these demands, and with what political consequences.

The argument proceeds in two steps. I first account for the way in which central governments respond to instrumental – particularly fiscal and economic – demands. This is the *political economy story* with which this project began. Over the course of my research, the instrumental factors on which I initially focused proved incapable of explaining additional theoretically important observations. Why did minority representatives not stop if and when their calls for fiscal and economic autonomy were met? Why did they escalate their demands? What accounted for the pattern of government responses to those newly articulated claims? Under what conditions did these dynamics lead to secessionist crises? To answer those questions, I found it necessary to broaden the scope of the inquiry and explain how symbolic claims and counter-claims of majority and minority communities influence both the process of accommodation of institutional demands and the political consequences of that process. This part of the argument constitutes the *symbolic politics story*.

The Political Economy Story

The politics of territorial accommodation do not play out in a political vacuum. In addition to addressing the demands for greater autonomy and recognition, central elites must engage in day-to-day policy-making. If accommodation undercuts their ability to deliver on policy commitments to state-wide constituents, they will resist demands for greater autonomy and may reverse earlier concessions. Conversely, they will be more willing to broaden fiscal and economic autonomy if doing so does not threaten the policy-making capacity of the central state apparatus. The disruptive potential of autonomy is a particularly salient political issue since a government's effectiveness in the provision of public goods influences the elites' ability to maintain their hold on power.[9]

The risk posed by greater autonomy of minority regions to state capacity depends on the *alignment between the broad and enduring policy paradigms*, or *strategies of governance*, adopted by the central government and the government of the minority territorial unit. In the interest of parsimony, I distinguish between *state-interventionist* and *pro-market strategies*.[10] Granting greater policy autonomy to a region whose government pursues a radically different strategy of governance may undermine the centre's ability to address its own policy priorities. On the other hand, alignment on policy goals makes greater decentralization of fiscal resources and economic policy more acceptable to the central government. For example, a centre committed to a pro-market, fiscally conservative strategy will be less likely to grant substantial spending or revenue-raising autonomy to a state-interventionist territorial government for fear of undermining

state-wide macroeconomic stability. Such concerns will be less pronounced with respect to autonomy demands of a pro-market region.
By contrast, a state-interventionist centre will find it difficult to accommodate a pro-market minority region since such accommodation will
weaken the centre's ability to develop comprehensive and costly government programs. Conversely, the alignment of state-interventionism at
both levels will facilitate accommodation of claimant governments.

I compare the processes of institutional accommodation in four
cases, each of which approximates one of the configurations outlined above: Canada, Spain, socialist Yugoslavia, and post-socialist
Czechoslovakia. In social science terms, the cases were selected on the
independent variable, each exhibiting a unique combination of governing strategies adopted by the central and regional governments.[11]
To ensure that I am comparing like with like I selected cases from
the "global North." While the countries covered in the book differ
from one another in some important aspects, they are closer to each
other than they are to other multinational states in terms of degree
of stateness, the persistence of multinationality, population size, and
international standing.[12]

In all four cases, existing autonomy arrangements were challenged
by elites claiming to represent the largest minority nation in each
country: Quebeckers, Catalans, Croats, and Slovaks.[13] While the
motives behind these challenges varied, the demands themselves were
broadly similar. The elite of each territorial unit pursued greater fiscal
resources and more comprehensive control over economic/social
policy. In each case, these demands were accompanied by claims for
greater recognition of the national status of the minority community
in question, and of the state's multinational character.

The evidence presented in Chapters 4 to 7 largely supports the
hypotheses I outline here. Where the central and regional strategies
of governance aligned, significant new powers were devolved to the
claimant unit. Where the claimant and central government clashed
on policy, accommodation was more limited. Only in Czechoslovakia
did the misalignment on policy endure, contributing to the country's
break-up. Yet, important as the political economy story is for understanding the patterns of accommodation, it is incomplete. Central
governments are further constrained in their ability to accommodate
minority demands by the symbolic logic of majority and minority
nationalism. Thus, even under a propitious alignment of policy

paradigms, central governments will not be free to accommodate minority demands as they please.

The Symbolic Politics Story

State institutions are not only instruments for the pursuit of collective and individual goals, but also potent political symbols with *either positive or negative valence*.[14] The clear – if underappreciated – implication is that institutions are symbolically salient for both minority *and majority* communities.[15] Minority demands for recognition seek to redress the perceived injustice of the symbolic-institutional status quo. Beyond claiming organizational and financial resources with which to protect their interests, minority nationalists seek to transform the common state from one that is an expression of a single political community into one that acknowledges and accepts its national diversity.[16] At the same time, such demands may be seen by members of the majority community as corrosive of the symbolic-institutional order embedded in their own national narratives. As a result, *satisfying minority symbolic demands may foster resentment among members of the majority nation.*

This interplay of symbolic logics shapes both the patterns of accommodation and the likelihood of major political crises in multinational states. Central governments are aware of the potential political cost of symbolic recognition of minority nations – in the form of majority political backlash and possible loss of support and power. For the purpose of analytical simplicity and clarity, I divide the political process through which this dynamic plays out into two rounds. In Round 1, in response to early demands for greater fiscal autonomy *and* recognition, the centre tends to grant the former – provided the political economy configuration permits it – but not the latter. As the examples of Spain and Canada demonstrate, even policy decentralization unfolded in a *formally* symmetric manner so as to avoid the appearance of symbolic recognition of national specificity for minority regions.

This partial accommodation of minority demands has contradictory political consequences. On the one hand, it provides moderates among minority political elites with discursive ammunition with which to argue against more radical options such as secession. Initial concessions are both inherently valuable and an indication of the possibility of future gains. On the other hand, the absence of recognition provides the impetus to continue pressing for greater symbolic concessions in the future and to mobilize on those grounds. Thus, partial accommodation early on is likely to result neither in elimination of minority grievances, nor in their extreme escalation, but rather in the continuing political relevance of the national question.

This ambiguous situation ushers in Round 2, during which minority nationalists increase political pressure on the central government through greater mobilization and/or more far-reaching political demands. Facing a more serious political challenge, the centre combines instrumental concessions with symbolic recognition. This recognition, however, may foster resentment among the majority population and create the conditions for a majority backlash. If enterprising majority politicians use this reservoir of resentment to mobilize their constituents against the recognition of minority nationhood, such backlash can nourish a far more serious minority reaction, leading to a full-blown secessionist crisis. I define such crises as junctures during which support for independence approaches or exceeds 50 per cent, and where regional governments take up the cause of independence, normally through the pursuit of a referendum on the region's status (Basta 2017, 55–6).

Majority backlash makes secessionist crises more likely thanks to three interlinked mechanisms. First, it increases the odds that attempts at recognition will be rescinded or that already granted recognition will be reversed. Second, it demonstrates – much more openly and conclusively than any arcane technical policy measure could – the majority's opposition to the recognition of minority nationhood. Third, demonstrations of this kind empower minority radicals and may lead to outbidding spirals among minority political elites.[17] Put differently, central governments' attempts to rein in minority regions through, for example, extensive use of their spending power (as in Canada) or overbroad application of framework legislation (as in Spain) are less politically combustible than open mobilization against the symbolic recognition of minority nationhood by majority populations and political elites.

Caveats and Scope of Analysis

Clarity of exposition requires that complex realities be packaged into overly neat and seamless narratives. This necessitates several caveats.

First, because my argument is structuralist – it is developed around constraints on political action – the framework might appear theoretically overdetermined. Yet the empirical chapters that follow repeatedly demonstrate the (bounded) contingency of the outcomes covered here. While I do identify regularities across the four cases, I consider these regularities to be "soft" (Almond and Genco 1977, 494). There is no *automatic* translation of "structural constraints" into "outcomes" here. There are greater or lesser costs associated with particular decisions (and even these costs must themselves be discursively "calibrated," a contentious process even under the best of circumstances), but these constraints can be reshaped by political actors in inventive and unexpected ways. That is to say, while the argument at the core of this book does not formally account for agency, political actors' agentic potential is the background assumption.

Second, a quick read of this chapter might lead to an erroneous assumption that I am trying to develop a *general* theory of accommodation in multinational states. My theoretical framework is based on the examination of a small number of fundamentally comparable cases and should be applied beyond these with great care. This has less to do with methodological than ontological considerations, an issue to which I return in the concluding chapter. Briefly, I do not believe that a theory of all multinational states across time and space is possible. The multinational states of continental Europe (and North America) in the late twentieth and early twenty-first centuries are far too different from, say, the multinational states of Sub-Saharan Africa or even those of late nineteenth-century Europe for similar political dynamics to apply. Thus, the argument is both temporally and geographically bounded. This is not to say that some of the factors identified in this book may not be transposable to other contexts. They may, however, combine in different ways in different contextual circumstances, necessitating distinctive theoretical frameworks.

Finally, the scope of this study is limited to the politics of institutional development in states that had already established a minimal level of territorial autonomy. I set aside the question of institutional origins: multinational federalism emerges under such vastly different circumstances that a convincing general theory likely remains beyond our reach.[18] I also do not explain secessionist outcomes, since these are subject to different causal patterns. Rather, I outline the *political dynamics* that are often a critical condition for state fracture.

A METHODOLOGY FOR A DYNAMIC PHENOMENON

Accommodation of demands for greater autonomy and recognition is the kind of dynamic, large-scale political phenomenon that has typically been the subject of comparative historical analysis (Mahoney and Rueschemeyer 2003b; Thelen and Mahoney 2015; Katznelson 1997). Three of its characteristics make it particularly suitable for comparative, process-based methodological treatment (Bennett and Checkel, eds., 2015; Bengtsson and Ruonavaara 2017). Territorial accommodation is a *process* rather than a one-off event; it is *causally dynamic* because it is shaped by shifting configurations of interacting causal factors and multiple feedback processes; and is *variable* from context to context. These features require a careful analytical treatment of processes occurring in a small number of comparable cases.

Both institutional change and the ensuing political dynamics are *inherently processual outcomes*. Rather than being snapshots – temporally condensed events – they unfold over long time periods, often years (Pierson 2004, 81). Cross-sectional comparisons are by their very nature insensitive to the dynamic character of such processes, since they compare cases at a specific juncture rather than through time. As importantly, the coding necessary for large-*n* cross-sectional studies, and the conceptual compression such coding implies, can prove dangerously reductionist if it results in the analyst overlooking important qualitative aspects of the phenomenon to be explained. For example, looking only for the specific policy responses to the demands of Québécois or Catalan politicians at any given time without noting the processes through which these responses materialized would have led me to omit the inclination of Canadian and Spanish governments to symmetrize these institutional concessions. Yet this important insight provides additional leverage for the second part of the argument concerning the symbolic politics of accommodation and is thus akin to auxiliary outcome causal-process observations (Mahoney 2010, 129–31). In other words, process tracing is a methodological tool appropriate not only for the identification of causal mechanisms (Bennett and Checkel 2015, 3–4) but also for a more sharply calibrated assessment of the phenomena we seek to explain. In this particular case, additional detail is not an embellishment that adds the vaunted "nuance" to the argument; rather, it is new evidence that qualifies the initial thesis in fundamental ways.

Even more importantly, institutional change in multinational states, along with its political consequences, is characterized by complex feedback loops. This is more than just a matter of complex interaction of different causal layers *at a given point in time* (Falleti and Lynch 2009; Katznelson 1997). The very political process one is examining changes the context in which it unfolds, so that the same set of causal factors produces different outcomes at different points in time (P. Hall 2003, 385; Pierson 2004, 170; Büthe 2002). In multinational contexts, a particular concession that might alleviate political tension at one point may not do so, or may produce the opposite outcome, at subsequent points in the causal chain. This is why increasing the number of observations through, for example, pooled time series analysis is not a viable research strategy here. Subdividing a process of accommodation into single-year observations would result in non-homogeneous units of comparison, compromising the validity of the conclusions issuing from such an exercise.[19] What is required, thus, is a process-tracing approach inherently suited for capturing trans-temporal complexities, one that conceives of the entire causal sequence as a single case (P. Hall 2003, 396–7; Büthe 2002, 484).

Finally, processes of accommodation vary across cases. The initial hypotheses that frame this study – under the heading of the political economy story – necessitate a comparison of at least four countries, each exhibiting one of the four configurations of strategies of governance.[20] Yet any such study would need to be particularly mindful of the problems of contextual equivalence and comparability (Adcock and Collier 2001; Falleti and Lynch 2009, 1144; Locke and Thelen 1995). While a significant number of modern states have faced self-determination movements of greater or lesser intensity, not all share the same political dynamics. The four cases selected for this study not only reflect the relevant political economy configurations but are also fundamentally comparable in terms of background nationalist dynamics.

In each case, the common state framework was subject to persistent demands for enhanced self-government of at least one territorially concentrated and demographically significant minority nation.[21] Moreover, in all four, institutions of territorial autonomy endured for a significant length of time.[22] In other words, all four are, or were, multinational states with a degree of self-government for the claimant communities. Additional contextual factors set them apart from other plural states: the absence of super-diversity;[23] the degree of stateness, in terms of both state capacity and state culture;[24] their relatively peripheral strategic status; and the absence of recent violent conflict. Cases that differed on any of these factors would exhibit qualitatively different patterns of politics and would thus be less comparable. Therefore, the logic of case selection also requires a qualitative comparison of a *small number* of processes (Slater and Ziblatt 2013, 1313).

Since the evolution of territorial autonomy in multinational states is relatively undertheorized, in this book the comparative process-tracing approach serves the simultaneous purpose of theory development and theory testing. While the starting point of the model is deductive, both cross-case comparison and within-case process-tracing contribute inductively to revisions of the initial model and to the generation of novel theoretical contributions (Falleti and Mahoney 2015, 229–30; Bennett and Checkel 2015b, 8). The final product is an example of iterative interplay of theory and evidence (Mahoney and Rueschemeyer 2003a, 13), producing new insights into the dynamics of multinational statehood and challenging existing theoretical claims.

CONTRIBUTION AND POLICY RELEVANCE

The theoretical contributions of this work should by now be clear. Most broadly, the book is an act of *conscious* (sub)disciplinary creation: it carves out and names a new subfield – the comparative study of multinational states. Of course, scholars have been developing theoretical accounts of such polities for decades. Yet their efforts have been subject to the intellectual pull of other subfields (e.g., comparative federalism, ethnic conflict, nationalism studies, comparative party politics), resulting in a fragmented and truncated body of knowledge.[25] This book gathers existing theoretical strands into a coherent block while at the same time identifying the thematic domains they leave untouched. More importantly, it points to the unique dynamics and issues *particular to multinational states*, in effect vertebrating the study of the phenomenon. The goal is to focus future scholarly work in the service of more comprehensive and productive analytical efforts at understanding one of the most vexing and important issues in modern politics.

At the same time, the volume's theoretical claims move the *existing* scholarship on the multinational state a few important steps forward. First, the book adds to the small but important literature on the institutional development of multinational polities. As noted, most of the institutional conflict-management literature has tended to ignore this side of the ledger. This is a twofold problem. For one thing, proposing institutional solutions (e.g., power-sharing or power-dividing arrangements) makes little sense if we do not know how politically feasible those solutions are in the first place. This book addresses the need for theories that explain how institutions develop and whether they are politically sustainable. More importantly, however, we should not assume that institutions are timeless, exogenous devices that can be transposed from context to context with similar results – as much of the accommodative and integrationist literature does. This volume demonstrates that *institutional impact cannot be understood apart from the specific patterns of institutional development.* It endogenizes institutional effects to the modalities of institutional change and shows the mutual interplay of the two phenomena.

Second, the book champions the role of institutional symbolism in understanding the political dynamics of multinational states. The vast majority of the conflict-management literature views institutions through an instrumental prism – they are tools for the achievement of various national goals – political or physical protection, economic advancement, or the preservation of one's own language and culture. I demonstrate the importance of the symbolic and expressive aspects of institutions. While struggles over relatively obscure and complex administrative details *do* matter, especially to the politicians themselves, big changes, particularly secessionist crises, are a consequence of shifts in the domain of institutional symbolism. Put differently, rather than being important for what they *do*, institutions in multinational states are crucial because of what they *mean*. This reorientation is critical in getting the story of the link between territorial autonomy and political instability right.

Finally, the volume foregrounds the interaction between minority and majority nationalist projects as *the* engine of political conflict in multinational states. A significant proportion of the work on institutional impact tends to focus on the way in which institutions and institutional change affect the political actions of minority communities. The integration–accommodation debate, for instance, revolves almost entirely around the best way institutions can placate restive minorities. The effect of institutions on majority communities is rarely discussed or integrated into theoretical models. Here, I show that it is difficult to grasp minority claims and actions without paying attention to what happens on the other side of the fence, so to speak.

Given this work's skepticism regarding sweeping explanatory claims, the reader will likely not be surprised by the paucity of fine-grained policy recommendations. I nevertheless do believe that the arguments developed here hold important implications for the institutional management of conflict in multinational states. Most obviously, any effort to accommodate demands for greater autonomy and recognition should proceed with an awareness of both policy and political obstacles to such efforts. While I foreground the constraints that political economy may impose on the sustainable accommodation of demands for greater autonomy, different contexts might throw up limits in other policy areas, including, for example, external security. As importantly, attention to the instrumental implications of institutional change should not crowd out the significance of institutional symbolism, particularly among segments of the majority population. Symbolically salient issues are far more politically bankable for majority counter-elites than are arcane policy matters. Both policy and political constraints can provide central elites with incentives to reverse earlier concessions. Prospect theory suggests that such reversals are more likely to result in conflict escalation than outright refusal to concede (Mercer 2005).[26]

PLAN OF THE BOOK

The following two chapters form the theoretical core of the book. Chapter 2 identifies the gaps in the scholarship on the multinational state. It outlines a list of major themes that ought to be of interest to students of that institutional formation, and shows that only a few have been systematically explored. It also shows why, for those themes that remain underexamined (e.g., state formation and institutional development), insights of theories developed with reference to the nation-state simply cannot apply to the multinational polity. With this in mind, Chapter 3 lays out the theoretical framework and summarizes the findings. I proceed in two steps. I first outline the deductive framework linking the political economy of multinational states to the accommodation of minority claims for fiscal and economic autonomy. In the second step, I broaden the analytical aperture to explore the ways in which symbolic aspects of state institutions shape the demands by minority nations, the responses by central governments, and the likelihood of secessionist crises.

Chapters 4 through 7 test the book's hypotheses against empirical findings. Each chapter is a self-contained case study, a choice dictated by the need to maintain the integrity of the causal narrative for all four countries. However, because my goal is not only to develop stand-alone causal narratives but also to compare the four processes of accommodation, claims in each chapter are checked against those in the others. In other words, each process serves as a counterfactual to the others. Chapter 8 brings the findings together and outlines the implications of the study for cases beyond the four examined here. I am particularly careful to note the limits to generalizability of the claims made in this book. As I see it, that does not point to a weakness of the argument; rather, it serves as a cautionary note and an antidote to the theoretical overreach of recent work in comparative politics.

2

Theoretical Bottlenecks

The comparative explanatory study of the multinational state is at once under- and over-developed. It is underdeveloped because many – indeed most – of the aspects of this multifaceted historical phenomenon are poorly understood. Yet it is overdeveloped because those lines of inquiry that *have* been pursued – notably the effectiveness of power-sharing and federal institutions in ensuring multinational state stability – have resulted in a disproportionately large body of work focused on an exceedingly narrow set of issues. The subfield thus looks like a desert encroaching on a few unusually fecund oases. The problem with this state of the subfield is not only the lack of theoretical knowledge about a broad range of important issues, but also that the active domains of inquiry have been limited by the lack of attention to other aspects of multinational statehood.

This state of affairs requires the mapping of the relevant thematic domains, the assessment of the literature as it pertains to each, and the illumination of paths for future inquiry. I therefore start this chapter with a brief and preliminary list of key themes relevant to the study of the multinational state:

- **State origins:** How and why do multinational states come to be? This question is, at least indirectly, related to the issue of the genesis of national groups, their merger (or "national integration") in some cases, and their persistent differentiation in others. But it is a question that brings together the study of state formation, political identity, and institutional legitimacy.
- **Institutional development:** How and why do institutions – particularly those related to the management of difference –

develop in multinational states? This question relates to
the politics of institution-building, institutional change and
resilience, deliberate institutional design, and institutional
breakdown. Here, scholars ought to examine the development
of various territorial forms of organization, and the links
between societal organizations and networks and those of the
state, as well as the structuring of central state institutions.

- **Institutional meaning:** What is the ontological status of state
  institutions in multinational settings? What kind of political
  work do they do? How does their meaning emerge, and
  how does it change? This is particularly important in light
  of the tendency of institutional scholars to overemphasize
  the instrumental functions of institutions at the expense of
  their meaning.
- **Institutional impact:** How do specific institutional models
  contribute to the management of the political conflicts that
  emerge in multinational states? Are specific "recipes" effective?
  Why, or why not, and under what conditions?
- **Nationalist mobilization and secessionist crises:** How and
  why do national communities in plural states mobilize to make
  claims? Why does their mobilization take the particular shape
  it does (sometimes violent, sometimes not), and why do the
  specific claims vary (at times for more or less autonomy or
  different policies, at times for independence). Why does
  secessionist support vary? If and once secession is mainstreamed,
  what accounts for success or failure in gaining independence?
  If secession is unsuccessful, what is its impact on the political
  dynamics of the state? While there is obvious overlap between
  these concerns and those relating to institutional impact, they
  are not the same.
- **Generalizability:** This is an ontological issue with profound
  methodological implications. Are insights about one set of states
  generalizable across space and time? If they are, to what extent is
  this the case, and in what domains? If they are not, why? Moreover,
  which themes are particularly resistant to generalization? This is
  possibly one of the most far-reaching issues and goes to the heart
  of how we think about the modern state as such. I pay more
  attention to this issue in the concluding chapter.
- **Meta-thematic concerns:** The primary issue here concerns the
  linkages between the various thematic concerns. I address one

of those linkages in this book – the relationship between institutional development and institutional impact – but there are others that merit exploration. Just as important is the question that overlaps with the study of nationalism in nationally homogeneous polities, but that assumes a different dimension in the multinational state – the intensity, resilience, and "viscosity" of "identities" (Oklopcic 2018, 164).[1] This issue overlaps in part with Brubaker's emphasis on the temporal situatedness of nationalist claims and "identity," but it also relates to the intensity of emotion felt for a particular political project and the community that is linked by it. Furthermore, it concerns the qualitative difference of the very practice of nationalism at different times and in different places. Thus, it is quite possible that there is a different *kind* of national identity that we might point to, say, among urban Nigerians in the 1960s, as opposed to rural inhabitants of Austria-Hungary in the late nineteenth century. Such differences may have profound implications for the degree of generalizability of our theories.

Some of these themes have received hardly any scholarly attention at all,[2] whereas others have been the subject of intense, multi-decade inquiry, producing a very large and self-sustained body of work. Table 2.1 summarizes the state of scholarship for each theme. The result is an image of a field dominated by concerns about the impact of power-sharing and autonomy arrangements on the stability of multinational states and, to a lesser degree and more recently, by secession. The preoccupation with institutional impact is understandable. Since we cannot easily change the political culture, social structure, or economic features of a country, institutions beckon as the one reasonably malleable lever with which to manage identity-based conflict. Indeed, much of the practice of post-conflict management revolves around institutional design, so it is important to know which options are most likely to yield peace and institutional sustainability.[3]

Yet there are at least two problems with this relentless pursuit of institutional remedies to conflict. First, no matter how appealing a particular conflict-management "recipe" may be, it is of little use if we do not know whether it is politically feasible in the first place. This is putting the prescriptive cart before the analytical horse. Second, there is little willingness in the extant literature to entertain the possibility that a specific pattern by which an institution develops may

Table 2.1
Theories of multinational state: The state of the field

Theme	Scholarly coverage	Comment
State origins	Low	Remarkably little has been written about the origins of multinational states. The most notable exception is the work of Stein Rokkan (Rokkan and Urwin 1983; Rokkan 1999) and to an extent, that of Juan Linz (1973). More recent contributions examine sources of politicized ethnic diversity, as with Wimmer (2011; 2018), Robinson (2014) and Darden and Mylonas (2016). Part of the problem with some of the more recent contributions is the exaggerated emphasis on generalizability – an issue I return to in the conclusion.
Institutional development	Low/moderate	The issue of institutional development has received increasing attention over the past two decades or so, but it is nevertheless underdeveloped relative to the theme of institutional impact. As importantly, the contributions hardly speak to one another. For a sample, see Cunningham (2014); Loizides (2016); Mylonas (2012); O'Leary (2001); Swenden and Toubeau (2013); Wolff (2009).
Institutional meaning	Low	There is very little systematic work that examines not only the various lines of institutional meaning in multinational states, but as importantly, where that meaning comes from, how it is produced and perpetuated, and what effect it has on the politics of those states. Exceptions include works on the expressive role of institutions and institutionalized policies in multinational states, but the focus here tends to fall on minority nations, rather than on all the relevant communities. See, for example Béland and Lecours (2010); Gagnon (2001); Keating (2001); Requejo (2001).
Institutional impact	High	This theme has motivated a multi-decade effort resulting in virtually hundreds of books and articles. Extends from the Lijphart, Nordlinger, and Horowitz's work, through the 1990s, all the way to the present. For further references and detail, see this chapter.
Mobilization/ crises/secession	Moderate	The past two decades have seen the rise of a fairly well-integrated literature on secession, falling into three strands: structural factors accounting for secessionist outcomes; literature on voting behaviour in secession referenda; and the international relations of secession. For references and more discussion, see this chapter. Less work has been done on the dynamics of secession, notably the sources and modalities of mobilization. For exceptions, see Beissinger (2002); Giuliano (2011); Huszka (2014) and, most recently, Roeder (2018).

influence its effectiveness in managing conflicts. The very same institutional "device," for example, might be perceived as adequately
addressing one community's needs and grievances but as wholly
inadequate in another context. Much depends on the character of the
political process through which that institution develops. Both issues
should encourage us to open the analytical aperture and consider a
much broader set of concerns related to multinational states. We
should also be more attentive to how various themes relate to one
another. To these can be added the purely scholarly motive – we simply
ought to know more about what makes multinational states work.

Each of the under-studied themes outlined in Table 2.1 has been
addressed by discrete subfields of political science and sociology.
However, scholars in those subfields have developed their insights by
reference to the nation-state. As the next section demonstrates, that
theoretical genealogy makes those insights ill-suited for an understanding of the multinational state. The discussion of the applicability of
these and related fields could span an entire volume, so I consider
only a few examples that are most directly relevant to the issues
flagged in Table 2.1.

THE MULTINATIONAL STATE
IN EXISTING SCHOLARSHIP

State Origins

The question of multinational state genesis ought to have been considered by the literature on modern state formation. Yet most of this
scholarship, from the classical contributions (Tilly 1975; 1992;
Skocpol 1985), through the 1990s (Centeno 2003; Ertman 1997;
Ikegami 1995; Spruyt 1996) and beyond (Grzymała-Busse 2007;
Slater 2010), has accepted the assumption that the modern state model
is inherently national. A key issue with that particular literature has
been its excessive emphasis on institutional creation as a result of war
or market-making, with little attention paid to sources of state legitimacy (Vu 2010). But even those scholars who have explored that
question have trained their sights on the nationally homogeneous
states (Loveman 2005; Gorski 2003). While there are some elements
that students of the multinational state can borrow from this field,
most of the concerns relating to the multinational polity are not
discussed at all.[4]

Institutional Development

Because the defining feature of the multinational state is conflict over self-government, and because the claims for self-government often take a territorialized form, the central institutional question is one of appropriate territorial organization. Scholars of federalism and regional politics have written extensively about the emergence and evolution of territorial institutions. But because those insights have been developed with reference to national federations, they do not always apply to multinational ones. Consider two major contributions to the study of federal origins. In his foundational work, William Riker argued that federations are in part a product of external threats that facilitate their integration even once they have been established (Riker 1964). Apart from the fact that many multinational federations are created not through merger of pre-existing units, as Riker presumes, but rather through the reform of previously centralized states, attempts to address external threats may *undermine* their unity. This is particularly likely if representatives of different national communities view the external threat differently or if they clash over the consequences or appropriateness of measures adopted to meet that threat.[5]

In a more recent contribution, Ziblatt explains the divergent outcomes of German and Italian unification by showing that Italian state-makers were as keen to build the new state as a federation as were their German counterparts but were unable to do so because of the weak governing capacity of the prospective federal units (Ziblatt 2006). Ziblatt's argument is convincing, but the dynamic he analyzes may not be operative in most multinational settings. Those who see themselves as members of a distinctive community seek autonomy even when their regions lack the elementary prerequisites for self-government. Refusing to grant autonomy on institutional capacity grounds in a multinational state may not be politically feasible, as it would violate the basic principle of national self-government. A more likely outcome is limited autonomy combined with central government assistance in shoring up organizational resources.[6]

Scholarship on the sustainability of federal bargains similarly offers few insights that are transferrable to multinational contexts. Jenna Bednar outlines five interlocking institutional features that preclude mutual encroachment between the central and constituent unit governments as well as unproductive burden-shifting among the constituent units (Bednar 2009, 68). She argues that where the dysfunctionality of a federal system passes a certain threshold, secession becomes less costly relative to the maintenance of the federation. She simultaneously acknowledges that secession is not equally likely across cases while suggesting that essentially all federal systems are subject to it (Bednar 2009, 84). This type of calculus, however, is hardly imaginable in a consolidated nation-state characterized by a hegemonic state idea. While Bednar does periodically recognize the situational differences between multinational and national federations, she seems to imply that the differences are a matter of degree, not of kind.

Tulia Falleti, for her part, foregrounds the role of institutional sequencing in explaining federal dynamics. She demonstrates that the agent facilitating institutional change (the central or sub-state government) influences the ordering of decentralizing reforms (whether they start with political or administrative devolution), which, in turn, affects the extent of decentralization (Falleti 2005; 2010). When driven by central governments, decentralization starts with administrative concessions and results in more modest decentralization than when the process is initiated by the regions. Again, this valuable insight is not easily transposable to multinational settings. Because minority calls for autonomy are at bottom demands for political *recognition*, decentralization in multinational states almost always begins with concessions that go beyond administrative devolution.[7] Moreover, even when the effective power of minority units is initially quite limited, this need not preclude quite far-reaching devolution of power down the road, contradicting Falleti's expectations.

Patterns of *political economy* have also been found to influence the sustainability of federal bargains. Jonathan Rodden argues that territorially uneven distribution of wealth tends to produce greater centralization. Politicians in the more numerous and populous poorer regions will push for centralization in the interest of redistribution of wealth (Rodden 2006, 265–6).[8] Obversely, a more even distribution of wealth should be more conducive to a decentralized federation. Eric Wibbels suggests a different pattern, one that focuses on the combination of factor endowments and regional wealth inequalities. Where regions diverge in terms of factor endowments, they will demand a decentralized federation in order to constrain the central government's ability to implement policies inimical to their economic interests. More homogeneous production profiles, by contrast, should produce a more centralized system. Conversely, high levels of regional inequality will lead to demands for redistribution (Wibbels 2005, 168–9).

Some federations might thus be characterized by both high levels of decentralization and high levels of redistribution. Pablo Beramendi's comprehensive study complicates matters further. Heterogeneous economic geography steers actor preferences toward decentralization, whereas greater economic equality among regions has the opposite effect (Beramendi 2012, 33).[9] The translation of these preferences into political outcomes depends on pre-existing institutions – foremost on the ability of the constituent units to influence central government policy (Beramendi 2012, 211).

Again, these arguments cannot be easily applied to multinational federations. For example, regardless of their relative economic position, few minority regions would openly demand greater fiscal centralization, even if it carried the promise of fiscal side-payments. Instead, the more likely outcome, and one that can be observed in several of the cases covered in this book, is the demand for both decentralization and redistribution. Furthermore, it would be difficult to imagine a wealthy minority region in a country with regionally even factor endowments accepting a centralized federal system. Both Rodden and Beramendi acknowledge the role played by identity politics in federal states but do not weave it into their analytical frameworks.[10]

Issues of institutional development and change in multi-level systems (including multinational federations) are tackled by scholars of *party politics*. Both William Riker (1964) and Filippov et al. (2004) see self-sustainable federalism as a product of an integrated political party system in which politicians at both the federal and regional levels depend on each other for electoral success. This assumption about integrated political space also informs the more fine-grained arguments about federal political dynamics. For Dickovick (2011), decentralization is a tool of political survival. Where the party of the executive faces the loss of power in state-wide elections, it decentralizes in order to strengthen regional bases of its power. Díaz Cayeros examines the process of centralization through a similar prism of inter-party competition. Here, lower-level governments surrender their (fiscal) autonomy in exchange for the central government's help in warding off regional challengers (Díaz Cayeros 2006).

Such arguments run aground in democratic multinational settings. In minority federal units the party system is normally regionalized: it contains both parties developed with the express purpose of articulating and defending minority national interests, and regional brands or federates of state-wide parties that must pay significant attention to the (minority) national question.[11] Examples of the latter include the Liberal Party of Quebec and the Socialist Party of Catalonia.[12] In other words, integrated party systems that are supposed to sustain federal bargains seldom emerge in multinational states.[13] By extension, this also means that the kinds of party-system safety valves theorized by Dickovick and Díaz-Cayeros are also less likely to occur. A state-wide party seeking regional refuge while in opposition is unlikely to find it in minority regions. Conversely, a minority nationalist party surrendering regional fiscal autonomy in exchange for central government's backing in local political battles would court tremendous political risks.

A growing subset of party politics literature sensitive to the regional dimension of politics has emphasized the relative parliamentary weight of regional parties in accounting for the willingness of state-wide parties to decentralize power (Meguid 2008; Toubeau and Massetti 2013; Toubeau and Wagner 2016; Verge 2013). Briefly, state-wide parties decentralize power when it helps them win office or form government. However important party-political considerations are in understanding the institutional dynamics of multinational states, there is a danger of overemphasizing the role both of that particular domain of politics and of strategic action within it. Structural factors can place definitive limits on how far partisan actors can go in pursuing their electoral advantage (Rovny 2015). For one thing – and this is an issue almost completely untouched by this literature – there is an underappreciation of the potential majority backlash to major constitutional change in multinational states.

Institutional Meaning

Despite the proliferation of institutionalisms in social science, with the three original varieties (rational choice, historical, and sociological) yielding a multitude of others, the understanding of institutions in multinational states has been rather reductionist.[14] Most explanatory work in nationalism and ethnic conflict (including the vast majority of works on institutional impact, which I reference in the next section) has understood institutions through a predominantly instrumental prism. They are either uncertainty-reducing or trust-building devices of rational choice, levers that privilege certain projects over others in path-dependent ways (according to historical institutionalists), or, more prosaically they are means through which particular communities secure or safeguard their economic, political, and cultural interests. The problem with such approaches, particularly in the context of multinational states, rests in their neglect of institutional meaning. As sociological institutionalists argue, institutions can be prominent and emotionally evocative symbols.[15] In multinational states in particular, institutions can embody the often-conflicting visions of what kind of state one is inhabiting and what kind of political community is encapsulated therein (Basta 2016, 2020c).

A subset of nationalism studies does pay attention to the symbolic dimensions of nationalist politics, from the ethno-symbolist approach of Anthony Smith (2009), through Billig's discussion of everyday nationalism (Billig 1995),[16] to Elgenius's discussion of symbols as constituting nationhood (Elgenius 2011) and Kaufman's study of ethno-nationalist conflict (Kaufman 2015).[17] Yet all of these works tend to neglect the symbolic role of *institutions*, focusing instead on what I would label *decorative* symbols of nationhood. These are material, visual, or aural phenomena, such as flags, monuments, and anthems that do not serve a function other than to represent the *signified*. While this understanding of nationalist symbolism helps us understand how identities are constituted and "grounded" in everyday life to the point of invisibility (Malešević 2019, 12–14, 19, Ch. 9), it screens off the link between the quotidian practice of nationalism and its "high" politics.

Only a few studies of the multinational state recognize the symbolic baggage and import of formal institutions (Dieckhoff 2016; Gagnon 2001; Gagnon and Tremblay 2020; Keating 2001; Popelier and Sahadžić 2019; Requejo 2001). Yet, even here, one notices a reticence to conceptualize institutions as symbols.[18] Moreover, most of this work tends to explore institutional meaning among minority communities, rather than focusing on the meaning that specific institutional modalities come to take on among all relevant societal segments.[19] Given the importance of this issue for the question of multinational state formation (particularly regarding the problem of legitimacy [Lemay-Hébert 2009]), institutional development, impact, and mobilization dynamics, the lack of attention to institutional symbolism constitutes a significant theoretical opening.

Institutional Impact

In contrast to the other themes outlined in the introduction to this chapter, the question of institutional impact has received an inordinate amount of scholarly attention. Over the past five decades, students of ethnic conflict, nationalism, and consociationalism have been trying to figure out whether territorial arrangements and the organization of the central government affect the political stability of multinational states, and if so, how. While broad-ranging in its theoretical scope and empirical reach, this literature can be divided into roughly three branches: the accommodative, which holds that political stability requires the recognition and institutionalization of national difference; the integrationist, which argues that such institutionalization subverts the political viability of multinational states; and the "situational," which elucidates the specific conditions under which particular institutional configurations produce stabilizing or destabilizing outcomes.

According to accomodationist scholars, national difference should be institutionalized through multinational federalism, with territorial boundaries reflecting national pluralism and consociational arrangements granting all constituent groups access to central executive power as well as veto over key decisions. Arend Lijphart conceives of consociationalism and multinational federalism as defences against enduring political exclusion of minority communities in nationally heterogeneous societies (Lijphart 1977). Lihpart's insights have been extended by other authors who view accommodative institutions as instruments that non-dominant communities can use to preclude their political, economic, and cultural marginalization.[20] Integrationist scholars, by contrast, argue that such institutional concessions only exacerbate conflict, entrench separate identities, and provide potential secessionists with the institutional means with which to accomplish their goals. Instead, they favour integrative or power-dividing institutions, such as centripetal electoral systems, regional federalism, and other measures that purportedly activate cross-cutting cleavages and thus diminish the political prominence of separate national identities.[21] The middle ground is occupied by "situational" scholars, who identify either extra-institutional circumstances or institutional specifics that shape the ability of accommodative and integrative institutions to alleviate conflict in plural states.[22]

Despite their diversity, these works share three important drawbacks. The first is a *static understanding of institutions*. Most of the contributions referenced here assume that the political process through which a particular institution is developed has little bearing on how effective it is in containing conflict. The causal weight of institutions is instead thought to reside in their inherent features – possibly in combination with contextual factors. If an institution protects a community's interests, for example, it is likely to deradicalize the demands and behaviour of members of that community. Little thought is given to the possibility that the perception of a particular institution's legitimacy, inclusiveness, or even effectiveness may be associated with the process through which it was developed. This understanding clashes with accounts that emphasize the temporal contextuality of political phenomena (Büthe 2002; Pierson 2004; Sewell Jr 1996). Those accounts imply that the same institution may not have the same meaning at different points in time, indicating that we may consider extending our scope of inquiry to institutional development if we wish to better understand institutional impact.

The second drawback of the literature on conflict management concerns the *excessively instrumental view of institutions*, alluded to in the section on institutional meaning. The dominant understanding of institutions in this scholarship has its roots in either rational choice or historical institutionalist traditions (Hall and Taylor 1996). Both traditions are, of course, quite distinctive, with the former foregrounding institutions as solutions to problems of coordination and collective action, and the latter focusing on the way institutions privilege some political projects at the expense of others in path-dependent ways. They nevertheless share the instrumental view of institutional rules that finds its way into scholarship on the multinational state. Specific federal and power-sharing arrangements are foregrounded for their instrumental role in accomplishing particular goals. They are generally not seen as important in their own right, as expressions of identity narratives pertaining to particular communities. This reductionism is especially problematic in multinational states, where political conflict is at its root about different meanings of fundamental political concepts such as democracy and self-government. Future research must address this problem by refocusing attention to the symbolic aspects of institutions.

The third problem with works on institutional conflict management is that they *overemphasize the impact of institutions on the actions of minority communities*. The overwhelming majority of the works I cite tend to assume that political crises issue from the demands and activities of minority nationalists. For accommodationists, conflict emerges from minority communities' dissatisfaction with the protection of their interests. For integrationists, it is those same minority communities that resist political integration into the broader community and wield institutional power to destabilize the state. As I show in this book, this is far from the entire story. It is, rather, the interaction between claims and counter-claims of distinctive national communities, and the intra-community politics surrounding those claims, that link institutions to political outcomes.

Nationalist Mobilization and Secessionist Crises

Nationalist mobilization in multinational states, including its modalities (repertoires of mobilization and collective action, including peaceful and violent ones), goals (e.g., autonomy or independence), and outcomes (in terms of institutional, policy, and political change, as well as the reconfiguration of public discourses), has also been inadequately addressed.[23] I consider the issue of mobilization to be separate from that of institutional impact for both theoretical and methodological reasons. Institutional impact literature is largely structural, emphasizing the features of particular contexts that make specific types of mobilization more or less likely. This tells us little about the actual politics of mobilization – in all of its dynamism, strategic intentionality (including attempts by societal agents to transcend structural limits to change), and unpredictability. Moreover, addressing the politics of mobilization entails very different methodological tools, including methodologies sensitive to temporality, social psychological dynamics, emotions, and meaning. This calls for a multidisciplinary inquiry that includes methodological tools used not only by political scientists and sociologists but also by social psychologists, historians, and anthropologists.

Literature on social movements is best suited to providing insights about nationalist mobilization. Yet, paralleling the situation prevalent in the scholarship on state formation, there has been very little interaction between authors writing about social movements and those exploring the dynamics of multinationality, as McAdam, Tarrow, and Tilly acknowledged in their field-shaping volume (2001, 9). Circumstances had not changed much a decade later: witness a lone chapter dedicated to the issue of nationalism and ethnic conflict (not exclusively in multinational states) in the *Oxford Handbook of Social Movements* (Muro 2015). A major exception to this rule is Mark Beissinger's remarkable work on nationalist mobilization in the USSR, which demonstrates how collective action transforms the context in which it unfolds and creates feedback loops that transform the very assumptions guiding political behaviour (and assumptions that guide scholarly inquiry into it) (Beissinger 2002). My own contributions examine the role of event-making in the process of building support for Catalan secession (Basta 2018, 2020a). Works by Giuliano (2011), Huszka (2014), Roeder (2018), and Porta, O'Connor, and Portos (2019) have also broadened our understanding of mobilization for secession and its consequences.

Examining nationalist mobilization in multinational states will require more creative and interdisciplinary approaches. The assumption underpinning much of the existing work on nationalist mobilization and secession (see below) is that people are moved to action through individualized avenues of influence. A particular political shift – say, the loss of autonomy – is perceived by each member of the community individually and potentially transforms those individual perceptions until a critical mass is reached that leads to mobilization. This largely implicit conjecture ignores work in social and political psychology showing the role of social pressures and conformity in accounting for outcomes. Both Moscovici and Noelle-Neumann, as well as those who came in their wake, suggest that while some segment of the population may be influenced directly by external events, many are swayed by their perceptions of what others in their midst are doing (Moscovici 1976; Noelle-Neumann 1974; Noelle-Neumann and Petersen 2004). In political science, the issue was taken up by Timur Kuran in his explanation of sudden change at the end of communist era, and subsequently refined and challenged by Lustick and Miodownik (Kuran 1991; Lustick and Miodownik 2020). In other words, explaining nationalist mobilization requires understanding how it may be shaped by the emergent properties of the situation. To the best of my knowledge, few studies of mobilization in multinational states have incorporated these insights into their theoretical models.[24]

The study of secession is in significantly better shape. The institutional impact literature covered in the previous section had secession as its background motive, but it did not treat it as an analytical theme in its own right.[25] This changed with the turn of the twenty-first century, when three distinctive strands of inquiry emerged: the dataset-driven cross-sectional studies of factors increasing the likelihood of secession (Sambanis and Milanovic 2011; Sorens 2005; 2012; Siroky and Cuffe 2015); the voting behaviour literature, focusing on determinants of voter choice in independence referendums (Cuadras-Morató and Rodon 2018; Hierro and Queralt 2020; Liñeira, Henderson, and

Delaney 2017; Muro and Vlaskamp 2016; Mendelsohn 2003; Nadeau, Martin, and Blais 1999); and, finally, works on the international relations of secession, probing the conditions behind levels of success for state-seeking movements (Coggins 2014; Griffiths 2014; 2016; Fazal and Griffiths 2014). More remains to be done, however, especially in light of the shortage of accounts of mobilization flagged above and the overemphasis on structural factors driving mobilization.

Generalizability

Scholars of the multinational state will have to reckon with the pressure to produce theories that are as general as possible. Comparative political science has been particularly influenced by the notion that a more general theory is more useful and "scientific" than a less general one. According to Gerring, "if the fundamental purpose of causal argument is to tell us about the world, then it stands to reason that a proposition informing us about many events is, by virtue of this fact, more useful than a proposition applicable to only a few" (Gerring 2005, 173).[26] This logic has legitimized the construction of large datasets, and subsequent statistical analysis, as the most desirable form of systematic political research (Schedler and Mudde 2010).[27] For both methodological and theoretical reasons, scholars of the multinational state ought to meet this challenge with a healthy dose of skepticism.

The insistent pursuit of generalization provides scholars with the incentive to increase the number of observations even when that choice is analytically unjustifiable. We see this in recent studies of nationalist and ethnic conflict. Here, sophisticated methodological exercises rest on conceptually problematic foundations. For instance, Bonnie Meguid shows that decentralization of power by state-wide parties can undercut the strength of "ethnoregional parties" in general elections (Meguid 2015). Her dataset includes both nation-states, such as Germany, Denmark, Norway, and Finland, and multinational ones – Spain, Belgium, and the UK. Her conclusions about the effectiveness of decentralization are problematic, for in most of her cases – the nationally homogeneous ones – ethnoterritorial parties are marginal curiosities rather than the important elements of political systems they are in the multinational states she covers.

Massetti and Schakel, as well as Rode and co-authors, assess the influence of decentralization on the support for secession, proxied by vote for secessionist parties (Massetti and Schakel 2016; Rode et al.

2018). They too include a slew of nation-states in their datasets. Yet neither the nature of political competition nor the role of ethnoterritorial parties is the same in Spain or the UK on the one hand, and France, Germany, Netherlands, or the Czech Republic on the other. An ethnic party claiming to represent a small ethnoterritorial community, most of whose members either do not conceive of themselves as a distinctive nation, or who perhaps do but are politically and demographically marginal, is incomparable to a party representing a relatively large, nationally conscious community that can conceivably make the claim to either internal or external self-rule in the context of a state characterized by contingent legitimacy. In a similar vein, Deiwiks and co-authors examine the link between regional economic inequality and secessionist conflict (Deiwiks, Cederman, and Gleditsch 2012). Their dataset also includes national and multinational federations, despite the fact that secession is practically inconceivable in nation-states such as Argentina, Austria, or Mexico.

Because the territorial framework of a nation-state is beyond question, any challenges to it can be expected to produce "not vigorous intra-institutional competition, nor polarized and possibly violent political struggle, but a discourse marked by all but universal rejection of the idea as impossible, unimaginable, absolutely unacceptable, and *certainly irrelevant*" (Lustick 2001, 85, emphasis added). This is why any study of secession or secessionist politics that analyzes both national and multinational states is sidestepping what Mahoney and Goertz have labelled "the possibility principle." This is the injunction to select as negative cases (those where the phenomenon of interest does not occur) only those where that phenomenon is *possible* in the first place (Mahoney and Goertz 2004). Studying the importance of secessionist parties in nation-states where such a phenomenon is all but inconceivable is equivalent to starting one's desk with a car key – it just doesn't work. This is yet another reason for a separate study of the multinational state.

Yet even if more care were to go into case selection, the problems with generalizability would not disappear. There is no *a priori* reason to assume we can develop covering law models – articulating specific correlations between specific social phenomena (Hempel 1962) – that apply to all or even most multinational states. One reason for this is the normative orientation that particular populations might develop toward the concept of the state as such. It does not require much effort to imagine that the attitudes toward the state might differ between, for instance, Indigenous populations of Latin America or

post-colonial Africa and those of continental Europe or parts of the
Middle East. This may be for a variety of reasons, including the patterns and time-scales of modern state formation, the intensity of
inter-state warfare and scope of mobilization, and the degree of state
responsiveness to the population. Whatever the reason, if there is
great variation among different populations in the ways in which they
perceive the state as such, then the political dynamics in multinational
states in different parts of the world or at different times might be
qualitatively different, precluding easy theoretical generalization across
contexts. I return to this point in the concluding chapter.

FROM CRITIQUE TO THEORETICAL SYNTHESIS: LOOKING TO CHAPTER 3

This chapter paves the way for the theoretical work that follows in
three ways. First, it maps the thematic concerns of interest for students
of the multinational state. Second, it shows that most of those concerns
have received scant scholarly attention.[28] Third, it demonstrates why
insights from adjacent thematic subfields of social science may not
be useful in analyzing multinational political systems. It thus points
to the pressing need for a separate field of inquiry dedicated expressly
to the study of the multinational state. This does not imply that one
should not compare nationally homogeneous and heterogeneous
states. Indeed, answering some of the questions raised in the chapter's
introduction demands such comparisons. Nonetheless, advancing our
understanding of the multinational state requires that we stop closing
our eyes to the fact that it is subject to political dynamics of its own.

That realization is the starting point of the present book. It is on
that foundation that I build an explanatory account that combines
several themes flagged in Table 2.1. I start by explaining institutional
development (why and how central governments respond to demands
for greater autonomy and recognition by representatives of minority
nations) and then demonstrate how that development (the specific
patterns of institutional accommodation, notably with or without
major symbolic concessions) affects institutional impact, including
the conditions under which it may lead to secessionist crises.
Underpinning the causal narrative is the understanding that institutional meaning is crucial in accounting for the political dynamics of
the multinational state. The next chapter develops these elements in
greater detail.

3

Decentralization, Symbolic Recognition, and Secessionist Crises

Minority elites in multinational states almost invariably demand some form of territorial autonomy.[1] This demand has two dimensions: the instrumental and the symbolic. The *instrumental dimension* relates to the utility of territorial autonomy in achieving other goals, such as the protection of cultural, economic, or political interests of a particular community.[2] This dimension predominates in the extant literature on multinational states. The *symbolic dimension* is not only expressive of the community's identity, but also constitutive of the very national difference in the name of which instrumental claims are made. In other words, the very fact of self-government, *if appropriately signalled* in the formal organization of autonomy and the state's constitutional framework, marks off one national community from another. The institutional denial of that fact causes anxiety among members of the claimant community since it *misrecognizes* their status as a nation (Taylor 1994).

While the instrumental dimension may be important for a community's ability to sustain and protect itself, the symbolic dimension delineates the boundaries of that community, making the instrumental demands intelligible in the first place. For example, if a person considers themselves to be a member of a state-wide political community, then their region's economic underdevelopment does not register as a politically existential threat. That person can move to a different part of *their* country in pursuit of opportunity and feel as much at home *politically* as they would in their place of origin. By contrast, if the same person feels that they belong to a political community *apart*, then the economic underdevelopment of the region in which most of that community resides becomes an issue of political survival.

Seen from this perspective, migration to other parts of the country is a loss of the community's demographic substance, while permanent underdevelopment implies the inability to maintain one's own culture. Autonomy might foster economic development and the community's reproduction.[3] Yet this instrumental claim makes sense only in the context of the more fundamental symbolic demand that marks a cluster of people as a distinctive nation, apart from the rest of the country's population.

The distinction between the instrumental and symbolic dimensions of institutional claims and responses has two important corollaries. First, the two institutional dimensions are separable. Instrumental demands can be met without symbolic concessions. A community might be self-governing and in position to protect its interests without being formally recognized as a nation. The reverse is possible too: a population might be acknowledged as a nation without having recourse to extensive self-government.[4] Pointing to this separability is important because it reveals the limits of the purely instrumental view of institutions that dominates political science. As I show in the rest of the book, some of the most consequential political conflicts in multinational states result from clashes over the symbolic, rather than instrumental, properties of institutions. Second, I do not wish to overstate the distinction between the two aspects of institutional claims. An institution or a policy might be both instrumental and expressive. However, I argue that the formal architecture of the state constitutes the *dominant expression of identity*. It is, in other words, a meta-symbol, unlike other elements of the institutional landscape.

This chapter develops a model that explains how and why central governments in multinational states respond to institutional demands on both the instrumental and symbolic dimensions, and with what consequences for political stability. I start with the observation that most governments in multinational states will meet initial demands for autonomy with important but limited concessions. These will include the establishment of the institutions of self-government (parliament/executive/bureaucracy), but with limited fiscal autonomy and modest symbolic recognition.[5] Both limitations provide minority nationalists with the incentives and the discursive material with which to press for more on both scores – more autonomy, notably in the fiscal and economic domain, and more recognition, ultimately to the point of full, constitutional, and formal equality of the constituent nations.

Central governments in multinational states face two major sets of considerations when deciding how to respond to minority claims for greater autonomy and recognition. When it comes to the instrumental aspects of autonomy, particularly in the domain of fiscal and economic policy, they have to consider *whether devolving more resources and decision-making powers will influence their ability to govern* and deliver on their commitments to a broader set of constituents (i.e., beyond the minority nation). At the same time, they must be mindful of how symbolic concessions to minorities might play among the majority population. Relatively minor or discreet concessions will likely cause little consternation. But if symbolic recognition of minority claims is seen to violate the symbolic order internalized by an important segment of the majority population, such concessions can pave the way for majority backlash. This is particularly likely if said concessions entail a wholesale symbolic reconfiguration of the state. Majority backlash will then increase the likelihood of minority radicalization and secessionist crises.

A THEORY OF THE MULTINATIONAL STATE

The Political Economy Story

The starting point of this project is the recognition that levers of fiscal and economic power are a crucial object of the political struggle in multinational states. Central governments are not eager to share these levers with minority nationalists, while the latter are keen to acquire them. Minority elites insist on fiscal and economic autonomy for both policy and political reasons. Without an independent source of funding, a government's autonomy in developing its priorities and providing public goods is sharply curtailed. In addition, regional political elites will find it more difficult to build their power bases if they cannot dispense patronage and jobs, all of which hinges on their ability to obtain revenue and make distributive decisions.

Central governments, for their part, seek control over fiscal resources and economic powers the better to meet strong political cross-pressures. On the one hand, they cannot ignore minority demands for more autonomy for fear of escalating political conflict. On the other, they must be able to deliver goods to their constituents in the rest of the country.[6] If territorial autonomy of minority groups impinges on the policy-implementing capacity of the central government, demands for more self-government may go unheeded. Conversely, if enhanced fiscal autonomy for minority regions does not damage the centre's policy-implementing capacity, it is more likely to be granted.

How far territorial autonomy compromises central government goals depends on the *alignment between the strategies of governance of territorial and central governments.*[7] I define strategies of governance as durable programmatic ideas held by governing elites (Schmidt 2008, 306), together with broad policy orientations that those ideas influence. Strategies of governance determine the extent of the state's involvement in society. In the interest of parsimony, I distinguish between state-interventionist and pro-market alternatives. This corresponds to the traditional division in party politics between the left and right economic dimensions (Huber and Inglehart 1995). As a matter of political practice, these ideas and the policies they inform are far from clear-cut. Nevertheless, it is possible to identify whether a strategy of governance tends to either extreme on the basis of programmatic statements, key indicators such as public expenditure trends, and qualitative assessments of those strategies in secondary materials.

What accounts for the choice of strategies of governance? Because central government strategies are historically contingent, their origins are not easily susceptible to generalization. In all four cases examined in this book, they are a product of the idiosyncratic combination of external and internal developments. In socialist Yugoslavia, central strategies were a consequence of a heterodox approach to socialism that developed in opposition to the Soviet experience, shifting from a state-interventionist to a laissez-faire socialist model in mid-1960s. During the 1960s and 1970s the Canadian federal government pursued a qualified Keynesian strategy, influenced by the country's socioeconomic features with roots in the Great Depression and the Second World War, as well as policy solutions pursued in the United States and United Kingdom. Spanish governments of the post-Franco era were constrained both by the turn to neoliberalism in the early 1980s and by the subsequent demands of the European currency project. Finally, the strategy of governance developed by the post-communist Czechoslovak federal government was shaped by the dysfunctionality of communist political economy and the ascendant neoliberal ideas of the 1980s.

Strategies adopted by minority governments are more predictable (Massetti and Schakel 2015). Multinational states, like nation-states, tend to exhibit geographically uneven levels of economic development.

Economists explain this outcome by reference to the positive externalities resulting from economies of scale and scope.[8] Where the most important business activities, such as research and development, finance, and production, are all located in one place, the costs of doing business are lower and productivity tends to be higher. As a result, new investment usually flows to the already developed regions (Hirschman 1958; Krugman 1991; Kaldor 1972; Myrdal 1957). These developmental differences tend to correspond, however imperfectly, with national divisions, so that minority regions are generally either better or worse off than the country average in terms of key indicators such as per capita GDP, investment activity, and unemployment rates.[9]

These differences influence the strategies of governance pursued by minority governments. Elites in relatively wealthy minority regions tend to endorse pro-market policies. They do so for two reasons. First, those regions feature larger upper and middle classes that typically endorse pro-market positions (Andersen and Curtis 2015). Second, these elites understand that the cost of statist policies at the state-wide level will fall disproportionately on the residents of their region.[10] We see this pattern in both Yugoslavia and Spain, where leaders in Catalonia, the Basque Country, Croatia, and Slovenia favoured market-oriented policies. On the other hand, governments of minority regions that are less well-off relative to the country average normally endorse state-interventionist policies. These policies are meant to address the persistent underdevelopment of the regions in question, as was seen in Quebec in the 1960s and Slovakia in the early 1990s.

These policy orientations are important because they shape the *purpose* of fiscal and economic autonomy as demanded by minority nations. Enhanced fiscal and economic autonomy will serve to further the strategies of governance adopted by regional governments. The centre's willingness to accommodate demands for greater fiscal and economic autonomy hinges on whether that concession will undermine the central government's own policy-implementing capacity. Minority regional and central government strategies of governance combine in four configurations, outlined in Table 3.1. Each configuration has different implications for the possibility of accommodation, as outlined in the hypotheses that follow.

INTERVENTIONIST CENTRE, INTERVENTIONIST REGION
Governments in relatively underdeveloped regions can be expected to endorse broadly statist solutions to the economic challenges facing them. Regional state intervention aims to address persistent economic

Table 3.1
Argument outline: The political economy story
,

		Claimant government	
		Pro-market	State-interventionist
Central government	Pro-market	Aligned strategies (Facilitating accommodation)	Conflicting strategies (Hindering accommodation)
	State-interventionist	Conflicting strategies (Hindering accommodation)	Aligned strategies (Facilitating accommodation)

deficiencies of such territories, enhancing the prosperity of members of the minority nation. Far-reaching fiscal and economic autonomy is seen as indispensable for the achievement of that goal.[11] If the central government adopts a statist strategy of governance as well, the likelihood of concessions increases. The relative underdevelopment of the minority region implies the prosperity of majority regions. Forgoing fiscal resources in favour of a minority region is thus not as daunting as it is where the majority regions are relatively poor and thus where minority regions are wealthy (see *statist centre/pro-market region* configuration). This is because the central government's core programs can be funded by the tax base of the more developed *majority* regions, whose populations identify with the common state project and are more likely than a wealthy minority to accept the burden of state-wide redistribution.[12] In addition, alignment on the same policy paradigm means that while there can be conflict as to the specifics of program implementation, there is overall agreement on broad policy goals.

PRO-MARKET CENTRE, INTERVENTIONIST REGION
Where a relatively underdeveloped statist regional executive faces a pro-market central government, its demands for greater fiscal and economic autonomy are unlikely to be met. Pro-market governments emphasize fiscal restraint, low taxation, and relatively low government spending, all of which are meant to facilitate the workings of the market mechanism. Extensive fiscal autonomy for a statist regional government entails public spending patterns that are likely to undermine the fiscally conservative project of the central government.

Consequently, the central government can be expected to either pre-clude far-reaching decentralization or to try to undermine it should it be granted.

INTERVENTIONIST CENTRE, PRO-MARKET REGION

Wealthier minority regions tend to be led by governments that endorse pro-market strategies of governance. Minority elites under this con-figuration are especially sensitive to the redistributive consequences of central government policies, aware that their regions will make disproportionate contributions to the central budget. The goal of their demands for fiscal and economic autonomy – normally implying the retention of a greater proportion of revenues in the territory in which they are raised – is to scale back this inter-territorial redistribution. Statist central governments will view autonomy for pro-market minor-ity regions as a direct danger to their ability to implement their strate-gies of governance, since it will entail a loss of crucial revenue for the implementation of state-wide policy initiatives. This is so because the minority region is wealthier than the country average, an issue that is amplified if the region in question accounts for a large propor-tion of the overall tax revenue.[13]

PRO-MARKET CENTRE, PRO-MARKET REGION

Pro-market governments in wealthy minority regions can expect an easier path to accommodation if the central government adopts a similar strategy of governance. As noted, a pro-market central govern-ment will endorse relatively low (or declining) levels of taxation and expenditure and emphasize balanced budgets. Extending greater fiscal and economic autonomy to a similarly market-oriented minority government is unlikely to undermine the central government's fiscally conservative strategy of governance. However, central government's pro-market stance will be tempered by the demands for redistribution emanating from the less developed regions of the country that con-stitute the bulk of the population.

Findings

The four configurations of governing strategies of central and claim-ant governments have been approximated in four multinational states since the second half of the twentieth century: Canada, Spain, the former Yugoslavia, and the former Czechoslovakia. While these cases

Table 3.2
Case selection

		Claimant government	
		Pro-market	State-interventionist
Central government	Pro-market	Spain/Catalonia (1980–) Yugoslavia/Croatia (1964–)	Czechoslovakia/Slovakia (1989–92)
	State-interventionist	Yugoslavia/Croatia (1950s–1964)	Canada/Quebec (1960–1984)

do not fit the model perfectly, one would be hard pressed to find real-world instances that come as close. The cases are classified in Table 3.2, where they replace the abstract configurations of Table 3.1. The summary of the findings related to the book's instrumental argument is presented in Table 3.3. In most cases, major policy-related demands have been rejected or accepted in line with the theory's expectations. In cases where strategies of governance were aligned, the accommodation process was fairly extensive, with key policy competencies and resources transferred to the claimant territorial governments, though not without exceptions. Where the strategies clashed, accommodation was less far-reaching. Nevertheless, the causal pattern is more complex than suggested by this static representation. A key factor complicating the picture is the role played by the symbolic meaning of the institutions in question.

The Symbolic Politics Story

Institutions are clearly important for what they *do* to and for the political actors in multinational states. This extends not only to the resources they might funnel to minority nations, as is the case with fiscal and economic autonomy, but also to social models (autonomy over social policy), physical security (jurisdiction over regional security forces), and the protection of culture (control of education and language policy). As noted in the previous chapter, most scholarship on the multinational state focuses on these instrumental aspects of institutions.

Table 3.3
The political economy story: Summary of findings

Case	Core policy demand	Expectation	Outcome confirmed?	Comment
Canada (aligned)	Program opt-outs with fiscal compensation	Accommodation	Yes	Pension opt-out but Victoria Charter demands rejected
Czechoslovakia (clashing)	Greater fiscal and monetary autonomy	Rejection	Yes	Initial increase in fiscal autonomy due to democratization
Spain (aligned)	Greater fiscal autonomy, creation of new fiscal system	Accommodation	Partially	Gradual transfer of tax revenue, but rejection of separate fiscal structure (2005)
Yugoslavia to 1964 (clashing)	Greater fiscal autonomy, transfer of investment decisions	Rejection	Yes (prior to late 1960s)	Limited fiscal/ investment autonomy prior to late 60s
Yugoslavia after 1964 (aligned)	Greater fiscal autonomy, investment decisions, foreign currency	Accommodation	Yes	In parallel with transfer of authority, establishment of an investment fund

Much of that work reflects the assumptions of historical and rational choice institutionalists. For the former, institutions are "formal rules, compliance procedures, and standard operating practices that structure the relationship between individuals in various units of the polity and economy" (Thelen and Steinmo 1992, 2). Institutions channel and privilege certain political options in path-dependent ways.[14] Rational choice institutionalists also view institutions as rules, albeit of a different nature. For North (1990), they are "rules of the game in a society or, more formally ... the humanly devised constraints that shape human interaction," a view shared by others (North and Thomas 1970, 5; Ostrom 1986, 5). Here, however, institutions are deployed to resolve the central issue of coordination – the collective action problem.[15] They reduce transaction costs (facilitating cooperation that would otherwise not take place), or signal credible commitment to cooperation (North and Weingast 1989). This understanding of institutions is unduly restrictive, standing in the way of a more acute understanding of the politics of multinational states.

Sociological institutionalists work with a more expansive understanding of institutions as both rules and *symbols*.[16] Institutions regulate and structure political action and are in this sense instrumental, but are simultaneously expressive and *constitutive* of a particular reality. For Friedland and Alford, "institutions are supraorganizational patterns of human activity by which individuals and organizations produce and reproduce their material subsistence and organize time and space. They are also symbolic systems, ways of ordering reality, and thereby rendering experience of time and space meaningful" (1991, 241). Institutions are also myths that "reflect widespread understandings of social reality" (Meyer and Rowan 1977, 343) and act as "receptacles of group idealism" (Scott 1987, 494). Indeed, the *formal* organization of an institution can express specific visions of society (Meyer and Rowan 1977, 346). Institutional innovation can lead to loss of institutional legitimacy when it departs from the societal "script." It need not be the instrumental disutility of the proposed institutional change that causes opposition, but a violation of the symbolic order that such a proposal might entail (Friedland and Alford 1991, 250–1). This dynamic is at the core of the conflict in multinational states.

Sociological institutionalists base their claims about the symbolic role of institutions on the contradiction between their expressive purpose and the instrumental ends they purportedly serve. A symbolically appropriate set of rules might be downright wasteful from the instrumental perspective (Meyer and Rowan 1977, 355). This means that institutions often formally express one kind of reality while informally functioning in ways that directly contradict that expression (357). Finally, in their symbolic role, institutions *constitute* the social world. The enactment of institutional rules serves both to manifest the collectively agreed-upon social reality and "create the subjectivities" at its root, *and* to reproduce its symbolic order (Friedland and Alford 1991, 248–50). More specifically, institutional roles as they are enacted can constitute the very identity of those who perform them (Clemens and Cook 1999, 454).

The distinction between the instrumental and symbolic dimensions of institutions is about the *difference of institutional purpose*. From the instrumental perspective, an institution is *a means* to an end. Viewed from the symbolic standpoint, an institution is *an end in itself*. Rather than a lever with which one accomplishes specific goals, it is an expression of a particular value or identity. Scholars of voting behaviour have developed a similar dichotomy juxtaposing instrumental and expressive voting (Hamlin and Jennings 2011). One who votes instrumentally is doing so in order to induce secondary outcomes – the act is not meaningful in itself. Conversely, one who votes expressively is doing so primarily because the act conveys meaning. In her contribution to the study of self-determination struggles, Kelle similarly differentiates between the symbolic dimension of territory on the one hand, and its strategic and material value on the other (Kelle 2017). The difference between the symbolic and instrumental dimensions of institutions echoes these dichotomies. While political actors may invoke either or both of the two institutional dimensions in political contests (e.g., this institutional proposal harms or advances our interests versus this institutional proposal denies or advances recognition of our identity), their ability to do this depends on the *a priori* availability of these two categories. The *political instrumentalization* of the two dimensions, in other words, presupposes their existence.

An institution can, of course, serve a dual purpose: it may be both an instrument and a symbol. These two dimensions are separable, however. An institution may provide members of a community with the means to protect their interests while failing to express their collective identity.[17] It is also possible for an institution to express collective identity without facilitating interest protection. These possibilities are important to consider because of what they tell us about the political effects of institutional change and continuity. *Institutional change that appears to misrecognize a particular community may produce a vehement reaction even if it means relatively little in instrumental terms.*

These insights are of profound relevance for the politics of the multinational state. In a nation-state, the symbolic order expressed in the polity's organization and codified in its constitution is, in the public narrative, deproblematized to the point of invisibility. In a multinational state, the symbolic order as expressed in state institutions can antagonize members of minority nations if it fails to express the minority's vision of a plurinational political reality and, by extension, its status as a full-fledged national community.[18] At the same time, attempts to align the state's symbolic order with the plurinational vision endorsed by members of minority nations may be seen as illegitimate by members of the majority.

Majorities are more likely to identify with the common state than are minorities (Elkins and Sides 2007; Staerklé et al. 2010). This is because overarching political identity and state institutions normally rest on the historical experience, symbols, and organizations of majority communities.[19] As the empirical chapters will show, majorities are also more likely to adopt a monist political view of both the state and the political community therein. They tend to resist the notion that "their" state is an institutional expression of multiple national projects. System justification theory offers additional psychological mechanisms accounting for majority opposition to attempts to alter the symbolic configuration of the state. Those who see the existing system as legitimate – "system justifiers" – not only oppose changes to the existing state of affairs but also disparage the perceived initiators of that change (Jost, Ledgerwood, and Hardin 2008, 174). Where the majority is open to including minorities in the superordinate identity (e.g., Canadian, Indian, British), members of majority communities become less able to perceive the residual unfairness of the system (Dovidio et al. 2016, 26).[20]

Simply put, political conflict in multinational states is about *whose story gets institutionalized*. Institutionalizing the majority story may be interpreted as a misrecognition of the minority's view of themselves and of the state. By the same token, institutionalizing the minority narrative can be interpreted as a misrecognition of the majority's view of themselves and of the political community. Moreover, as I show in the case of Yugoslavia, even if the majority elite accepts the idea of the state as nationally plural, there is always the issue of fair and appropriate expression of that multinationality. A key symbolic element in three of the four cases covered in the book is the question of formal territorial a/symmetry. It was accompanied, in all four cases, with a clash over formal constitutional, or quasi-constitutional, recognition of minority nationhood.

None of this means that conflicts over instrumental issues, such as the division of powers or resources, are unimportant. However, two features of the symbolic aspect of institutions make them more politically combustible – and thus more likely to stimulate broad-based and enduring conflict – than instrumental ones. First, *symbolic issues are more cognitively accessible* – easier to grasp – than are instrumental ones. Instrumental matters such as the division of powers between levels of government, rules over fiscal redistribution, and patterns of bureaucratic staffing are complex and difficult to make sense of.[21] Their consequences for the distribution of power among levels of government are ambiguous. An instrumental institutional reform can simultaneously strengthen and weaken a particular government (Broschek, Petersohn, and Toubeau 2017), and decentralization might undercut rather than strengthen the effectiveness of a regional government (Falleti 2005). Even politicians and legal experts frequently find it difficult to know whether a reform helps or hurts their cause over the long run.

By contrast, the meaning and importance of the symbolic aspects of institutions are far easier to apprehend. The significance of calling one group a nation, and giving it "special status," or refusing to do so, is much more apparent than the intricacies of, say, a federation's fiscal redistribution formula. These assertions are borne out by the voting behaviour literature. Voters are more easily motivated by the "easy issues," which are at once symbolic (rather than technically demanding), concern outcomes rather than (complex) processes, and are usually familiar to the general public, having been "on the agenda" for prolonged periods of time (Carmines and Stimson 1980, 80).

Second, *symbolic aspects of institutions are more likely to be emotionally evocative* than instrumental ones and can therefore facilitate political mobilization more easily. Since institutional symbols speak to the very identity of entire communities, the perceived erosion of symbolic recognition is simultaneously a blow against collective selfhood. Recent work in social psychology and international relations addresses this erosion as a challenge to ontological security – a consistent sense of one's own identity necessary in order to ward off anxiety about the uncertainty of the world (Kinnvall 2004, 746; Mitzen 2006, 344; Rumelili 2015, 4). This is why symbolic issues are such potent motivators of political action, as both social psychologists (Sears 1993, 121; Huddy 2003) and scholars of ethnic and nationalist politics note (Horowitz 1985; Kaufman 2001, 2015; Anthony Smith 2009).

This is not to say that instrumental issues cannot foster mobilization. However, because of their complexity and their seemingly mundane and undramatic quality, they are less likely to gain emotional traction. Of course, arguably all aspects of institutions or policy could be converted into symbols. Still, not all are *easily* convertible into symbols, and not all symbols are *equally potent*. The more cognitively demanding a policy issue, the more difficult it is to present it as a politically potent symbol, as research on voting behaviour suggests. More importantly, the organization of the state is a political meta-symbol, far more important than most others. This is because the state is arguably the highest expression of the political community (Walzer 1967).

This view of institutions as symbols informs the hypotheses developed for the second part of the argument, expressed graphically in Figure 3.1. The causal narrative is as follows. Because of the limited fiscal autonomy and symbolic recognition in the early stages of autonomy, representatives of a minority nation advance their claims for greater decision rights and recognition. In this first phase of the process (Round 1), the central government weighs the instrumental demand, and if the political economy configuration allows it (see previous section), it grants substantial new resources to the claimant government. At this stage, the symbolic demand remains unaddressed.

This has an ambiguous effect on minority politics. The concession makes it possible for minority moderates to argue that further accommodation is possible. At the same time, the lack of recognition strengthens minority radicals, though not to the point of dominance. The competition between the two camps results in the escalation in the scope of minority demands and in the character of the mobilization, which gains broader support and may involve extra-partisan activism. The pursuit of symbolic recognition assumes greater prominence and is more forcefully pressed, alongside renewed instrumental claims for more powers or resources. The looping shape of Figure 3.1 suggests this return to the initial claim, albeit one that is now of greater intensity.

An important corollary is that the absence of symbolic concessions to the minority position during Round 1 makes it difficult for the "defenders" of the majority vision of the state to mobilize. I therefore *do not expect to see majority backlash during this stage*. While the instrumental concessions might provoke a degree of resentment among those identifying primarily with the common state, that resentment will lack the potency needed to power sustained political mobilization – either among the general population or among state-wide parties – against the minority national project. Instrumental concessions are not likely to threaten the idea of the state as an expression of a single political community that majorities tend to endorse.

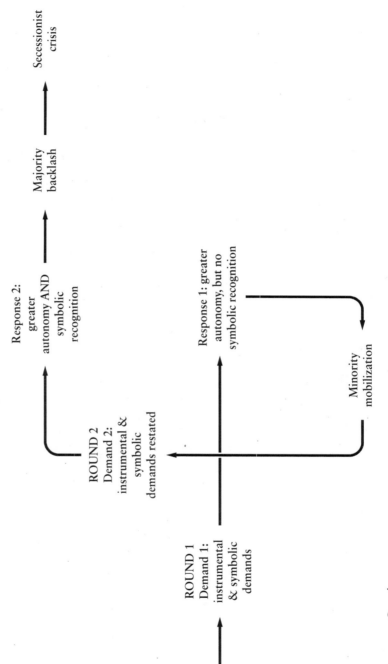

Figure 3.1 Causal process summary

The ramped-up minority mobilization for more autonomy and recognition leads to *Round 2* of the process. The escalation in claims and mobilization becomes a more serious threat to the political stability of the state, increasing the likelihood that the central government will now combine instrumental and symbolic concessions. If and when this happens, the stage is set for majority backlash. Symbolic concessions are normally simpler, more visible, and more emotionally evocative than instrumental ones. The expression of nationhood for the minority nation in the constitution or a quasi-constitutional text, combined with clearly asymmetric treatment of the minority territorial unit, results in a reconstitution of the symbolic order that many members of the majority may not be willing to condone. The rising resentment clears the path to open political mobilization among the majority population and political elites against this concession.

Once this opposition materializes, it contributes to the radicalization of the minority population through three mechanisms. First, open opposition to the symbolic recognition of minority nationhood is qualitatively different from opposition to technical issues such as decision rights or fiscal redistribution. It is a direct and explicit repudiation of the minority's self-conception as a nation and their view of the state as a multinational community. Second, that mobilization will increase the likelihood that the initial symbolic concession will be rescinded, resulting in an obvious loss for the minority nation. The psychological effect of this can be devastating, as suggested by prospect theory (Mercer 1995). Third, these developments will weaken the moderates among the minority and may set in motion an outbidding spiral among minority parties, leading them to more radical positions. This is likely to result in an increase in support for secession and in the greater willingness of minority political parties to take steps toward independence.

In three of the cases – Canada, Spain, and Yugoslavia – during the first round the centre yielded on instrumental demands without moving on symbolic ones. At this stage in none of the cases was there concerted politicized majority backlash against minority claims. The government of Quebec obtained some of the key instrumental concessions during the 1960s and 70s, but there was little by way of explicit recognition of Quebec as a "distinct society." Indeed, the concessions were frequently symmetrized in order to avoid the appearance of Quebec's exceptionality. As expected, there was no major political mobilization among Canada-wide parties against this. Likewise, the government of Catalonia won more power and resources during the 1980s and 90s, though not as much of either as it demanded. Again, there was little explicit symbolic recognition here, and unsurprisingly, no majority backlash. Finally, in the Yugoslav case we see Croatia and Slovenia gaining ground on instrumental demands during the second half of the 1960s and early 1970s, once the federal strategy of governance changed. No major symbolic concessions were made during the 1960s, and we also do not see concerted mobilization among members of the largest nation, the Serbs, against these concessions.[22]

In all three cases, we see increased minority mobilization in Round 2. In Quebec, that mobilization culminated in the election of the sovereignist Parti Québécois in 1976, followed by the 1980 referendum on sovereignty-association. In Catalonia, the largest political parties, secessionist and non-secessionist ones, stepped up their demands for a new Statute of Autonomy in the early 2000s. In Croatia, a similar scenario played out during the late 1960s and particularly in 1970–71, during the Croatian Spring. At this point, the cultural society Matica hrvatska played the role of a *de facto* opposition party, pushing the Croatian League of Communists to more radical positions.

As expected, during Round 2 in all three cases the central government moved to accommodate both instrumental and symbolic demands. In Canada, the core symbolic issue was the constitutional recognition of Quebec as a "distinct society," something that the federal government accepted in the Meech Lake (1987) and Charlottetown (1992) accords. In Catalonia, the central government recognized Catalonia as a "nation" in the new statute adopted by the Spanish Socialist government in 2006.[23] In Yugoslavia, constitutional reforms between 1970 and 1974 in effect converted the country from a federation to a confederation; they also constitutionalized the status of the republics, including Croatia, as national states. This abandonment of official Yugoslavism was exacerbated by the asymmetric arrangement under which the largest nation's republic – Serbia – was the only one that was itself internally federalized.

In all three cases, symbolic concessions – or attempts to implement them – would foster majority political mobilization. In Canada, this was manifested in the rise of the Reform Party, explicitly opposed to Quebec's distinct status, and in opposition to the Meech Lake and Charlottetown accords by an important segment of the Liberal Party of Canada and key provincial leaders. Provincial opposition precluded the passage of both accords. This led directly to growth in support for independence in Quebec to a point not seen during the 1970s. In Spain, the reference to Catalan nationhood in the new regional statute prompted the opposition Popular Party to mobilize both in the parliamentary arena and through highly visible extra-parliamentary initiatives (demonstrations, petitions) against the statute's passage. Ultimately, the Popular Party would sponsor a court challenge that would reduce the scope of Catalonia's autonomy and, notably, interpret the reference to nationhood as lacking legal force. This opposition helped mainstream Catalan secessionism by 2012, eventually leading to the attempt to hold a unilateral referendum on independence in 2017.

In Yugoslavia, Serb backlash developed more slowly, in part, though not entirely, due to the authoritarian character of the regime. Many Serbs found the changes of the 1970s doubly problematic. The symbolic concessions granted to the republics undermined the idea of Yugoslavism that was particularly resonant among the Serbs. At the same time, for many Serbs the promise of national equality under the more explicitly multinational framework appeared unfulfilled because of the asymmetry it engendered, with Serbia being the only internally divided republic. The political mobilization against the new institutional status quo first took place behind closed doors, subsequently made its way through the Serbian intelligentsia, and emerged in the public arena in the second half of the 1980s in the person of Slobodan Milošević. Milošević would move against the institutional order created by the 1974 constitution, thereby boosting support for independence first in Slovenia and then in Croatia.

Czechoslovakia offers a useful counterpoint. Here, the period under examination is much shorter – three years between the end of communism in 1989 and the dissolution of the country in 1993. By contrast to the other cases, the strategies of governance adopted by the centre and the claimant government continued to diverge. As a result, the central government refused to accommodate some of Slovakia's more far-reaching instrumental demands for fiscal and economic autonomy. The response to Slovak elites' symbolic demands was more equivocal. On the one hand, in the negotiations on the future constitutional agreement, the federal (and Czech) elites regularly acknowledged the country's multinational character and recognized Slovakia as the state of the Slovak nation. This recognition did not elicit majority backlash since it did not deviate significantly from the symbolic logic already institutionalized in the 1968 federal reforms. By contrast, the federal elites rejected Slovakia's new symbolic claim – that democratic Czechoslovakia's constitution be rooted in a "state treaty" between the Czech and Slovak Republics.

The Czechoslovak case corroborates the model's theoretical expectations. In the absence of comprehensive symbolic reconfiguration of the state framework, no majority political party mobilized against the Slovak demands. As expected, without majority backlash, support for secession among members of the minority nation remained low. Public opinion surveys conducted during this period never showed more than 20 per cent of Slovaks supporting independence. As significantly, Slovakia's largest political parties did not adopt independence as their immediate policy goal. The country's break-up was a result not of a secessionist crisis, but rather of elite agreement devised to resolve a political impasse over clashing institutional and policy goals.

This argument covers some of the same ground as two recent contributions to the debates on secessionist mobilization, complementing them in important ways. Philip Roeder's book explains how secessionist movements mobilize otherwise heterogeneous populations behind a single goal – independence (Roeder 2018). The "platform population" that the secessionists seek to win over consists of enthusiasts, or true believers in independent statehood; expressionists, motivated primarily by participation in campaigns; and pragmatists, individuals who are largely indifferent to secession but who could be persuaded to endorse it if properly motivated (2018, 10). Since enthusiasts and expressionists constitute only a fraction of the relevant population, the key challenge is to bring the more numerous pragmatists on board (2018, 156).

That challenge can be met by convincing enough pragmatists that independence will address their individual *material* aspirations (Roeder 2018, 51, 71, 75). Thus, rather than being motivated by high-minded considerations or by grievance, most eventual supporters of independence are likely to be won over if they can be persuaded that independence is going to make their lives better. Given enough time and resources, most of those people could be converted into true believers. Since resources are scarce, the instrumental sales pitch is likely to be the second best (and the only optimal) solution for advocates of secession (2018, 75). In addition to being motivated by material "carrots," members of the minority nation will support independence if they believe that most of their compatriots will do the same (2018, 8) and if they face social, economic, or political pressures to give up on the common state (2018, 118).

There is a problem here that cannot be undone from within Roeder's argument. The conversion of pragmatists to independentists through the above-outlined mechanisms presupposes that a critical mass of such individuals has already been won over. For independence to appear as a viable solution to most people's parochial problems, it must already be seen as a likely prospect. That is to say, it must already have attracted a substantial and visible proportion of the "platform population." This is even more important if social pressure is to be exerted on members of the minority nation who might support the status quo. That mechanism cannot be operational unless a significant part of the population is already hostile to the territorial/institutional status quo and thus sufficiently powerful to effectively penalize "defectors" from the secessionist project.

This book furnishes the missing ingredient by showing how and why such intermediate mobilization may occur. Note, though, that the argument inverts Roeder's logic. It is not the parochial material issues that sovereign statehood promises to satisfy, but the reversal of direction on symbolic institutional concessions, that explains the surge in support for independence. To the extent to which material arguments are used in order to support the political breach that secession constitutes, they may be more important in rationalizing what are fundamentally emotional and non-material motives. I do not claim that beyond that point Roeder's mechanisms may not be operational, but they require the prior massification of support for independence in order to do the work Roeder expects them to.

André Lecours's upcoming book similarly addresses the rise in support for secession over time (Lecours 2020; forthcoming). Here, it is the inflexibility of central governments in allowing for further accommodation of minority claims that makes it possible for secessionists to win more adherents. Lecours's argument is thus similar to the one advanced in this book in that its focus is on collective grievance rooted in institutional politics. In those cases where the claimant community's demands for more extensive autonomy continue to be met, secessionism does not stand much of a chance, as in Flanders and South Tyrol. However, if the central government places an upper limit on further gains in autonomy, it creates conditions for resentment among members of claimant nations and thus prepares the way for an upsurge in support for independence. Lecours uses the Catalan and Scottish cases to make his point.

There are several points of productive complementarity and tension between Lecours's work and the argument advanced here. Both accounts foreground the role of *institutional dynamics* in accounting for the rise in support for secession. Moreover, both emphasize the importance of interaction between claimant communities and central governments in explaining secessionist dynamics. The distinguishing feature of this book is the distinction it draws between the symbolic and instrumental aspects of institutional change and the ways in which these drive the conflict between the minority and majority/state-wide national projects. The book thus offers additional insights into the limits of accommodation of nationalist claims that drive secessionism, complementing Lecours's work.

METHODOLOGY, CASE SELECTION, AND EVIDENCE

The Political Economy Story – Methodological Note

Each of the two arguments developed in the previous section required a distinctive methodological approach. The study's starting point is a model addressing the link between the political economy of multinational states and the ability of central governments to address minority demands for greater fiscal and economic autonomy. To assess the model's validity, I opted for a standard structured, focused comparison (George and Bennett 2004, Ch. 3). The comparison required at least four cases, which were selected according to two criteria. First, each case reflected one of the four combinations of policy strategies adopted by the two orders of government (central and claimant). In other words, I selected these cases on the independent variable for the purposes of testing the political economy hypotheses, and then continued to explore the symbolic logic of accommodation in each instance.

Second, I selected cases that were sufficiently comparable and that thus minimized unit heterogeneity. Given the complexity and sociopolitical idiosyncrasies of multinational states, no case selection will be problem-free. Nevertheless, the four cases compared here are similar in some fundamental ways that set them apart from other multinational systems. These similarities allow for the necessary minimum of comparability as well as the elimination of at least some competing explanations. All four of the cases in this study are unambiguously multinational states, with each containing at least one minority nation with a long-standing self-determination claim. This is not a characteristic of many countries that have experienced fleeting demands for self-determination.[24] Broad institutional features provide further grounds for comparability. All four of the minority nations at the centre of this study possessed some minimal level of territorial autonomy at the beginning of the periods examined. In addition, all of the cases are similar to one another in terms of "stateness."[25]

In demographic terms, all of the minority nations included in this study form a significant proportion of their state's population (between 15 and 30 per cent). This distinguishes them from smaller groups with a history of self-determination claims that can be more easily accommodated and more easily sidelined.[26] All four countries are also moderately sized and populated (from Czechoslovakia's 15 million to Spain's 47 million), with two accompanying implications. First, none are characterized by the super-diversity of an India or a Nigeria.[27] Second, since none of the countries under study are major powers, all are foreign policy takers.[28] Consequently, they are unable to dominate minority movements in the way that some of the larger powers could. While it would be difficult to demonstrate decisively that these factors have not played a role in accounting for the differences between these cases, the similarities reduce this likelihood.

Despite the parallels, each case has its idiosyncrasies. The most obvious difference is between Yugoslavia and the other three countries. It is possible that Yugoslavia's authoritarianism accounts for the pattern of institutional development one can observe there. However, the Yugoslav case is a puzzling example of an authoritarian regime that was willing to tolerate the emergence of alternative centres of power through political decentralization during the 1960s and 1970s. The advantage of including Yugoslavia in the study is that the regime shifted from a state-interventionist to a pro-market strategy of governance during this time period, providing a within-case counterfactual. So, if anything, the Yugoslav case provides an important test of the propositions articulated in this book. Moreover, if a similar dynamic related to the symbolic importance of institutions can be observed across regime types, the utility of the theoretical framework should be greater. The Czechoslovak case is distinguished both by the transitional character of its democracy and by its brief duration compared to the other three cases. The explanatory narrative in Chapter 7, and the comparison with the other three cases, will, nevertheless, demonstrate that the process of (non)-accommodation of Slovak claims and the resulting political outcome were both strongly influenced by the factors outlined in this chapter.

Another key difference concerns the institutional framework that distinguishes Spain and Canada from Czechoslovakia and Yugoslavia. The first two cases are what Broschek (2011) calls "self-rule" territorial regimes, with the latter two being "shared-rule" federations. In the former, the constitution does not provide for the formal inclusion of territorial units in the central decision-making process. In the latter, the units are an inherent part of the central decision-making mechanism. While these differences have invariably influenced the pattern of accommodation, especially in Czechoslovakia, where shared-rule institutions preceded the start of negotiations, the differences should not be exaggerated. In Canada, for instance, the institutional framework allowed the provinces a degree of control over the development of federal policy initiatives that replicated to a certain extent the kind of power that Slovak MPs had over federal legislation in Prague. Yet the differences in outcomes on political economy issues in particular are quite stark.

The four cases also diverge in terms of the number of self-determination movements. Where Spain contained at least three, and Yugoslavia potentially six, Canada and Czechoslovakia had only one movement each.[29] One might expect that the political elites in states with a larger number of minority nations would be more cautious in extending territorial autonomy for fear of contagion.[30] However, no such correlation held in the four cases analyzed in this thesis. Though containing only one minority nation, Czechoslovakia and Canada displayed different accommodative patterns. Spain and Yugoslavia, each containing several minority nations, also exhibited divergent trends in decentralization at different times.

The Symbolic Politics Story – A Methodological Note

While a static comparison between four cases sufficed to ascertain whether or not specific political economy configurations shaped instrumental concessions as predicted, a different approach was needed in order to test the hypotheses associated with the pattern of symbolic concessions outlined in Figure 3.1. I chose the same cases to assess whether the predictions about the process of accommodation I make in the model are valid. This is a major methodological strength of the study. The cases were selected on the independent variable on a once-removed set of hypotheses. In other words, they were chosen in order to test propositions unrelated to the symbolic politics argument. This *case recycling* ensures that the conclusions are not biased as a result of either conscious or subconscious cherry-picking of cases.

The approach I deploy is comparative process tracing. Process-tracing is a method of causal inference based on testing hypotheses about dynamic historical processes. It consists of three elements. First, it requires the development of a clear, explicit set of hypotheses about causal mechanisms that induce particular outcomes (Bennett and Checkel 2015b, 9). These mechanisms are by definition not one-off events, but rather sequences of occurrences that constitute temporally extended social developments. Second, the method entails the identification of observable implications of those hypotheses. The researcher must outline what they expect to find if the hypotheses are correct, as well as what would count as disconfirming evidence (Bennett and Checkel 2015, 18). Third, it requires the researcher to gather empirical material and identify *causal process observations* (cpos) – that is to say, the instances of those observable implications – in the process constructing an explanatory narrative and assessing the degree to which that narrative conforms to the theory's expectations (Rohlfing 2013). Key to this enterprise is ascertaining whether the evidence supports the researcher's theory or an alternative account of the same developments. This approach is normally used to develop and test hypotheses against a single historical process. In this case, the method is used comparatively (Bengtsson and Ruonavaara 2017), in part because I believe that a successful test of the model's hypotheses against a larger number of processes would increase my confidence in the strength of the theoretical framework.

Since I emphasize the importance of symbolic over instrumental aspects of institutions in accounting for the political dynamics of multinational states, the observable implications I identify relate to both perspectives (see Table 3.4). On the majority side, I expect that instrumental concessions to minority nations without accompanying symbolic shifts should not result in majority backlash. Obversely, major symbolic concessions to minority communities ought to spur majority mobilization. The absence of those outcomes should weaken my hypotheses, and if these outcomes were to be disconfirmed in all cases, the

Table 3.4
Summary of causal process observations

Expected observable implications	Theory-confirming CPOs	Theory-disconfirming CPOs	Ambiguous CPOs
No symbolic concession, no majority backlash	Canada Round 1 Spain Round 1 Yugoslavia Round 1	None	None
Symbolic concession, majority backlash	Canada Round 2 Spain Round 2 Yugoslavia Round 2	None	Czechoslovakia (symbolic recognition granted *and* withheld – no majority backlash)
No majority backlash, no secessionist crisis	Czechoslovakia	None	Canada Round 1 (No majority backlash, but a referendum held, support of 40%)
Majority backlash, secessionist crisis	Canada Round 2 Spain Round 2 Yugoslavia Round 2	None	None

hypotheses should be rejected. Thus, an instrumental concession not accompanied by a symbolic one, followed by open, politicized majority backlash, would constitute theory-disconfirming evidence. Likewise, a major symbolic concession not accompanied by majority backlash would constitute a disconfirming causal process observation (CPO).

Moving to the minority side of the ledger, I anticipate that majority backlash against symbolic concessions to minority nations will stimulate minority secessionism and lead to a secessionist crisis. The absence of such backlash, by the same token, ought not to be followed by a secessionist surge. A CPO where majority backlash was not accompanied by a rise in support for secession to near or above 50 per cent, and minority political parties did not engage in a sustained campaign for independence, would count as disconfirming evidence. I would likewise consider a spike in secessionist support in the absence of majority backlash as a disconfirming CPO.[31] Table 3.4 compares the theory's expectations to the findings detailed in the causal narratives in the next four chapters. The table formalizes – albeit in a static manner – the findings that in the empirical chapters take a narrative, dynamic form. The results are striking – there is not a single theory-disconfirming CPO in any of the four cases. By contrast, nearly all relevant CPOs corroborate the theory's expectations.

The empirical work produced two ambiguous CPOs. First, the Czechoslovak context featured fairly extensive symbolic concessions to the Slovak side, but majority backlash predicted by the theory failed to materialize. This finding could count as a disconfirming CPO, but I characterize it as an ambiguous observation for two reasons. First, the symbolic concessions did not constitute a departure from previous political practice. Certainly, each round of constitutional negotiations recognized the Slovak and Czech Republics as homelands of their titular nations, and Czechoslovakia as a federation of the two republics. However, this principle of binationality was already institutionalized in the 1968 federal constitution. The Czech elites and the population at large had two decades during which they were socialized into the formal recognition of the country's binationality. Second, the qualitatively new Slovak demand for a state treaty as the basis of a new constitution was rejected repeatedly by the federal and Czech negotiators. The Czech elites' attitude to this new claim was, in fact, reflective of the Czech population's preference for a more integrated state framework, as revealed in opinion surveys at the time. Overall, the partial accommodation of Slovak symbolic demands did not constitute a comprehensive symbolic reconfiguration of the state.

The second ambiguous CPO concerns the developments in Quebec between 1976 and 1980. The model predicts that, in the absence of majority backlash, there will be no spike in support for independence among the minority population. Likewise, minority political parties should not adopt independence as their immediate policy goal. The election of the secessionist Parti Québécois in 1976, and a referendum on independence in 1980 during which 40 per cent of the population supported sovereignty, could, in the absence of majority backlash, be interpreted as a disconfirming CPO.

I consider these outcomes to be ambiguous for the following reasons. First, the election of the PQ in 1976 did not reflect a rise in support for independence, but rather the deep unpopularity of the incumbent federalist Liberal Party of Quebec. Indeed, the PQ managed to win only after it moderated its stance on secession – promising it would negotiate sovereignty-association with Canada rather than proclaim independence in the event that it won in any future referendum. In fact, the party's electoral fortunes might have been even greater had it not pursued a constitutional break with Canada. Second, the 40 per cent that the sovereignty-association option attracted in the 1980 referendum should be viewed with some skepticism. Support for outright independence in Quebec never exceeded 20 per cent during the 1970s. The sovereignty-association on which the provincial population voted was a compromise version of independence that would have combined political separation with continued economic integration with Canada. The contrast with early 1990s Quebec could not be more stark – support for sovereignty-association exceeded 60 per cent, and close to 50 per cent of Quebeckers actually supported independence.

GUIDE TO EMPIRICAL CHAPTERS

All but one of the empirical chapters are organized on the same template, outlined in Figure 3.2. Following the introduction, each features a brief historical sketch of the nationality question, leading up to Round 1 of the causal narrative. The remainder of every chapter is divided into two sections, one covering each round. The section covering Round 1 features an outline of the minority government's demands, followed by the central government's response. The latter is divided into two sub-sections, one dealing with the instrumental response (the political economy story), and the other outlining the symbolic response (the symbolic politics story). The section covering Round 2 likewise features a sub-section on the renewed minority demand, and the centre's response. I then I cover the political consequences of that response – notably the conversion of the majority backlash into rise in secessionist support among the minority population and political elites.

The only exception to this is Chapter 7 on Czechoslovakia. Here, I begin similarly, with an introductory section and historical background. However, the Czechoslovak case covers a much shorter period and thus contains only one "round." Nevertheless, this round is treated similarly, beginning with a discussion of the Slovak demands, followed by the "response," one that is divided into the political economy and symbolic sections.

Introduction

Historical Background

Round 1

 The demand
 The response
  Political economy story
  Symbolic politics story

Round 2

 The demand
 The response
 Political consequences

Conclusions

Figure 3.2 Chapter layout

4

Canada and Quebec from the Quiet Revolution to the 1995 Referendum

The 1960 provincial election was a watershed moment in Quebec's history. Prior to that year, the provincial political elite subscribed to a minimal role for the state, in a society dominated by a reactive and traditionalist nationalism. By contrast, the Liberal government elected in 1960 was anything but quiescent. It saw the provincial state as an instrument of both national affirmation and rapid socio-economic development. In order to meet that ambition, the provincial government required more powers and resources than it had at its disposal at that point. While Quebec was already equipped with political and administrative autonomy, its fiscal and policy capacity was hamstrung by the spending power of the federal government.[1] Moreover, though the province enjoyed certain constitutional exemptions, Quebeckers were not explicitly recognized as a nation.[2] As a result, the provincial government began demanding greater fiscal and policy autonomy, along with the formal acknowledgment of Quebeckers' distinctive status.

This chapter explains Ottawa's response to Quebec's demands and links this pattern of accommodation to the 1995 referendum on the province's sovereignty. The causal process covered here started with *instrumental* demands for greater fiscal autonomy as well as for opt-outs from social programs initiated by the federal government in the first half of the 1960s ("Round 1 – Demand 1" in Figure 4.1). These were accompanied by demands for Quebec to be recognized as a distinct society. Canada's political economy configuration during the 1960s facilitated partial accommodation of the instrumental demands ("Round 1 – Response 1"). Quebec was granted greater power over its fiscal affairs, as well as the right to opt out of a range of social programs. Both had important knock-on effects for the policy capacity

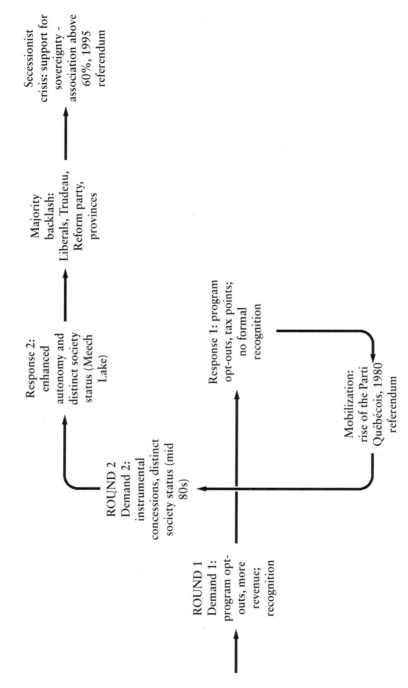

Figure 4.1 Canada 1960–1995 causal process summary

of the provincial government. However, the demand for symbolic recognition was not met. Indeed, even when instrumental concessions *were* made, the federal elites insisted that they be formally available to all provinces, so as to preclude the appearance of symbolic recognition of Quebec's national specificity.

This pattern of accommodation had two important consequences. First, the instrumental concessions made to Quebec did not provoke open backlash from outside the province. What reaction there was largely took the form of low-key policy initiatives. Second, the partial accommodation of Quebec's demands helped the provincial federalists and secessionists alike. While the provincial Liberals continued pressing for more autonomy and recognition within Canada, the secessionist Parti Québécois gained strength, winning power in 1976 and holding a referendum on sovereignty in 1980 ("Round 1 – Mobilization"). The sovereigntists lost the referendum, but the pressure drove the federal government to consider more comprehensive accommodation. Federal Prime Minister Pierre Trudeau committed himself to constitutional renewal, but his constitutional patriation project in 1981 was interpreted in Quebec as an assault on the province's autonomy and status.

The combination of the referendum and constitutional reform resulted in a renewed round of demands by Quebec ("Round 2 – Demand 2"). This time, the provincial government scaled up its symbolic claims, presenting the formal acknowledgment of Quebec as a distinct society as the prerequisite for signing on to the Constitution. During this round, the federal elites accommodated both the instrumental demands and the symbolic ones. The federal government of Brian Mulroney made two attempts to adopt Quebec's claims, via the Meech Lake and Charlottetown rounds of constitutional negotiations. Both packages recognized Quebec as a distinct society and included a number of instrumental concessions ("Round 2 – Response 2").

Formal symbolic recognition proved too much for English Canada. Meech Lake provoked an open political backlash against what was perceived as "special treatment" for Quebec, among both the population and the political and intellectual elites ("Round 2 – Majority Backlash"). Ultimately, both accords were defeated, demonstrating the unwillingness of a substantial proportion of the English Canadian population and political elite to accept the vision of Canada championed by a wide swath of Quebec's political and intellectual leadership. In this context, support for Quebec's sovereignty now exceeded 60 per cent, leading to the second referendum, which the sovereignist side lost by a mere 0.6 per cent of the vote ("Round 2 – Secessionist crisis"). The rest of the chapter accounts for these outcomes in greater detail.

THE BACKGROUND: QUÉBÉCOIS NATIONALISM BEFORE THE QUIET REVOLUTION

Francophone inhabitants of what is today Quebec became British subjects after the conquest of New France in 1760.[3] This defeat, and the subsequent political, economic, and demographic dominance of the anglophone population, coloured the French-speakers' perception of what would become Canada. Military loss and subsequent humiliation contributed to the idea of "la survivance" – the notion that the survival of francophone Canadian culture was perpetually in question (Gingras and Nevitte 1984, 5). This mistrust was reinforced by the outcome of the 1837–38 rebellions in Lower and Upper Canada. Both uprisings sought to break the stranglehold of entrenched oligarchies and to liberalize politics.[4] It was the Lower Canada Rebellion, centred on today's Quebec, that presented the more serious challenge to the colonial regime, being both longer lasting and better organized. In addition, it had an ethnolinguistic component reflected in the ample support it received among the francophone population.

In response, Lord Durham, the Governor General of British America, decided that the future stability of the colony required the assimilation of the French Canadian population (Durham 1963; McRoberts 1997, 5–6). He amalgamated the provinces into a legislative union meant to ensure the political marginalization of the francophones. That scheme proved so dysfunctional that it led to the increasing acceptance of the federal concept among the anglophone elites and to the federal bargain of 1867 (Ormsby 1969). The 1867 agreement established the Dominion of Canada, and with it the province of Quebec with its own legislative and administrative institutions.

The federation was a compromise between the advocates of legislative union, concentrated among the anglophone elites, and the federalists of Lower Canada, who favoured the institutional recognition of separate cultural identities (Ajzenstat et al. 2003, Ch. 9). The product of this compromise was a centralized federation. Yet between the end of the first Macdonald government (1871) and the Great Depression, power gradually shifted from Ottawa to the provinces (Simeon and Robinson 1990, Ch. 4). This trend was reversed by the convergence of Canada's rapid industrialization, the Great Depression, and the Second World War. The federation was recentralized, primarily through the assertion of the federal government's spending power, and continued to be so into the 1950s (Simeon and Robinson 1990, Ch. 8).

French Canadian nationalism of this era was clerical and conservative. It was also fundamentally apolitical, emphasizing cultural aspects of the national question. Monière summarized its elements thus:

> The ideas of liberation and independence [of the early nineteenth century] were replaced by the idea of survival. The objective was not now to build an independent nation and a democratic state, but to rely on a French and Catholic provincial government for the preservation of faith, language, and traditional institutions. ... With the clergy in the ascendant, Quebec withdrew into itself, and lay still under the domination of a conservative ideology whose main themes were anti-statism ... the worship of agriculture and the French colonial past, the rejection of industrialization, progress, and all the modern freedoms. (1981, 288)

This nationalism was not the potent force that would shake the foundations of the Canadian state in the 1970s and beyond. Its protagonists dominated Quebec politics well into the 1950s. During the first two decades following the Second World War, the province was governed by Maurice Duplessis's conservative Union Nationale. Duplessis clung to an anachronistic political vision of limited government at the precise moment when most Western states were becoming more interventionist.[5]

By the end of Duplessis's last mandate, however, postwar industrialization had already transformed Quebec's economy and society beyond recognition. Between 1945 and 1960, the province saw rapid economic growth, urbanization, and a general increase in prosperity (Linteau et al. 1991, Chs. 16; 17; 20; 23). At the same time, the traditional ethnic division of labour persisted, with the local anglophones constituting the business elite and francophones supplying cheap labour and filling clerical positions (Canada, Royal Commission on Bilingualism and Biculturalism 1969). Furthermore, Quebec itself, though not a poor province, lagged behind the industrial powerhouse of Ontario. Meanwhile, the Canadian federal government was becoming increasingly assertive, expanding its reach through its spending power and new social programs (Banting 1987). The tension between Quebec's traditionalist politics, rapid social change, and the federal government's activism gave birth to a new, modern, Québécois nationalism.

For Quebec's new nationalist leaders, limited provincial government in the context of an unequal ethnic division of labour and relative economic stagnation was detrimental to the interests of the Québécois nation. The social and economic modernization of Quebec was both inevitable and irreversible, but if unguided it would lead to the loss of francophone identity through the gradual assimilation of workers into the anglophone culture (Behiels 1985, 39–40). Moreover, the domination of the provincial economy by outside players would ensure permanent underdevelopment. The solution to both problems was an activist provincial government. The province would foster the formation of large-scale public enterprises, which would then provide managerial opportunities for upwardly mobile francophones (Breton 1964). Such opportunities were not available in the anglophone-dominated private sector. At the same time, the government would develop a provincial welfare state to protect workers from the whims of the market. The national and social elements would need to be welded together if the government was to mobilize the population behind the nationalist cause.

While neo-nationalists struggled to transform Quebec from within, they also became concerned about the federal government's growing interventionism. To the extent that Ottawa usurped provincial legislative and fiscal powers, it would prevent the transformation of the provincial state in Quebec and ultimately undercut the neo-nationalist project. Underpinning all these instrumental concerns was the belief that Quebeckers constituted a distinctive national community and that this fact ought to be formally acknowledged by the rest of Canada. These ideas informed the demands that successive governments in Quebec would press in Ottawa. The transformation they ushered in became known as the Quiet Revolution.

ROUND 1 – QUIET REVOLUTION TO CONSTITUTIONAL PATRIATION

The Demand

On 22 June 1960, the Liberal Party of Quebec (PLQ), led by Jean Lesage, won the provincial election. The PLQ government became the political vehicle for the neo-nationalist agenda, demanding greater fiscal and policy autonomy along with some form of recognition of Québécois nationhood. Claims for greater control over the province's revenues were already emerging in the first half of the 1950s. In 1954, the provincial government unilaterally imposed an income levy in the amount of 15 per cent of the federal tax, while demanding equivalent credits for its taxpayers so that the move would not amount to double taxation of Quebec's residents (La Forest 1981, 29).[6]

In 1964, the provincial Liberals called for further fiscal concessions, this time in the form of the transfer of tax room by the federal government – notably, for 25 per cent of both personal and corporate income taxes, and all of the succession duties (Simeon 2006, 51). During a series of federal–provincial meetings on social policy in 1963 and 1964, Lesage pressed for more control in a number of policy fields, demanding the right to opt out of federally funded programs while receiving corresponding fiscal compensation. This compensation would take the form of tax abatements rather than direct transfers from the federal government. In other words, the federal government would yield a portion of the taxes it raised that would otherwise be used to pay for the program in question (Simeon 2006, 47–56).

When the federal government initiated work on a new Canada-wide pension plan, the Lesage government produced its own alternative ahead of the federal–provincial negotiations. The federal team believed that Lesage might present problems in the formulation of the Canada Pension Plan, but they were unprepared for a fully developed alternative, which Quebec unveiled at the conference of March 1964 (Simeon 2006, 55). A provincial pension plan was important for both political and policy reasons. A successful opt-out would prevent the federal government's intrusion in this field of public policy and present the PLQ as a competent defender of Quebec's interests.[7] At the same time, the savings generated by the provincial plan would be mobilized for accelerated economic development in the province. The Caisse de dépôt et placement du Québec, the managing arm of the fund, was going to foster investment into those sectors that would otherwise be neglected by foreign-owned private capital, thus boosting economic growth (Brooks and Tanguay 1985, 103).

These instrumental demands were reinforced by the claims for the symbolic recognition of Quebec. Such assertions were already developed in the 1950s. The 1956 Tremblay Report commissioned by the provincial government couched the instrumental demands for greater

authority over fiscal, social, and industrial policy in the language of
binationalism. The authors "sought to define Quebec's *special role*
within the Canadian Confederation, insofar as it constitutes the *national
focus* of French-Canadian culture" (Quebec, Royal Commission of
Inquiry on Constitutional Problems 1973, 209; emphasis added). The
centralization of the Canadian federation stemmed, the authors argued,
from the monist interpretation of the Canadian state and the political
community it contained. The remedy to this problem, as they saw it,
was to reaffirm the binational character of the Canadian state.

The understanding of Canada and of Quebec's place in it articulated
in the Tremblay report would inform, to varying degrees, the demands
of all Quebec governments during Round 1 and beyond.[8] For Lesage,
Quebec was "asking for the equality of Canada's two founding ethnic
groups ... seeking a status that respects its special characteristics."[9]
Indeed, he affirmed the symbolic roots of his government's instrumental demands, noting that "for Québec, autonomy is the vital
condition of its affirmation as a people [*sic!*] *rather than of its survival,
which is now secure.*" The PLQ would endorse the principle of
Quebec's special status at its conference of October 1967, calling for
the "*formal recognition* of the presence of two nations in Canada and
on the clearly demonstrated will to make French Canadians full
members of a new Canadian confederation" (Saywell 1977, 16;
emphasis added).

The Response

THE POLITICAL ECONOMY STORY

During Round 1, successive federal governments accommodated some
of Quebec's key instrumental demands while avoiding formal symbolic
recognition. The province's 1954 imposition of a 15 per cent personal
income tax was followed by the federal government vacating tax
room so as to prevent an overall increase in Quebeckers' tax burden
(Simeon and Robinson 1990, 147). Quebec's demand for a greater
share of income taxes during the early 1960s was also accommodated,
with the federal government ultimately yielding 24 per cent of personal
income tax to all provinces (Simeon 2006, 59). In addition, Quebec
refused the federal government's offer of tax collection, choosing
instead to raise its own personal and corporate income taxes though
a revenue agency established in 1962 (Boadway and Watts 2000, 91).
As importantly, in 1965 the federal government acceded to Quebec

opting out of a range of federal social programs, with fiscal compensation (Boadway and Hobson 1993, 47). The most notable opt-out
concerned Quebec's 1965 decision to establish a separate pension
plan (Simeon 2006, 45–46). This forward march of autonomy was
largely arrested by the 1970s. By that point, the province was equipped
with far more power than it had possessed a decade before.

This *relatively* far-reaching accommodation of Quebec's demands
was made possible by the alignment of policy strategies deployed by
the governments of Canada and Quebec. Quebec's strategy of governance was shaped by Canada's economic geography. The province's
relative underdevelopment in the 1960s was an outcome of a gradual
shift in Canada's centre of economic gravity (Naylor 1972, 9).[10]
Between the two world wars, the country reduced its reliance on the
declining British imperial economy and aligned itself more closely
with the booming giant to the south. As a result, patterns of trade
and foreign direct investment shifted from the previously dominant
Montreal toward Ontario (1972, 22–3; Norrie and Owram 1991,
446–52, 458, 580). The Second World War led to yet another spurt
in Canadian industrial growth, further exacerbating the differences
in regional economic development, with Ontario benefiting from
wartime opportunities much more than Quebec.[11]

Quebec's relative underdevelopment came with an intra-provincial
twist: an ethnic division of labour, with francophones disproportionately confined to the more marginal employment and business opportunities. Though the share of anglophones in Quebec's total population
had been declining since the mid-nineteenth century, they retained
their dominant economic position into the 1960s. Their early commercial and financial advantage was reinforced during the industrialization of the first half of the twentieth century (Coleman 1984, 26;
Renaud 1987, 56). In the mid-1960s, the Royal Commission on
Bilingualism and Biculturalism found a pervasive pattern of marginalization of francophones in the provincial economy in terms of
income, educational attainment, representation in professional and
managerial occupations, and ownership in the most profitable and
dynamic branches of the economy (Canada, Royal Commission on
Bilingualism and Biculturalism 1969, 17, 43, 53–60).

These socio-economic patterns shaped Quebec's demands for greater
fiscal and policy autonomy. Lesage and his team were committed to
building a strong and interventionist provincial state for three reasons.[12] First, they sought to speed up the province's economic growth

and catch up with other parts of Canada, notably Ontario (Colgan 1993, 70; 72). Second, they wanted to undo the prevailing division of labour by developing a *francophone* capitalist economy, with francophone ownership, management, and technical know-how (Colgan 1993, 70; Fournier 1978, 17–18). Finally, they wanted to construct a welfare state managed by the provincial rather than the federal government (1978, 17). The Lesage government's interventionism is evident in public spending figures. The Union Nationale governments had increased government expenditures by 2 per cent of GDP between 1940 and 1960; under the Lesage Liberals, that figure grew from 15 per cent of the provincial GDP to more than one third (1978, 17).

The interventionism of Quebec's provincial elites was matched by that of the federal government. The Great Depression and the Second World War facilitated the expansion of the federal government's reach. The Depression legitimized interventionist ideas among future policymakers, people who would shape the character of the Canadian state during war and in its aftermath (Granatstein 1982; Owram 1986). The war also provided the federal government with the political opening it needed to enhance its power vis-à-vis the provinces and increase the state's presence in society. Two major policy documents, the Rowell–Sirois Report (1940) and the White Paper on Employment and Income (1945), pointed to the pressing need for extensive government intervention in order to buffer the working population from the worst excesses of the market. Both documents called for the implementation of a range of programs, as well as for deficit spending in order to finance them and to act as a counter-cyclical measure (Canada, Royal Commission on Dominion–Provincial Relations 1940, 270; Canada 1945, 1, 21). For political and constitutional reasons, however, Canada's Keynesian moment would have to wait (Guest 1980, 140, 142). In the first decade and a half following the Second World War, federal public policy was at best haltingly Keynesian (Campbell 1987; Gordon 1966).

It was only in the 1960s that Canada saw a concerted and massive expansion of the state's role in society and the economy. The federal governments of Lester B. Pearson oversaw the implementation of the Canada (and Quebec) Pension Plan (1965), the Canada Assistance Plan[13] (1966), and the Medical Care Act (1966), which greatly expanded access to health care (Guest 1980, Ch. 10). In addition to socially redistributive policies, the federal government implemented programs of territorial redistribution, such as the fiscal equalization scheme, established in 1957 (Clark 1988, 84–6). Finally, both the federal and provincial governments expanded their participation in the direct provision of goods and services by broadening state ownership of enterprises during the 1960s (Langford and Huffman 1983, 297). These policy priorities meant an increase in both federal and provincial spending. Between 1960 and 1984, total government expenditures grew from approximately 29 to 44 per cent of GDP (Huber et al. 2004). The federal government alone increased its spending by two thirds between 1960 and 1980 (Di Matteo 2017, fig. 3). While Canada was not a developmental state during this time, it was increasingly interventionist.

The alignment of strategies of governance, combined with the particular territorial distribution of wealth, worked in favour of accommodation of Quebec's demands for more fiscal responsibility and greater policy autonomy.[14] The accommodation of opt-outs during the 1960s was facilitated by the fact that both governments sought to expand social programs. This is all the more important because the federal government agreed to opt-outs on the condition that provincial governments implemented a similar version of the programs they were opting out of (Telford 2003, 37). Had the government of Quebec pursued a strategy of governance substantively different from that of its federal counterpart, the incompatibility of policy goals would have made accommodation more difficult.

The federal government's concessions on *fiscal* autonomy (both through tax abatements and the transfer of tax revenue) also relate to the alignment of the two governments' strategies of governance. As I showed earlier, Quebec's interventionism was shaped by that province's relative underdevelopment. Economic geography also shaped the province's fiscal preferences. Namely, no Quebec government during Round 1 advocated full fiscal autonomy whereby it would collect most revenues raised in the province and fund its priorities that way.[15] It is easy to see why this is the case if we consider the full range of revenue sources at Quebec's disposal. Namely, after the late 1960s, Quebec was a net beneficiary of federal spending, its taxpayers contributing less to the federal purse they were getting out of it. In fact, Quebec was a beneficiary of both transfer payments meant to shore up the fiscal capacity of "have-not" provinces, and of federal transfers for provincial programs in health, welfare, and education (Government of Canada 1975; Mansell and Schlenker 1995, Table 1).

By contrast, the "have" provinces, notably Ontario, along with Alberta and British Columbia, underwrote the expansion of social programs and government intervention during this era, with their taxpayers contributing more to Ottawa than they got from it. Insisting on full fiscal autonomy across the board would have implied a lower degree of inter-territorial redistribution and a loss of revenue for Quebec. The fiscal demands Quebec made were thus relatively modest and easy to accommodate, because they did not compromise the federal government's ability to deliver on its priorities.

The situation would have been different had Quebec's per capita GDP exceeded the Canadian average. Under this scenario, Quebec elites would have been more likely to support a less interventionist strategy of governance, thus leading to sharper conflict with an expansionist federal government. A wealthy Quebec, rather than Ontario, BC, or Alberta, would have shouldered the cost of equalization and federally developed programs. It follows that the provincial government would likely have asked for more extensive fiscal autonomy precisely in order to limit Quebec's redistributive load, while the interventionist federal government would have resisted these demands since they would have hamstrung its redistributive capacity.[16]

This counter-factual is not purely speculative. In both Spain and Yugoslavia, governments of more developed minority regions resisted bankrolling state-wide redistribution. This was the case in Yugoslavia during the interventionist period, but it happened under market-oriented Spanish central governments as well. Catalonia would eventually demand the authority to collect all revenues raised in its territory, while repatriating a pre-agreed sum to the central government. There were hints of such resistance to redistribution in Ontario, in fact. Ontario's leaders were fully aware of their province's disproportionate contribution to the Canadian project, and they did occasionally voice their displeasure (Simeon 1980, 186). Nevertheless, Ontario's elites were, and continue to be, invested in the Canadian national project, often seeing their interests as overlapping with those of Canada as a whole (Young, Faucher, and Blais 1984, 790).[17] The purpose of their province's autonomy is fundamentally different from that of Quebec, which is why they opposed the erosion of federal economic power and never demanded complete fiscal autonomy (Simeon 1980, 186).

THE SYMBOLIC POLITICS STORY
The story of relatively successful accommodation of instrumental demands in a propitious structural context is incomplete unless we

consider an additional dimension. Concessions extended to Quebec from the 1950s onwards were made *formally* available to every other province. This was the case with the aforementioned income tax reform of 1954. The federal government offered tax room not just to Quebec but to *all provinces* that decided to opt out of tax rental agreements, "wishing to avoid any appearance of recognizing special status for Quebec" (Simeon and Robinson 1990, 147).[18] Similar measures followed in the 1960s. After Quebec opted out of the Canada Pension Plan, the federal government extended opt-outs "to all provinces for all major programs, without their ever having asked for it" (Simeon and Robinson 1990, 201). This pattern extended to other policy areas. During the 1970s, Quebec acquired an unprecedented degree of control over immigration. Yet the legislation that formed the basis of the Cullen-Couture Accord of 1978 granted the right to similar kinds of bilateral immigration accords to *all* provinces, though none asked for that right. Indeed, the federal government actively invited other provinces to seek similar accords, as it "did not want it to appear that Quebec was the only province with an immigration agreement" (Vineberg 1987, 315).

Extending *de facto* asymmetric autonomy while insisting on *de jure* symmetry was an attempt to meet Quebec's instrumental demands while precluding the perception that Quebeckers were a distinctive *political* community. This can be inferred from the following statement by the leader of the opposition Progressive Conservative Party, Robert Stanfield, during a televised electoral debate in 1968:

> I am not in favour of one province being granted powers that are not offered to all the provinces. On the other hand, I recognize that Quebec has its special interests and aspirations by virtue of being something over 80% French speaking. ... But, if the Continuing Committee of the prime minister and the premiers ... should consider that requests from a province could be met without infringing on the essential powers of the federal government, I would want this power offered to all the provinces, *although it might not be of equal interest to all of them.*[19]

The principle according to which Quebec is a province like all others has as its corollary the understanding that Quebeckers, for all their differences, do not constitute a separate nation. This issue, as much as any other, served to help secessionist political elites mobilize support during the 1970s.

What, then, was the political consequence of the pattern of accommodation outlined above? In the immediate term, the partial accommodation of Quebec's demands indicated that further accommodation was possible. Lesage was pleased by his government's ability to wrangle concessions out of Ottawa and presented the Quebec Pension Plan as the *de facto* recognition of Quebec's special status (Simeon 2006, 59). The PLQ lost the 1966 election but returned to power in 1970. While it continued pressing for more autonomy and formal recognition, the party argued that the way forward was through continuing engagement with the Canadian elites and a continuation of Quebec in a renewed Canadian federation, rather than through secessionist "adventurism" and "leaps into the unknown" (Shames 1974, 182–3).

On the other side was the sovereignist Parti Québécois (PQ), established in 1968. Its leader, René Lévesque, quit the provincial Liberals in 1967 when they refused to endorse his call for a sovereign Quebec (Hagy 1971, 55). His outsized role in the sovereignty movement calls for a closer examination of his understanding of Quebec's future. Unlike his Liberal counterparts, Lévesque believed that Quebec stood to gain little from any future attempts at accommodation within Canada. He argued that the resources and policy levers that were the absolute minimum necessary for the free development of the Québécois nation constituted an "unacceptable maximum" for English Canada (Shames 1974, 262–3). The events of the 1960s were, for Lévesque, the end rather than the beginning of the process of negotiation for more self-government and recognition.

Lévesque's new party would pursue what he would come to define as sovereignty-association – a status that would have combined political independence with economic integration with the rest of Canada (Lévesque 1973). This created a bridge that nationalist Quebeckers who feared the economic consequences of independence could use to cross over to his party. Prior to the 1980 referendum, support for independence in Quebec had never exceeded 19 per cent; yet in a poll conducted in 1980, sovereignty-association attracted 42 per cent of respondents (Pinard 1992). The Parti Québécois would gather strength during the 1970s. Its third electoral showing, in 1976, would prove to be the charm ("Round 1 – Mobilization" in Figure 4.1).

Sovereignty-association did attract adherents over the course of the 1970s, but it was not the only factor accounting for the PQ's 1976 victory. The remarkable unpopularity of the provincial Liberals and the moderation of the separatist and class-based message of the PQ were as important (Saywell 1977, 140–2). If anything, the pursuit of sovereignty-association may have done the party more harm than good (Pinard and Hamilton 1978). At any rate, Lévesque delivered on his promise, holding a referendum in 1980. The vote was a major event in Canadian political history, even though the sovereignist camp fell short of the 50 per cent mark (winning 40.4 per cent of the vote) (McRoberts 1997, 159).

The institutional change during Round 1 thus cannot be said to have produced a decisive outcome. On the one hand, there was no open majority backlash against the concessions made to Quebec during this period.[20] I argue that part of the reason was that those concessions, far-reaching as they may have appeared to many English Canadians, did not imply a wholesale symbolic reconstitution of the Canadian state. On the other hand, neither was there a decisive turn to secessionism. Outright independence never commanded more than 20 per cent of popular support, and even sovereignty-association arguably did not come close to being supported by half the province's electorate. I do not wish to overstate this point. Any argument about what constitutes a result "close" to 50 per cent will be at least somewhat arbitrary. But it is clear that the support for both independence and sovereignty-association during the 1970s, in the absence of majority backlash, did not approach the levels seen in the early 1990s, in the midst of such backlash. The electoral victory of the Parti Québécois in 1976 was only partly a secessionist affair, being a result of a confluence of context-specific factors, some of which had little to do with constitutional and identity politics. However, it is also clear that these events, and particularly the 1980 referendum, were interpreted as a wake-up call in the rest of Canada, leading to Round 2.

ROUND 2 – MEECH LAKE TO THE 1995 REFERENDUM

The Demand

In the lead-up to the 1980 referendum, Prime Minister Trudeau promised Quebeckers a change to the constitutional status quo, though this was only a vague commitment to "constitutional renewal." Indeed, instead of meeting the province's demands, Trudeau's project of constitutional patriation would end in a multiple defeat for the Québécois national project. The new constitutional package omitted the long-coveted veto for Quebec, ignored demands that the province's uniqueness be recognized, and was passed without Quebec's consent, which was deemed legally redundant as a consequence of a Supreme Court opinion (Russell 2004, 111–12; 116, 119–20). The combined result of the 1980 referendum and the 1981 patriation was contradictory. On the one hand, the sovereignist position seemed weakened by the referendum loss; on the other, the constitutional reform only broadened and deepened resentment in Quebec. This brought the demands of two major Québécois parties, the PQ and PLQ, in close alignment ("Round 2, Demand 2" in Figure 4.1).

After initial radicalization in response to the patriation, the Parti Québécois moderated its demands (Fraser 2001, ch. 18). It contested the 1985 provincial election, having replaced its traditional goal of sovereignty-association with constitutional reorganization (McRoberts 1993, 384). The PQ demanded a number of concessions in exchange for its endorsement of the Canadian constitution. Most fundamentally, it argued that "the recognition of the existence of a people of Quebec is an essential prerequisite in Quebec's agreement and participation in a new constitutional relation" (Government of Quebec 1985, 11). Symbolic recognition was the foundation upon which all other demands rested. Those included Quebec's primacy over language rights, supremacy of Quebec's Charter of Human Rights and Freedoms over the Canadian equivalent, veto power over the reform of federal institutions, the limitation of federal spending power, including the right to opt out of new federal programs with full fiscal compensation, and constitutional affirmation of Quebec's primacy over key policy areas (Government of Quebec 1985).

The Parti Québécois lost the 1985 election to Robert Bourassa's Liberals. But just as the PQ moderated its demands, so the PLQ escalated its own. In its policy paper of February 1985, the PLQ proposed constitutional changes virtually identical to those of its provincial adversary. As in the PQ document, the PLQ asked "that Quebec be given explicit constitutional recognition as a distinct society, with its own language, culture, history, institutions and way of life" (O'Neal 1995, 10). Just as the PQ did, the Quebec Liberals demanded a veto for Quebec, increased immigration powers, limits on federal spending power, and a say over Supreme Court appointments (Behiels 2007, 260). It is of particular note that, with the exception of the constitutional recognition of Quebec as distinct society, most of the instrumental demands had in one way or another been accepted by various federal governments in the past (MacDonald 2002, 249). Indeed, some of the concessions granted over the previous two decades – such as, notably, the establishment of a separate pension plan and the increasing influence of Quebec in the selection of immigrants – had far greater implications for the Quebec government's power to implement its key policy goals. Yet, as noted, none of these concessions had produced open *political* backlash outside of the province.

The Response

The 1984 federal election made possible the formal recognition of Quebec as a distinct society. The incoming Progressive Conservatives under Brian Mulroney campaigned on the reopening of the constitutional question. If they could win over those Quebec nationalists who were either federalists or disillusioned by the PQ, the party would be able to loosen the federal Liberals' grip on the province and re-establish its presence in Ottawa (Behiels 2007, 256). Mulroney's strategy was the work of his Quebec lieutenant, Lucien Bouchard. Bouchard was committed to recognizing Quebec's distinctiveness and providing Quebec nationalists with a strong incentive to buy into the Canadian federal project. He sought to do this through the symbolic reconfiguration of Canada from the state of a single, if diverse, national community to a binational polity.

This alignment of demands emanating from Quebec, and strategic considerations within the federal government, led to the Meech Lake Accord of 1987. The federal government and nine provincial leaders agreed to most of the demands made by the Bourassa government (Behiels 2007, 263–64) ("Round 2, Response 2" in Figure 4.1). The other premiers, reluctant though many have been, agreed to the deal in exchange for concessions to their own interests. Consequently, the agreement would have further decentralized Canada in a largely symmetrical fashion, but it would have done this along with asymmetric recognition of Quebec. The accord's "distinct society" clause stipulated that "the Constitution of Canada shall be interpreted in a manner consistent with ... the recognition that Quebec constitutes within Canada a distinct society" (Canada 1987). Initially, all of the relevant political players were on board. In addition to the prime minister and the ten premiers, this included the leader of the opposition Liberal Party, John Turner.

However, unlike in the previous rounds of concessions, Meech Lake resulted in an increasingly strident *political* opposition to the deal

("Round 2 – Backlash"). The agreement's most contentious element was the distinct society clause, not the instrumental concessions that would have reconstituted the power relations between the federation and the provinces. The opposition came from a number of quarters and manifested itself publicly, not only during the Meech Lake ratification process but also during the Charlottetown Accord negotiations that attempted to rescue the hope of rapprochement once Meech Lake had expired.

There was opposition within the federal Liberal camp, first among the party membership and caucus, then subsequently among high-profile former officials, with the by then retired Trudeau at the forefront. While Liberal leader John Turner continued to support the package, his party first tried to reverse course, and then countered the distinct society clause with its own constitutional resolution in November 1986. The resolution pointed to "the distinctive character of Quebec as the principal but not the only source of the French language and culture in Canada" (Liberal Party of Canada 1986, 4). It included a commitment to linguistic duality and "the multicultural nature of Canadian society, and in particular respect for the many origins, creeds and cultures and well as the differing regional identities that shape Canadian society" (1986, 4). In other words, the party diluted the reference to distinct society by equating it with other lines of Canadian diversity, reducing the national distinctiveness of the Québécois to a mere aspect of the Canadian national identity.

This internal opposition was accompanied by more visible criticisms of the accord by Pierre Trudeau and other Liberal patriarchs (Behiels 2007, 265). In late 1987, Trudeau penned a searing op-ed published in major papers in both official languages. A significant portion of it dealt with the instrumental danger of the accord, including how it might enfeeble the welfare state, endanger the Charter of Rights and Freedoms, and dismantle federal power (Trudeau 1987). However, special hostility was reserved for the distinct society clause, including its most fundamental implication: "those Canadians who fought for a *single* Canada, bilingual and multicultural, can say goodbye to their dream: we are henceforth to have *two Canadas*, each defined in terms of its language" (Trudeau 1987, emphasis added). The distinct society clause, along with the instrumental concessions, according to Trudeau, represented the destruction of the vision of Canada as a single political community and its replacement with a binational state.

The opposition to Meech Lake by the Liberal old guard was amplified by an important newcomer – the Reform Party. While this was a Western protest party, one of the central tenets of its program was opposition to formal recognition of Quebec's national specificity. In its 1988 and 1993 electoral platforms, the party denounced Quebec's status as a distinct society. The 1988 document featured an entire section on Meech Lake, challenging "the granting of special status to any group or party in Canada" (Reform Party of Canada 1988, 8). This position was reiterated in the 1993 platform, in which the party committed itself "to Canada as one nation, in which the demands and aspirations of all regions are entitled to equal status in constitutional negotiations and political debate" (Reform Party of Canada 1993, 3).

Ultimately, it was opposition from several provincial leaders that would kill the Meech Lake Accord. Premier Filmon of Manitoba was under pressure from his own party and the opposition over the distinct society clause (Behiels 2007, 269). His counterpart in Newfoundland, Clyde Wells, traditionally a strong advocate of provincial symmetry, would come to power in 1989 on the wave of anti-Meech sentiment (Behiels 2007, 270). While Wells was unhappy with the entire accord, he was particularly unsympathetic to its symbolic essence, the distinct society clause. He sought to move the clause to the constitution's preamble to forestall "a special legislative status for Quebec" (Coyne 1992, 26–7).

Opposition to Meech Lake was not confined to the political class. It was rooted in widespread *popular* hostility to the symbolic recognition of Quebec. Of all of the elements of the Meech Lake Accord, it was the distinct society clause that caused the greatest consternation in English Canada (Blais and Crête 1990). There was similar reaction to the clause's equivalent in the Charlottetown Accord. English Canadians were split on the support for the clause, but it was the most important motive for those who voted against the package in the 1992 referendum (LeDuc and Pammett 1995, 27). Indeed, there is a significant degree of consistency in English Canada's opposition to formal federal asymmetry. A poll commissioned by *Maclean's* in 1995 found that a majority of Canadians outside of Quebec opposed recognition of distinct society for that province (53%), with an overwhelming majority (88%) being against both special status and the concession of powers *not available to other provinces* (*Maclean's*

1995). In other words, when formal symbolic recognition of Quebec as a distinct national community was accompanied by asymmetric institutional architecture, it was opposed by almost the entire population of Canada.

Provincial opposition in Manitoba – shaped by First Nations' resistance to the deal – and Newfoundland and Labrador prevented the ratification of Meech Lake Accord by the 23 June 1990 deadline (Russell 2004, 141–53). Its replacement, the Charlottetown Accord, was defeated in a relatively narrow vote in a referendum in 1992. Quebeckers voted against it because it did not go far enough, and many outside of Quebec, particularly in Western Canada, voted against it because it was too far-reaching in its concessions (2004, 226).

Political Consequences

In stark contrast to the 1960s and 70s, the two accords provoked open political opposition to the accommodation of Quebec. Concessions during Round 1 changed policy and altered the *de facto* division of federal power, but they did not undermine the symbolic vision of Canada as the state of a single national community. The push-back took the form of policy and legislative measures that sought to prevent the appearance of Quebec having won recognition as a distinct society, but it did not amount to political mobilization.

The Meech Lake and Charlottetown accords, by contrast, provoked strident and openly political reaction. The instrumental aspects of Meech Lake, for instance, were not much more far-reaching than concessions that had been either granted or contemplated in decades past.[21] Where the accord differed from past attempts at accommodation was in the combination of instrumental gains and a formal recognition of Quebec's uniqueness. The inclusion of the distinct society clause in the symbolic sense would have converted Canada from a nation-state (of diverse individuals, linguistic and ethnic groups, regions, etc.) to a binational state.[22] *This* was the major difference between Round 1 and Round 2.

Majority backlash produced three interlocking effects. First, it ensured that the promises made to Quebec were rescinded, which was in and of itself a major potential cause of political volatility in the province. Second, it demonstrated, in a fairly convincing manner (not only in the actions of various politicians, but also among the population at large), English Canada's rejection of the Québécois vision of themselves as a distinctive national community. This is, in fact, how the major Québécois evening news program, *Le Téléjournal*, presented the rejection of the Meech Lake Accord. The program's framing implied "that rejecting the accord with its société-distincte clause was tantamount to refusing to recognize Quebec and its rightful place in the Canadian confederation" (Conway 2011, 107). Third, the defeat of Meech Lake weakened the hand of the federalist Bourassa. In response, his Liberal Party of Quebec escalated its demands for greater powers for Quebec and called for a referendum on sovereignty if those demands were not met (Behiels 2007, 276).

The defeat of Meech Lake coincided with a jump in support for sovereignty-association in Quebec to as high as 65 per cent in late 1990 (Pinard 1992, 480). In addition, it caused a reconfiguration in Quebec politics ("Round 2 – Secessionist crisis"). Mulroney's Quebec lieutenant, Lucien Bouchard, quit the Conservatives and formed a federal separatist party, the Bloc Québécois (Russell 2004, 149). Bouchard would be instrumental in the 1995 referendum campaign. Moreover, the political upshot of these developments was the re-election of the Parti Québécois, and the 1995 referendum, in which the sovereignists nearly won, with 49.4 per cent in favour of a sovereign Quebec and 50.58 per cent in favour of remaining within Canada (McRoberts 1997, 230).

CONCLUSION

The Canadian case closely follows the hypotheses developed in Chapter 3. During Round 1, from 1960 to about 1980, successive governments of Quebec pursued greater fiscal and policy autonomy (instrumental demands), alongside formal recognition of the province's distinct status (symbolic demands). The close alignment of the policy priorities of the Quebec and federal governments facilitated the accommodation of the province's instrumental claims. By opting out of federal social programs while simultaneously implementing a similar provincial version, Quebec had not compromised Ottawa's strategy of governance. Had the two governments been at odds about the appropriate role of the state in society, Quebec's demands for exemptions would likely have faced greater federal opposition. Perhaps as importantly, the relative underdevelopment of Quebec and the redistributive policies of the federal government that benefited the province moderated its fiscal demands, making them easier to accommodate.

While the federal government proved moderately accommodating of Quebec's instrumental demands during Round 1, it did little to recognize Quebec's distinctiveness. In fact, federal elites framed their *instrumental* concessions so as to prevent the appearance of distinctive status for Quebec. All major gains by that province were *formally* extended to all others, despite the absence of demands for such symmetry. Summing up, Round 1 combined instrumental accommodation with the lack of symbolic recognition. I argue that the absence of recognition explains the absence of political majority backlash to the gains made by Quebec, as predicted by the model in Chapter 3.

At the same time, partial accommodation of Quebec's demands provided fuel to both moderate and radical nationalists in the province. Support for sovereignty grew during this period, eventually resulting in the election of the sovereignist Parti Québécois in 1976. The new government then held a referendum on the province's status in 1980. While these events could be interpreted as a secessionist crisis, evidence suggests a different reading. First, support for outright independence during this period never exceeded 20 per cent. Second, the PQ had to moderate its sovereignist message in order win the 1976 election, and even then, it benefited from the remarkable unpopularity of the incumbent Liberal government. Finally, the sovereignists lost the referendum 40 to 60 per cent. In response to the mobilization of the late 1970s, the federal government of Prime Minister Trudeau initiated a process of constitutional change, the results of which would fail to satisfy Quebec's core demands. The upshot was a new constitutional settlement that the government of Quebec refused to sign.

The events of the late 1970s and early 1980s resulted in Round 2. By the mid-1980s, both major parties in Quebec, the PQ and the PLQ, were calling for more autonomy and an explicit recognition of Quebec as a distinct society. In 1987, the federal government, the other nine provinces, and Quebec agreed on a constitutional reform package – the Meech Lake Accord – that would have accommodated the province's instrumental and symbolic demands. Yet the agreement soon provoked open political backlash. It was the distinct society clause – the symbolic heart of the deal – rather than any of the instrumental elements of the package that proved to be most contentious. If James Bickerton is right and "'English Canada,' 'Canada outside Quebec,' or 'the Rest of Canada' ... has no sense of itself as a nation apart" (Bickerton 2011, 170), then the reason why is clear. The symbolic reconstitution of Canada signalled by Meech Lake would have redistributed the burden of identity adjustment from Quebeckers to anglophone and allophone Canadians, eroding their ontological security.[23]

Open majority backlash produced three interlinked outcomes. First, it demonstrated to Quebeckers that a large segment of the Canadian society and elite was unwilling to accept the idea of Canada as a binational state, rather than the political expression of a single state-wide nation. Second, it contributed to the failure of the reform, which, if we are to take prospect theory seriously, was more provocative than simple non-recognition would have been.[24] Third, both facts facilitated a radicalization of Quebec nationalism and directly contributed to an unprecedented rise in support for sovereignty-association *and* independence, and to a much closer referendum result in 1995 than was the case in 1980.

Thus, contrary to the expectation of much extant theoretical work, greater autonomy did not facilitate secessionism by itself. Concessions not accompanied by symbolic recognition had at best an ambiguous effect. They certainly did not lead to majority backlash. However, nationalist mobilization in Quebec during the late 1970s pushed the federal government to combine instrumental with symbolic concessions. It was the majority backlash to these that supercharged minority resentment and led to the secessionist crisis of the 1990s.

5

Spain and Catalonia from the Transition to the 2017 Secession Crisis

Catalonia's secession crisis of 2017 has its roots in Spain's transition to democracy in the late 1970s. Spain's democratic constitution opened the path for the re-establishment of Catalan autonomy in 1979. That reform included control over a range of policy areas, but little by way of fiscal autonomy. Over the next two decades, successive Catalan governments would call for greater powers in the fiscal sphere (instrumental demand), as well as formal recognition of Catalan nationhood (symbolic demand). This chapter explains the Spanish central elites' response to those demands and the ways in which that response fed back into the politics of nationalism in Catalonia.

During the first round of this process, from the early 1980s to the early 2000s, the Spanish leadership gradually broadened the fiscal autonomy of Catalonia and the remaining Autonomous Communities.[1] This outcome was facilitated by the alignment of the pro-market policy priorities of Spanish and Catalan governments. At the same time, however, the central leadership attempted to exert greater control over the process of decentralization through basic and framework legislation. What we see, then, is a process of simultaneous extension and contraction of autonomy. During this round, instrumental concessions were not matched by the recognition of Catalan national uniqueness. Indeed, the central government often generalized concessions granted to Catalonia by extending them to the remaining ACs, exacerbating Catalan demands for recognition ("Round 1 – Response 1" in Figure 5.1).

At the same time, Round 1 did not see open majority backlash as a result of the concessions made. I argue that the reason for this was, as in Canada, the lack of symbolic reconstitution of the state along

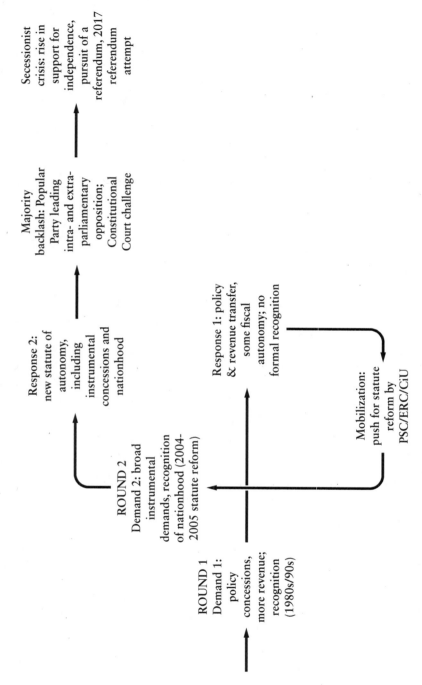

Figure 5.1 Spain 1980–2017 causal process summary

ROUND 1
Demand 1: policy concessions, more revenue; recognition (1980s/90s)

ROUND 2
Demand 2: broad instrumental demands, recognition of nationhood (2004-2005 statute reform)

Response 2: new statute of autonomy, including instrumental concessions and nationhood

Majority backlash: Popular Party leading intra- and extra-parliamentary opposition; Constitutional Court challenge

Secessionist crisis: rise in support for independence, pursuit of a referendum, 2017 referendum attempt

Response 1: policy & revenue transfer, some fiscal autonomy; no formal recognition

Mobilization: push for statute reform by PSC/ERC/CiU

the lines articulated by Catalan politicians as early as the constitutional debates of 1978. This pattern of accommodation encouraged more far-reaching demands by Catalan political elites during Round 2 ("Round 2 – Demand 2" in Figure 5.1). Catalan claims were further boosted by inter-party competition in an increasingly fragmented regional party system during the early 2000s.

The renewed push for accommodation was channelled through the reform of Catalonia's Statute of Autonomy. The new statute combined instrumental demands for, *inter alia*, comprehensive fiscal autonomy and protection of Catalonia's legislative and policy competencies from central encroachments with the formal recognition of nationhood. The election of a socialist central government in 2004 facilitated the centre's willingness to accede to some of these demands for both ideological and pragmatic reasons ("Round 2 – Response 2" in Figure 5.1). While the final version of the statute approved by the Spanish parliament did not accommodate Catalonia's most far-reaching instrumental claims, it did contain a reference to Catalan nationhood. As in Canada, it was this symbolic element of the package that proved to be particularly contentious.

In contrast to Round 1, the combination of instrumental and symbolic concessions gave rise to open political opposition to Catalan demands ("Round 2 – Backlash" in Figure 5.1). The state-wide opposition Popular Party would lead both intra- and extra-parliamentary mobilization against the statute, culminating in a 2006 challenge to its constitutionality. In 2010, the Spanish Constitutional Court annulled key elements of the statute and judged the reference to Catalan nationhood to be legally void. For many Catalans, this open political opposition and its juridical result constituted a repudiation of Catalan nationhood and of the idea of Spain as a multinational state. Majority backlash helped strengthen the more radical political factions in Catalonia, ultimately pushing support for independence to close to 50 per cent. Contributing to intense outbidding among Catalan nationalist parties, this shift culminated in the botched attempt to hold a unilateral referendum on independence in October 2017.

THE BACKGROUND:
CATALAN NATIONALISM BEFORE THE TRANSITION

Modern Catalan nationalism has its roots in the political and social turmoil of late nineteenth-century Spain. A number of scholars explain its emergence as a consequence of the failure of Spanish nation-building, itself rooted in the weak nineteenth-century Spanish state (Álvarez Junco 2013, 311; L. Balcells 2013; Linz 1973, 33). This, however, is an oversimplification. A broad-based Spanish national identity did in fact emerge over the course of the nineteenth century (Álvarez Junco 2013, 310; Smith 2014, 50), and it was shared by the majority of Catalan political and social elites of that era (Angel Smith 2014).

During the second half of the nineteenth century, narrow circles of intellectuals, clergy, political activists, and, in some cases, business-people started to call for the cultural, economic, and political auton-omy of Catalonia within Spain (Angel Smith 2014, chs. 5–7). They almost never demanded full Catalan statehood. Indeed, many of their proposals viewed Catalan autonomy as a way to reform and modern-ize Spain (Angel Smith 2014, 143, 159, 198). These efforts were largely ineffective until they received the support of the region's powerful bourgeoisie. For most of the nineteenth century, the Catalan industrial and commercial elite sought to influence Spanish policy through its representatives in established parties and lobbying organizations, showing little interest in the politics of Catalan regionalism. When in 1898 Spain lost its remaining colonies and their markets, Catalonia's business elites finally joined the autonomists to create a regional political movement, in the hope that autonomy would amplify their political influence in Spain (Ehrlich 1998, 401).

The movement's organizational manifestation was the conserva-tive, pro-business Lliga Regionalista. The Lliga won administrative autonomy for Catalonia in 1914 in the form of the Mancomunitat (Commonwealth) of Catalonia, but lost business support when it attempted to harness social unrest for political gain in the aftermath of the 1917 Russian Revolution (Ehrlich 1998, 406). It lost the last vestiges of its legitimacy through its association with the dictatorship of Primo de Rivera. That dictatorship, lasting from 1923 to 1930, was a reaction to political dysfunction, social instability, and the radicalization of Basque and Catalan nationalists (Ehrlich 1998, 414). Primo de Rivera closed down a number of Catalan cultural institu-tions, prohibited the public use of the Catalan language, and eventually dissolved the Mancomunitat (A. Balcells 1996, 83–5).

The dictatorship thus radicalized the Catalan nationalist movement further, and shifted its ideological foundations (A. Balcells 1996, 89). The Catalan left, otherwise disunited and politically weak, allied with their Spanish counterparts to establish the Second Republic in 1931.

This event coincided with the formation of the Catalan Republican Left (Esquerra Republicana de Catalunya – ERC), the party that would dominate Catalan politics during the Second Republic (A. Balcells 1996, 92). Catalan nationalism thus shifted from a largely right-wing phenomenon to one occupying the left of the political spectrum. During the brief republican era, Catalonia won its autonomy, only to see it extinguished with the victory of Francisco Franco's Nationalist forces in 1939. Nationalist rebels saw as great a threat in the putative Catalan separatism as they did in the social radicalism of the Spanish left (Conversi 1997, 41).

For this reason, Francoist repression was particularly severe in Catalonia. Public use of the Catalan language was banned, and Catalan political and cultural institutions were dissolved to facilitate the cultural assimilation of the local population (Conversi 1997, 109–13). Catalan identity would also come under pressure from the explosive economic growth of the 1960s. While the regime's early policies discriminated against the region's economic interests (Harrison 2009, 199), the liberalization of the 1960s fostered growth in wealthier parts of Spain, including Catalonia (Carr 1982, 747). Between 1950 and 1975, 1.4 million Spaniards from poorer areas made their way to the region in search of employment (Guibernau 2004, 67).[2] The presence of such large numbers of Castilian-speakers added another dimension to Catalan concerns.

The regime ultimately failed to contain Catalanist activity. The Catholic clergy, businesspeople, cultural and labour activists, and political dissidents all helped keep the national project alive (Dowling 2013, ch. 3). With Franco's death in 1975, the region's civic and political organizations united in their demand for self-government. On 11 September 1977, more than a million people came out in the streets of Barcelona to demand the restoration of Catalonia's autonomy (*La Vanguardia* 1977). In addition to the multitudes and the representatives of major social organizations, this manifestation featured leaders of all Catalan political parties. Autonomist ideas advocated in Catalonia and in other regions with historic national claims, such as the Basque Country, resonated in the rest of Spain as well. Pro-democracy politicians associated decentralization and autonomy for minority nations with democratization (López 1981, 196). This broad buy-in ensured that the 1978 constitution would facilitate the establishment of what would become the State of Autonomies: a system of decentralization that would culminate in the establishment of seventeen Autonomous Communities covering the entire territory of Spain.

ROUND 1 – TRANSITION TO THE 2006 STATUTE REFORM

The Demand

Even prior to the ratification of the 1978 constitution, the political process led to the establishment of "pre-autonomies," including a proto-government for Catalonia. The 1979 Statute of Autonomy formalized this state of affairs. For the next two decades, successive Catalan governments would demand the full development of self-governing capacities envisaged by the Spanish constitution and the statute. Those two documents already delineated a broad scope of policy capacity for the Catalan government.[3] The 1980s saw heated judicial conflict over the distribution of powers between the Autonomous Communities, especially Catalonia and the Basque Country, and the central government. These related to the interpretation of the constitution and the respective statutes for these ACs (Agranoff and Gallarín 1997, 16-17).

In addition, the Catalan government demanded the expansion of judicial and policy autonomy. For example, in 1987, the regional parliament called for the establishment of the Catalan High Court of Justice, expanded policing powers, the promotion of the Catalan language, and greater control over state subsidies and economic policy (Parlament de Catalunya 1987, 9543–4). The parliament also criticized the centre's legislative incursion into areas of exclusive autonomous competency, a drift that would motivate more far-reaching demands by the turn of the century. The Catalan elites also demanded more revenues and greater decision-making power over them (Parlament de Catalunya 1987, 9544).

In the 1988 and 1992 electoral campaigns, Convergence and Union (CiU), the federation that would govern the region between 1980 and 2003, called for the transfer of a share of personal income tax revenues, an increase in unconditional transfers from the central state, and a degree of participation in revenue collection and the management of whatever taxes were ceded to the ACs (Convergència i Unió 1988, 26, 29; 1992, 22, 26). In 1992, it also asked for the transfer of competencies over ceded taxes, that is, not only the revenues themselves but a degree of control over tax policy (Convergència i Unió 1992, 22–23). On both occasions CIU lambasted the central state's fiscal system for underprivileging Catalonia both vis-à-vis the ACs belonging to the Concierto Económico (the Basque Country and Navarra, with their comprehensive fiscal autonomy), and those in the Common Regime to which the remaining ACs belong. The former had the ability to collect all of the taxes on their territory and transfer a pre-agreed amount to the central government for joint services, resulting in lower contributions to the common budget. The latter, CIU charged, were benefiting from higher per capita revenue transfers relative to Catalonia (Convergència i Unió 1992, 21).[4]

In 1995, the demands escalated. CIU argued that Catalonia was still too reliant on state transfers and that it was contributing too much to the less developed ACs (Convergència i Unió 1995, 83–4). It urged greater equalization of resources among the communities, but also a greater share of state taxes, including not only the income tax but also the value-added and so-called special taxes (Convergència i Unió 1995, 85). To this was added a more vocal call for policy autonomy over the ceded taxes. The party noted that if per capita revenues received by Catalonia and other ACs were not equalized, it would prepare to switch to a Basque-style fiscal system (Convergència i Unió 1995, 86). This warning was accompanied in early 1996 by the creation of a parliamentary commission to study the possibility of Concierto Económico as a solution for Catalonia's fiscal challenges (Parlament de Catalunya 1996, 1533). During nearly the entirety of Round 1 the Catalan government did not demand exemption from the "joint fiscal regime" that all other ACs except the Basque Country and Navarra were subject to (Viver Pi-Sunyer and Grau Creus 2016).

In the 1999 regional electoral campaign, however, the party's discourse escalated. Grievances related to Catalonia's fiscal position were accompanied by a more specific outline of what was now called a "deficit" – the per capita difference between what each Catalan paid to the central government and what they received from those payments (relative to other Spaniards) (Convergència i Unió 1999, 41–3). As importantly, this was the first time the party had asked for a "fiscal pact" with the central government, one that would include an increasing share of state taxes (income, value-added, and special), policy autonomy over those taxes ceded to Catalonia, and, importantly, the ability of the Generalitat (the government of Catalonia) to collect *all the revenues* in Catalonia and pass along the central government's share (Convergència i Unió 1999, 45–7).

These instrumental demands were accompanied by increasingly vociferous appeals for the recognition of Catalan nationhood and the "plurinational" character of the Spanish state. This symbolic dimension was evident in the original demand for the reinstatement of Catalan autonomy during the constitutional debates of 1978. In heated discussions about the inclusion of the term "nationalities" in the constitution's Article 2 to refer to Catalonia, Galicia, and the Basque Country, representatives of all major Catalan parties (ERC; Democratic Convergence of Catalonia [CDC]; Catalan Communists [PSUC]); and the Catalan Socialists [PSC]) consistently articulated a vision of Spain as a multinational reality in which Catalans were not merely a part of the Spanish political community, but a nation in their own right.[5]

ERC's Barrera i Costa saw Spain as a "community of peoples" (Cortes Generales 1978a, 2162–3). For Roca i Junyent of CDC, one of the "fathers of the Constitution," there was no difference between the term nation (which the text reserved for Spain) and nationality, the only distinction being that the latter did not possess its own state (Cortes Generales 1978b, 2274–5). Solé Tura of PSUC, another member of the constitutional commission, argued that the right to autonomy for the three nationalities should not only be recognized but also be understood as *constitutive* of the Spanish state (Cortes Generales 1978b, 2313). Finally, the socialist Reventós i Carner saw the Spanish state as a product of the will of nationalities and regions (*sic!*) of Spain, not only of all Spaniards. He proposed an amendment according to which the 1978 constitution would *establish* the unity of Spain in a political-constitutional sense (Cortes Generales 1978b, 2299–2300).[6]

Catalan elites did not call for the explicit recognition of Catalan nationhood during the 1980s, but they began doing so over the following decade. The motive for this change was the institutional and policy symmetrization the central government promoted during the preceding period. In 1993, for example, the Catalan parliament called for the abandonment of symmetrization on the grounds that it clashed with the principle of recognition of Catalonia's uniqueness (Parlament de Catalunya 1993). Moreover, throughout the 1990s, the regional parliament enacted a number of resolutions using the language of nationhood and sovereignty to describe Catalonia (Viver Pi-Sunyer and Grau Creus 2016). As Round 1 drew to a close, the instrumental demands were thus increasingly accompanied by symbolic ones.

The Response

THE POLITICAL ECONOMY STORY

During the 1980s and 90s, Catalonia acquired control over a range of policy areas, within the boundaries set by the 1978 Constitution and the ambitions laid out in the 1979 Statute of Autonomy. This included *inter alia* policing, language and culture, education, and health. At the same time, the central government gradually symmetrized a number of these concessions, extending them to other Autonomous Communities, at times even when some of them preferred the status quo. In addition, the trend toward greater policy decentralization was countered by the central government's frequently overbroad use of the framework and basic legislation.

Catalonia's fiscal autonomy lagged behind its policy capacity. Its spending obligations increased as it took over costly policy responsibilities such as health care, but its revenues remained confined to conditional and unconditional transfers from the central government, along with a narrow set of its own taxes and fees (León 2015, 118–23). This started to change with the new fiscal deal in 1987, after which the ACs began receiving a higher proportion of their funds from unconditional central state transfers. In 1993, the central government transferred 15 per cent of the personal income tax to the ACs (León 2015, 129). Catalan elites acknowledged this and previous transfers and changes to the system as improvements in revenue autonomy (Parlament de Catalunya 1993, 10343). As the Catalan government sought more resources and greater control over ceded taxes, the central executive made further concessions. In 1997, the incoming Popular Party government transferred an additional 15 per cent of personal income taxes to the ACs, along with legislative autonomy over half of the personal income taxes ceded (León 2015, 131–3) ("Round 1 – Response 1" in Figure 5.1).

CiU continued, however, to press for greater control over fiscal resources. As noted in the previous section, during the 1999 regional election the party called for a more far-reaching autonomy through a bilateral "fiscal pact" with the central government, along with more resources. While the central government did not transfer revenue-raising responsibilities to Catalonia, it did expand regional fiscal room.

In 2002, the ACS again received a higher proportion of income tax
(33%), with decision-making power over the entire bundle, as well
as part of VAT and a number of other taxes (León 2015, 134–8).

The standard explanation for this gradual expansion of fiscal
autonomy for Catalonia is that it was a consequence of CiU's political leverage over minority central governments in 1993 (PSOE) and
1996 (PP) (Verge 2013, 325). While important in accounting for
those concessions, political leverage alone cannot explain them. As
important were the structural conditions – notably the alignment of
strategies of governance between the governments of Catalonia and
Spain – that made these dispensations possible in the first place. This
alignment had two interlinked implications. First, the pro-market
policy orientation of the Catalan government moderated its demands
with respect to fiscal matters. Second, the alignment of strategies
and the moderate demands for fiscal autonomy also meant that the
central government found fiscal devolution acceptable. Devolving
greater power to similarly pro-market jurisdictions did not endanger
the centre's strategy of governance. In what follows I account for the
sources of the strategies of governance of the Catalan government on
the one hand, and the central government on the other.

Catalonia's market-oriented strategy of governance is closely
connected to the region's relative prosperity. It was the first part of
Spain to industrialize, thanks to its proto-mechanization in the second
half of the eighteenth century, Spain's trade policies, and the ability
to absorb new machinery over the porous French border (Marfany
2010; Thomson 2005). Historians regard the opening of the first
steam-powered textile mill in 1833 in Barcelona as the beginning of
Catalonia's industrial revolution (Thomson 2003, Ch. 9). The region's
take-off widened the already existing economic disparity between
Catalonia and Castilian-speaking Spain. Economic divergence continued into the twentieth century (Tirado, Paluzie, and Pons 2002,
349). Catalonia suffered from the autarkic policies of the first two
decades of Franco's dictatorship but benefited from the economic
liberalization and growth of the 1960s. Moreover, it was among the
top recipients of foreign direct investment during the late Franco era
(Harrison 1985, 157). It maintained its economic advantage during
the 1980s and 90s.[7]

Catalonia's wealth, along with its large middle class and powerful
bourgeoisie, has shaped the strategy of governance pursued since the
transition. CiU found its core support precisely in Catalonia's sizable

middle and upper classes (small, medium, and large business) as well as in its professional elites (Marcet and Argelaguet 1998, 75–6, 79). Consequently, the party developed a largely non-interventionist economic policy (Keating 2001, 225), though generally supporting investment in supply-side policies in the interest of regional business (Güell et al. 2010). Relations between the Catalan government and its counterpart in Madrid tended to be amicable, since they had common economic policy goals (Agranoff and Gallarín 1997, 15).

During the 1980s and 90s, Spain's central governments also pursued a pro-market economic policy. This choice was a result of the confluence of the crisis of the economic model inherited from the Franco era, the international policy and ideational context in which pro-market ideas were ascendant, and the Spanish elites' embrace of the European integration project. The pro-market strategy of governance was deployed by both left- and right-leaning governments. In fact, it was the Spanish Socialist Party (PSOE), first elected in 1982, that laid the foundations of the country's contemporary political economy.

To broaden its electoral appeal and simultaneously reduce the possibility of political and social friction that might threaten the newly established democracy, PSOE decided to abandon its formal commitment to expansionary, pro-employment policy (Share 1988, 417).[8] Instead, it developed a model based on restrained public spending and macroeconomic stability (Boix 1998, 109; Recio and Roca 1998, 140; Share 1988, 417), rationalization and reorganization of public enterprises for future privatization (Etchemendy 2004), and the use of public investment not to reduce socio-economic inequalities but rather to bolster the economy's supply-side capacity (Boix 1998, 110–13). The goals were to attract investment and to prepare the Spanish private sector for increased integration with the European and global markets (Holman 1996).

At the same time, successive PSOE governments expanded social protections in order to soften the blow of their economic policies. The combination of industrial restructuring and restrictive fiscal and monetary policy resulted in high unemployment, with rates double the West European average (Share 1988, 417). The Franco-era social welfare system was not equipped to address these challenges. Thus, the Socialists were compelled to shore up unemployment insurance, expand pension coverage, and broaden health care protections (Hamann 2000, 1036–7). While seemingly expansionist, these policies were not part of a transformative statist strategy of governance.

Rather, they were meant to make a pro-market strategy more palatable to the electorate and thereby reduce the likelihood of social strife.

The market-friendly approach of the PSOE governments (1982–96) was continued by the Partido Popular (1996–2003). Prime minister Aznar's preference for a market-based economy and a small state was reflected in his government's reduction in public spending and control of social outlays (Murphy 1999, 66). The privatization of public assets, already initiated by the Socialists, accelerated under his government (Salmon 2001, 139). Thus, both left- and right-leaning governments deployed a market-oriented approach to economic governance, buffered by a modest social welfare state. Between 1980 and 1990, patterns of public spending reinforced this interpretation, despite a spike in public spending in late 1980s and early 1990s. Past this point, public spending tended toward 40 per cent of GDP and was frequently below that figure (OECD 2010).

This alignment of strategies of governance at the two levels facilitated the accommodation of Catalonia's demands for more fiscal resources in several interconnected ways.[9] For one thing, it moderated the demands for fiscal and policy autonomy emanating from the region during Round 1. For CiU, autonomy was not a means of economic transformation of the regional economy, as it was for the far more interventionist Liberal Party of Quebec during the 1960s. As noted, far from being an economic laggard, Catalonia ranks well above the Spanish average on a range of relevant economic indicators. Moreover, the regional ethnic division of labour favoured the Catalans, in stark contrast to the situation prevailing in 1960s Quebec. Here, it was the Catalans who owned and managed businesses and the migrants from other parts of Spain who supplied the labour (Conversi 1997, 208).[10] Thus, neither the relative nor absolute levels of development, nor the internal political economy, militated in favour of an interventionist regional state.

These factors were reinforced by the fact that the governing CiU's core constituency was the middle class and the business community (Marcet and Argelaguet 1998, 75–6, 79). These social actors were the least likely to support economic interventionism. To the contrary, they were inherently averse to risky public initiatives (S. Greer 2007, 174). Political and economic stability was all the more important for big business, which was traditionally well-connected with the centres of power in Madrid (Keating 2014, 329). CiU had little to gain from escalating its fiscal demands vis-à-vis the central government; indeed, it might have antagonized a core constituency if it did so. Certainly, Catalan business has been in favour of greater regional control of revenues and more infrastructural investment, but this did not amount to a demand that Spain's political economy be reconfigured (Keating 2014, 328).

Thus, even when the CIU held the balance of power in the central parliament during the 1990s, it did not use that position to wrangle more than fairly modest fiscal concessions from the PSOE and PP governments (G. Greer 2007, 133). As Greer notes, CIU faced a dilemma: how was it to satisfy the nationalist demands of its more radical members and constituents, as well as the requirements of political and economic stability of its business constituents (G. Greer 2007, 135)? This dilemma would not be too acute in Round 1; it would prove to be far more taxing in Round 2, as I show in the next section.

This relative moderation of Catalan fiscal demands cannot be divorced from the strategy of governance pursued by successive Spanish governments. As I noted earlier, the pro-market orientation of these governments emphasized macroeconomic stability and investment in supply-side factors to facilitate growth based on private initiative. Social spending was generally restrained, as was the state's intervention on the demand side and via industrial policy. This meant that the fiscal burden of the central government on the entire Spanish economy, but especially on wealthier regions such as Catalonia, was more moderate than it would have been under an expansionist centre. Under that scenario, the central government would have placed a greater tax burden on wealthier regions of the country and would have pursued industrial policies that likely would have met with hostility from the Catalan business community. To the extent to which Catalan business is not the dominant player in Madrid, this would have resulted in more strident demands for fiscal autonomy in Catalonia, sooner than this did in fact happen. In the scenario that it did obtain, the Catalan government's demands for greater fiscal autonomy were largely met by the centre during the 1990s, as they did not threaten to undermine the latter's market-based strategy of governance.

This explanation must be qualified by the acknowledgment that in the context of a lopsided economic geography in which large swathes of the country are relatively underdeveloped, even a non-interventionist central government can ill-afford to ignore demands for fiscal redistribution. This is particularly the case in Spain because both major state-wide parties, the PSOE and PP, rely for their electoral fortunes on large constituencies in less-developed regions of Spain. Consequently, both PSOE and PP governments have maintained a system of inter-territorial redistribution that has benefited the less developed ACs at the expense of wealthier ones (Beramendi 2012, 184–6). This redistribution was increasingly criticized in Catalonia over the course of the 1990s.

As noted, CiU started calling for complete fiscal autonomy along Basque lines in the second half of the 1990s. However, it was only the intensification of electoral competition at the turn of the century that pushed it to actually pursue such an arrangement as a policy option. Indeed, a new fiscal deal was the key driver of the escalation of Catalan demands during the 2004–6 revision of the Statute of Autonomy. While this takes the discussion into Round 2, it has to be mentioned in light of the response by the socialist central government to that demand. Namely, while the deal that the Spanish government struck with the Catalan negotiators included a greater share of the state's revenue, the Catalan demand for a Basque-style fiscal arrangement was shot down. This was despite the fact that PSOE depended on the Catalan nationalists in order to govern, and despite the party's nominal dedication to a more plural Spain. As the then Minister of Finance, Pedro Solbes, noted, accommodating Catalan demands for more far-reaching revenue-raising autonomy would have endangered the fiscal capacity of the (central) state (Solbes Mira 2013). Indeed, given the disproportionate contribution of Catalan taxpayers to the central government, full fiscal autonomy for Catalonia would have potentially deprived the central government of an important source of funds for redistribution.

THE SYMBOLIC POLITICS STORY

The concessions granted to Catalonia during Round 1 did not result in open majority backlash. There was no sustained political opposition by a major political party or societal organization to the autonomy initially granted to the region through the 1979 Statute, nor to any additional elements that would be won over subsequent decades.[11] I argue that the key reason for this was the absence of major symbolic concessions to Catalan demands beyond the statute itself. While far-right politicians opposed the decentralization of the country initiated by the 1978 constitution, even what would become the centre-right Partido Popular eventually internalized the "state of autonomies." This does not mean there was no opposition to decentralization, particularly for Catalonia. At different times during the 1980s and 90s, the central government attempted to symmetrize and constrain devolution of power to the AC s, sometimes precisely in order to avoid the perception that it was recognizing minority nations. As importantly, the government tended to place legislative limits on Catalan autonomy through the overly detailed use of framework legislation. However, most of this opposition was conducted through legal, legislative, and administrative acts rather than ostentatious political repudiation of the Catalan national project.

The 1978 constitution provoked debates about the character of the Spanish state during which Catalan politicians articulated a vision of a nationally plural polity. Their Spanish counterparts, particularly those on the right of the political spectrum, countered with a monist understanding of the political community. Representatives of the centre-right Union of the Democratic Centre (UCD) accepted the term "nationalities" in reference to the Catalans, Basques, and Galicians, but they made it clear that they did not conceive of Spain as a multinational state.[12] According to Arias-Salgado "the term nationality merely recognizes the existence of socio-historical formations with the right to autonomy, the limit of which, as a matter an inviolable principle, rests precisely in the sovereignty of the political unity that encompasses those formations" (Cortes Generales 1978b, 2269). On this reading, Spain might be *culturally* plural, but that plurality did not extend to constitutive principles that would make the state itself multinational. Both Arias-Salgado and his counterpart Cisneros Laborda, a UCD member of the constitutional commission of seven, conceived of the indissoluble unity of both the Spanish state and the Spanish nation as a meta- and pre-constitutional principle (Cortes Generales 1978b, 2269, 2302).

Nevertheless, UCD proved reasonably flexible on the specific institutional expression of Spain's "social" pluralism. Its sought to legitimize the new order among the minority nations and to preclude the escalation of minority nationalist demands in the future (Cortes Generales 1978b, 2267). Representatives of the far-right Alianza Popular shared UCD's stance on the indissoluble unity of the Spanish state and nation but rejected the term "nationalities" altogether. AP representatives called for the application of the term "regions" to all territorial units of Spain, including those inhabited by minority nations. Both the term "nationality" and the asymmetry between "nationalities" and "regions" in Article 2 suggested unequal status

of different segments of the Spanish population and, more importantly, a repudiation of the idea of a single Spanish people (Cortes
Generales 1978b, 2272–3). On the PSOE side, there was greater
willingness to accept the regionalization of Spain, though even here
there was no contemplation of plurinationalism. Indeed, over time,
the Spanish left (outside Catalonia, Galicia, and the Basque Country)
abandoned the notion of plurinationality altogether (Balfour and
Quiroga 2007, 73–5).

Once the system of autonomy was firmly established, with the entire
state subdivided into seventeen Autonomous Communities, opposition to asymmetry and the *de facto* – if ambivalent – recognition of
minority nationhood did not take open political form. What did
happen was a gradual process of symmetrization that would, by the
late 1990s, largely equalize the formal powers and autonomy held by
most autonomous communities. This process had several sources.
One was the transformation of Spanish nationalism. Because their
ideas had been delegitimized by their association with the dictatorship, Spanish nationalists reinvented themselves through regional
politics and discourse. Even those local politicians tainted by association with the regime were thus able to legitimize their political activism
and simultaneously reinforce the idea of a single Spanish nation
composed of diverse but ultimately equal territorial populations
(Núñez Seixas 2005, 114).

The second source of symmetrization was competitive pressure
emanating from regions other than Catalonia, the Basque Country,
and Galicia. That pressure started with Andalusia, the first region
to react to what its leaders saw as the unequal treatment afforded
by the constitutional compromise of 1978. Namely, while the regions
that were able to claim autonomy during the Second Republic were
allowed a "fast track" route to more comprehensive autonomy, the
remaining territories faced a slower process. This provoked consternation in Andalusia, where bottom-up political pressure eventually
led to that region also being afforded the status of a nationality
(Newton 1982). Jurisdictional jealousies would keep pushing various
regions to demand the same level of autonomy that minority regions
had been able to carve out, which served to "equilibrate" and homog-
enize the system (Moreno 1997). At the same time, those regions
outside of Catalonia and the Basque Country in particular would
frequently use discourse invoking a unified vision of Spain in their
claims (Núñez Seixas 2005, 114, 118). These competitive pressures

among the regions were fostered by the statewide political parties, PSOE and PP, when they found themselves out of power (Verge 2013, 324, 327).

The third impetus for symmetry came from the central government itself. In the early 1980s, it strove for greater control over the process of decentralization, in part in response to the February 1981 coup attempt. The 1982 Organic Law on the Harmonization of the Autonomy Process (LOAPA) had as its stated goal the rationalization and harmonization of the devolution of power to the Autonomous Communities. The initiative provoked broad-based opposition in Catalonia and the Basque Country, where it was seen as an assault on their only recently recovered autonomy. The law was therefore challenged at the Constitutional Court, which subsequently emptied it of content. The judges found that the law constituted an undue incursion into the competencies of the Autonomous Communities. Importantly, it decided that the law was unconstitutional because it intended to use the principle of individual equality of Spaniards in order to justify the equalization of autonomy of Spanish Autonomous Communities (*El País* 1983).

Despite this early defeat, the central government managed to symmetrize autonomy across ACs over the coming decade and a half through various policy measures. Among the major events in this direction were the "autonomy pacts" signed by the two main parties, PSOE and PP, in 1992. These agreements upgraded the powers of lagging ACs, thereby equalizing the level of autonomy among the regions on a range of policy issues (Agranoff 1993, 8). By 2002 the major policy areas of education and health care had been devolved to all ACs, including those that originally had not had control over them (Gallego, Gomà, and Subirats 2005, 107–8). Arguably this equalization was driven by concerns about the effectiveness of policy-making and by problems that might have arisen as a result of the coordination of two sets of policy frameworks (Aja 2014, 56–7; Maiz, Caamaño, and Azpitarte 2010, 66). However, the push was also nourished by objections from various regional governments about the "special treatment" extended to Catalonia and the Basque Country (Agranoff 1993, 8–9). In addition, the central government used its constitutional prerogative to establish framework legislation in areas of shared competence, certain organic laws, and its ability to ensure general economic coordination to limit and symmetrize the autonomy of ACs (Maiz, Caamaño, and Azpitarte 2010, 68–71).

Whatever the motives behind these equalizing tendencies, they met with consternation in Catalonia. In 1993, the Catalan parliament warned against the homogenization of autonomous competencies by the central state and urged the regional government to "deepen the development of the Statute of Autonomy ... *taking into account the constitutional principle of heterogeneity and the Catalan differential fact*" (Parlament de Catalunya 1993, 10343–4; emphasis added). Nearly ten years later, the parliament would advocate a new stage of the autonomy process for Catalonia because "the existing political framework fails to recognize the plurinational, pluricultural, and plurilingual character of the state," linking this further to the "progressive homogenization of autonomy" (Parlament de Catalunya 2002, 24). More politically visible was the signing, in the summer of 1998, of the Barcelona Declaration by the leading nationalist parties of Catalonia, the Basque Country, and Galicia.[13] The document observed a "notable lack of recognition of our respective national realities," lamenting that after twenty years of democracy the three "historical nationalities" were still waiting for the "articulation of Spain as a plurinational state" (Juan 1998).

The central government's encroachments on the Catalan government's legislative turf, and the symmetrizing thrust of autonomy reforms, would bring about nationalist outbidding among the major Catalan political parties ("Round 1 – Mobilization" in Figure 5.1). By the late 1990s, CIU was shedding votes to the Socialist Party of Catalonia (PSC), which was starting to play the Catalan identity card as part of its political strategy (Barrio, Teruel, and Fontaine 2014, 105–6). In the 1999 and 2003 elections, PSC called for institutional reform, at the forefront of which was recognition of Catalan national uniqueness and the plurinational character of the Spanish state. Its 1999 electoral manifesto called for "political federalism, proceeding from the recognition of the historic nationalities, converting the Senate into the chamber of representation of the plurinational reality of Spain" (Partit dels Socialistes de Catalunya 1999, 7). By 2003 the party was calling for the reform of the Statute of Autonomy. At the same time, the openly independentist Republican Left of Catalonia (ERC) increased its share of the vote (Barrio, Teruel, and Fontaine 2014, 113). The 2003 election ultimately produced a coalition among PSC, ERC, and the Initiative for Catalonia/Greens (IC-V), the so-called Tripartit. The coalition's central policy plank was statute reform.

ROUND 2 — STATUTE REFORM
TO THE 2017 REFERENDUM

The Demand

Round 2 of the causal process in Spain kicked off with two elections – the regional contest of 2003 that brought the Tripartit to power, and the 2004 Spanish election, won by PSOE. Socialist victory in Madrid was crucial if the Tripartit's statute reform was to see the light of day. Indeed, not only did the Socialist leader José Luis Rodríguez Zapatero support the reform – he infamously pledged to accept whatever statute draft came out of the Catalan parliament (Rusiñol and Cué 2003). The reform unfolded between 2004 and 2006, with the draft statute passing from the Catalan to the Spanish parliament and ultimately being ratified in a regional referendum.[14] The draft that would emerge from the Catalan parliament in September 2005 was in part a result of the outbidding between ERC and CiU. While in opposition, CiU was nevertheless a veto player because of the supermajority requirement for the law's passage in the Catalan parliament. CiU conditioned its support for the project on the acceptance of a much more ambitious fiscal arrangement than the one contemplated by the Tripartit. The statute would be ratified by an overwhelming majority of parliamentarians, with 120 out of 135 MPs voting in favour (*El País* 2005b).

The ratified document was in effect a far-reaching demand for instrumental and symbolic concessions ("Round 2 – Demand 2" in Figure 5.1).[15] It was significantly longer than the 1979 version (containing 227 articles, compared to the original 57), specifying in great detail the exclusive competencies of the regional government in order to insulate them from the central executive and parliament's encroachments (España 1979). It would have created a fully autonomous judiciary, elevated Catalan as the preferential language of administration, education, and public communication, and created an entirely new fiscal arrangement. Articles 204 and 205 essentially transferred the collection of all state taxes in Catalonia to a newly created Catalan revenue agency (Parlament de Catalunya 2005).

Its symbolic aspect, however, was arguably even more important. The very first article replaced the 1979 reference to Catalonia as a nationality with the simple and impactful statement declaring Catalonia a nation. Moreover, the document stipulated that the powers of the Catalan government emanated from the *Catalan* people, rather than, as in 1979, from the Spanish constitution, the statute, and "*the* people" (not specified by name). Finally, it established as one of the foundations of the political framework the principle of "the plurinationality of the [Spanish] state." In other words, the 2005 Statute implied a *de facto* symbolic reconstitution of the Spanish state on foundations that would prove unpalatable for a significant proportion of the Spanish political elite and population.

The Response

The response to these demands differed markedly from the pattern observed during Round 1. During the 1980s and 90s, regional leaders had often criticized what they portrayed as an unfair advantage for Catalonia (and the Basque Country). However, neither PSOE nor PP engaged in sustained political mobilization against the concessions made to either of the two regions. In fact, most of the response to what the central elites saw as undue concessions to Catalonia came in the form of legislative, legal, and regulatory changes, none of which were particularly symbolically prominent. Round 2 brought about a different pattern. Starting in 2005, the opposition PP ramped up its rhetorical and political action in explicit and open opposition to the Catalan Statute ("Round 2 – Majority Backlash" in Figure 5.1). The recognition of Catalan nationhood provoked particular hostility.

The first line of defence of the symbolic status quo was the Spanish parliament. The parliamentarians altered two notable features of the statute draft. First, they moved the reference to Catalan nationhood from the body of the text to the preamble. Second, the fiscal arrangement embedded in the 2005 statute was scaled down in conformity with the prevailing "common fiscal regime." In exchange, the PSOE government conceded greater resources to Catalonia (Colino 2009, 272–3). These changes alone would have been sufficient to provoke a reaction among the more radical segments of Catalan nationalist opinion. Indeed, ERC called on its supporters to vote against the revised statute in the confirmatory referendum in 2006 (*La Vanguardia* 2006).

Had this been the only response to the statute, it might not have amounted to much. However, the PP went further, spearheading an open *political* campaign against the new arrangement. In October 2005 it called on the legislatures of all ACs to pass resolutions opposing the statute (Marcos 2005a). In December of the same year, it held a large demonstration in Madrid, foregrounding the idea of a single Spanish nation in clear opposition to recognition of Catalan nationhood (Marcos 2005b). Finally, the party initiated a country-wide petition for a Spain-wide referendum on the Catalan Statute (Junquera and Tesón 2006). In a high-profile stunt, PP's leader Mariano Rajoy presented 4 million signatures in support of the proposed referendum. In Rajoy's words, the initiative was "in defense of the rules of the game from 1978, of the Spanish nation, and equality among all Spaniards" (EFE 2006).

PP's campaign constituted an explicit, and highly visible, political repudiation of the Catalan demand for recognition, one supported not only by a political party but also by a significant segment of the Spanish population. A survey in October 2005 demonstrated the degree of opposition to the statute. In an echo of Canadian opposition to the "distinct society" clause, Spaniards outside Catalonia were particularly resistant to the idea of Catalans as a nation, with 69.4 per cent opposing this element of the statute and only 23.3 per cent in favour.[16] A lower percentage of respondents, 53.2 per cent, rejected a separate fiscal arrangement for Catalonia, with 30 per cent in favour (*El País* 2005a). Once the statute was finally ratified, PP went further still, taking it to the Constitutional Court. While court challenges had been a prominent feature of Spain's multi-level politics, PP's 2006 appeal was unusually comprehensive and thus perceived in Catalonia as a major challenge to Catalan self-government (Casanas Adam and Rocher 2014, 52–3).

Political Consequences

The political mobilization against the recognition of Catalan nation-hood produced a counter-reaction in Catalonia that would lead to a massive shift in favour of secession in 2012. Between 2006 and 2009, the less patient secessionists within ERC and CDC attempted to move both parties to endorse independence as an immediate policy position in response to the developments related to the Statute of Autonomy. Their efforts were mirrored in extra-party secessionist activism, with small groups of activists fanning across Catalonia and making the case for independence.[17] Both sets of players argued that the events of 2005 and 2006 indicated that the negotiated path to an acceptable level of self-government and recognition was at an end (Basta 2018).

Both intra- and extra-party efforts failed to convert either of the two nationalist parties to the cause of independence. Support for secession among the Catalans was growing, but did not exceed 20 per cent during this period (see Figure 5.2). This prompted secessionist activists to change their strategy. In September 2009 they initiated what would become several waves of informal municipal-level referendums on Catalonia's independence (Muñoz and Guinjoan 2013). These events would put in place the organizational backbone for what would soon become a mass-based secessionist movement. During the first referendum, held at a small municipality of Arenys de Munt, two veterans of the pro-independence movement, Miquel Strubell and Pere Pugés, founded a non-partisan organization whose sole purpose would be to promote the idea of independence and, equally importantly, to change the calculus of the nationalist parties on the issue.[18] This effort would result in the formation of the National Assembly of Catalonia (ANC) in 2010.

In the midst of independentist mobilization, in June 2010, the Spanish Constitutional Court issued its verdict on the Catalan Statute. A number of important articles were struck down or reinterpreted in a more restrictive manner, including those related to the preferential use of Catalan over Castilian language in public administration and the media; autonomous judiciary; and fiscal competences. Most importantly, the judges stipulated that the reference to Catalonia as a nation in the statute's preamble had no legal effect (Delledonne 2011, 8). Their decision contributed to growing resentment in Catalonia. While it did not by itself transform Catalan politics,[19] it provided the pro-independence movement with a potent tool for mobilizing undecided Catalans. The explicit denial of Catalan nationhood was arguably more impactful than the changes in the instrumental features of the statute.[20] The slogan of the large demonstration against the verdict held two weeks later suggested as much: "we are a nation, we decide" (*La Vanguardia* 2010).

In September 2012, the now much stronger ANC led a massive demonstration for independence. The event coincided with, and arguably spurred, a sizable increase in support for secession, which now easily exceeded 30 per cent and would continue to grow. Catalonia's president, Artur Mas, made one last-ditch effort to obtain a new fiscal deal from the Spanish government but was rebuffed. In light of this outcome of the secessionist mobilization in the streets, and of the rapid increase in support for independence, the autonomist CIU made

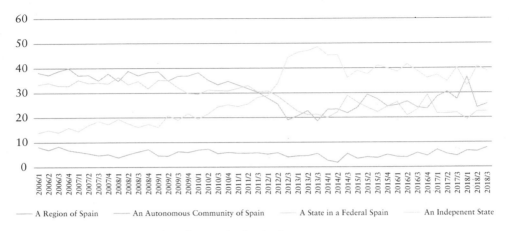

Figure 5.2 Institutional Preferences in Catalonia, 2006–2017

Source: Data from Catalan Government's Centre d'Estudis d'Opinió
(http://ceo.gencat.cat/ca/barometre/?pagina=1).

a secessionist turn ("Round 2 – Secessionist crisis" in Figure 5.1).[21] Mas called an early election in which he promised he would hold a referendum on Catalonia's status. It was at this moment that the support for independence registered its high-water mark, reaching 44.3 per cent (see Figure 5.2).

In the aftermath of the election, CIU and ERC formed an alliance based on a mutual commitment to the referendum. This commitment, along with the central government's refusal to permit such a vote, would mark the next five years of Catalan and Spanish politics. In the event, by mid-2013, close to 50 per cent of Catalans supported independence, and the regional government went from one clash to another in its attempt to stage a referendum. The entire 2012–17 period was a prolonged secessionist crisis, culminating in an attempt by the regional government to hold a unilateral referendum and then to proclaim independence in October 2017. When the central government suspended Catalonia's autonomy in response, it was the first and only suspension of its kind since the creation of Spain's system of territorial autonomy.

CONCLUSION

The Spanish case corroborates most of the predictions developed in Chapter 3. During the 1980s and 90s (Round 1), the governments of

Catalonia and Spain shared broadly similar, market-oriented strategies of governance. This alignment, along with the influence of the Catalan middle and upper class over the region's dominant party, CiU, moderated the Catalan government's fiscal demands. Throughout this period, the regional government called for a greater share of fiscal resources and a greater say over revenue policy. It did not, however, pursue comprehensive fiscal autonomy. Its demands were largely met by successive central governments.

At the same time, increasingly vocal demands during the 1990s that Catalan nationhood be recognized were disregarded. In fact, the Spanish central government passed institutional and policy reforms that were interpreted by key political actors in Catalonia as entrenching a vision of Spain as a nation-state rather than a multinational polity. These changes symmetrized the levels of autonomy available to all autonomous communities, thereby diminishing the institutional differentiation that minority political elites saw as an expression of the country's plurinationalism. Moreover, in order to control the decentralization process, central governments frequently overstepped their jurisdictional reach and intervened in the policy competencies of the Catalan government. Both these facts, combined by the increasing identity-based competition among Catalan political parties, facilitated the escalation of demands toward the end of Round 1. Thus, both CiU and the Catalan Socialists called for more powers and the explicit recognition of Catalan nationhood. At the same time, Round 1 did not feature open majority backlash against concessions made to Catalonia.

The competition between PSC, CiU, and the Republican Left (ERC) would eventually lead to the demand for a new Statute of Autonomy for Catalonia (Round 2). The proposed statute would have entrenched the existing powers of the Catalan government, given it new powers in legal, linguistic, and fiscal matters, and recognized Catalans as a nation. By contrast to Round 1, this time the central government proved willing to combine symbolic recognition with instrumental concessions. The result was political backlash spearheaded by the opposition PP.

As expected by the model outlined in Chapter 3, this opposition led to a partial reversal of concessions initially granted, notably through the 2010 decision of the Constitutional Court. In addition, the politicized backlash demonstrated the unwillingness of a significant segment of the Spanish political elite to recognize the Catalan claim to nationhood and to reimagine Spain as a multinational state.

This elite opposition was mirrored among the Spanish public. Opinion polls at the time showed very high levels of disapproval (around 70%) for the recognition of Catalan nationhood in the statute. This was higher than opposition to the other elements of the new institutional package.

These events strengthened the hand of independentists in Catalonia's political and civil society, as predicted by the model in Chapter 3. While the political leaders of major nationalist parties, CDC and ERC, initially resisted a turn to secessionism, extra-parliamentary mobilization shifted their electoral calculus, leading the autonomist CiU and the temporizing ERC to embrace the cause of independence in 2012. This shift in the party system was both encouraged by, and further stimulated, the rise in secessionist support among the population, which reached a high of 48 per cent in late 2013. The secessionist outbidding between CiU's dominant party, CDC, and ERC would lead to a unilateral attempt at independence in the fall of 2017 and to the suspension of Catalan autonomy by the central government.

6

Yugoslavia and Croatia from the Re-emergence of the National Question to the Break-Up

In the early 1970s, Yugoslavia experienced a series of seismic institutional shifts that would set it on the path to dissolution. These had their origins in the early 1960s. At that point, the political and intellectual elites in Croatia and Slovenia, the country's wealthiest republics, began advocating for greater autonomy over crucial investment funds and economic policy. Over the following decade, those instrumental demands were reinforced by increasingly vociferous claims for the recognition of the specificity of Yugoslavia's nations. This chapter tells the story of the response these demands elicited among the federal political elites and in Serbia – home to the country's most numerous national community.

As long as the strategy of governance adopted by Croatia and Slovenia clashed with the policy priorities of the federal elites, the latter resisted pressures for more comprehensive fiscal and economic autonomy. However, during the mid-1960s, the country's central party leadership shifted from statist to market-friendly policy orientation, opening the path for the accommodation of the Croat and Slovene demands ("Round 1 – Response 1" in Figure 6.1). Decentralization would be slow in coming: some of the reforms, instead of transferring investment decision-making from the federation to the republics, simply shifted it to a different set of centralized institutions. During this period the federal authorities made halting concessions to national particularism that fell far short of what the nationalist wing of the Croatian League of Communists, and especially the nationalist intelligentsia and students, had called for.

Federal foot-dragging on instrumental issues antagonized the Croatian party leadership. At the same time, regime norms against

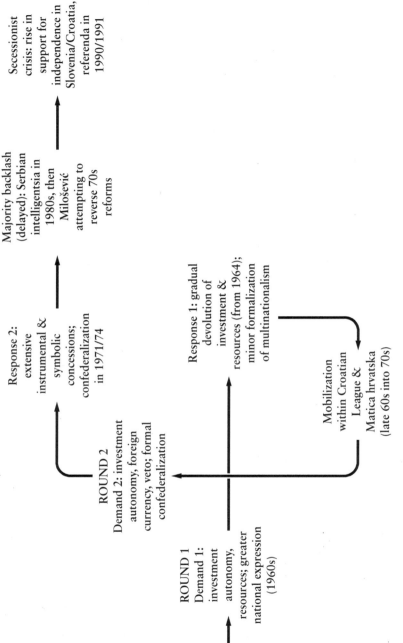

Figure 6.1 Yugoslavia 1960–1991 causal process summary

the public expression of national identity facilitated the mobilization of Croat nationalist opposition in the late 1960s ("Round 1 – Mobilization" in Figure 6.1). The extra-party nationalist pressure, combined with the negotiations with federal elites and other republics, drove the Croat leadership to escalate their demands during what would become known as the Croatian Spring. The new initiative included not only stripping the federal government of its investment role and acquiring greater control over foreign currency for Croatia, but also constitutional reform to convert Yugoslavia into a *de facto* confederation and to replace socialist Yugoslavism with explicit multinationalism ("Round 2 – Demand 2" in Figure 6.1).

The centre conceded on both issues ("Round 2 – Response 2"). Most of Croatia's institutional and policy demands were met through a series of institutional changes that culminated in the 1974 constitution. The Belgrade-based banks in charge of the country's investment funds were dismantled and their resources and decision-making authority were devolved to the republics. Croatia's enterprises were allowed to retain a significantly higher proportion of the foreign currency they earned. At the same time, a more far-reaching formal commitment to the principle of multinationality was expressed in the very institutions of the federal government – a collective presidency was established, the republics were constitutionally recognized as states and given *de facto* veto power over key areas of federal legislation. Croatia's triumph, however, came at a cost. In its reformist zeal, the republic's governing elite had fostered a degree of political pluralism that the federal party found intolerable. This prompted the country's leader, Josip Broz Tito, to replace Croatia's top leadership with a more pliable set of officials.

Because of the regime's authoritarian character, and the clampdown on nationalism in the wake of the Croatian Spring, Serb backlash against the new institutional framework took a decade to materialize ("Round 2 – Majority backlash"). Initially, opposition took place behind the scenes, with Serbia's political elite attempting to reverse the republic's internal fragmentation. In parallel, a segment of the Serbian intelligentsia began developing a comprehensive critique of the new institutional reality. They argued that the constitutional changes of the 1970s had undercut the supra-national aspects of Yugoslavism. Even on its own terms, they argued, the new multinational articulation of the state was unfair: since Serbia was the only republic subdivided into autonomous provinces, the Serbs had ended up being the only nation without a constituent unit truly of their own.

These grievances constituted the ideological backbone of the political program of Serbia's new leader, Slobodan Milošević, in the late 1980s. Milošević would begin reversing the institutional realities established in the early 1970s by changing the status of Serbia's provinces, and through direct political intervention in Montenegro. These actions, combined with the mass mobilization of Serbian nationalism, fuelled the secessionist movements in Slovenia and, later, Croatia ("Round 2 – Secessionist crisis"). Referendums on the status of those two republics in 1990 and 1991 would lead in time to the violent dissolution of the state.

THE BACKGROUND: NATIONAL QUESTION FROM FIRST TO SECOND YUGOSLAVIA

Yugoslavia was established in 1918 through the merger of the South Slav fragments of the defeated Habsburg Empire and independent Serbia and Montenegro.[1] Great Power politics played an important part in this outcome. Nevertheless, the new state also owed its existence to the nineteenth-century idea of South Slavic (Yugoslav) unity. Advocates of Yugoslavism were particularly active in the Habsburg lands. They viewed cooperation between the Serbs and Croats within Austria-Hungary as a means to achieve greater political influence and recognition, while increasingly looking to cooperation with Serbia itself (Gross 1979). In Serbia, which had been autonomous since the early nineteenth century and independent since 1867, the Yugoslav idea was less prominent, overlapping with the aspiration for the unification of Serbs in Serbia and those in the Habsburg Monarchy (Pavlowitch 2003, 59–60). The First World War brought the two sides together. The Yugoslav idea aided the strategic calculations of both the Serbian government and a narrow set of South Slav political elites in the Habsburg domains. The outcome was a hastily arranged unification under the Serb crown on 1 December 1918 (Banac 1984, 114–40).

National consolidation was already well advanced among the Serbs and the Croats before the war, with the result that the political elites claiming to represent those two communities harboured conflicting notions of the appropriate institutional organization of the Yugoslav state (Djokić 2012, 80). The leadership of the Croatian Peasant Party

(CPP), the pre-eminent political force among the Croats, advocated federalism as a way of maintaining Croatian statehood under the new circumstances (Biondich 2000, Chs. 5–7). The Serb political elite, however, had little patience for the principles of national pluralism. Apart from emphasizing the political and administrative benefits of centralization, the leaders of Serbia's major parties did not see Yugoslavia's communities as nationally distinctive. Members of the Radical Party saw all Štokavian speakers (including the majority of Croats) as potential Serbs, whereas for the Democratic Party all of the "tribes" of the new state were components of a single Yugoslav nation (Biondich 2000, 152–4).

These two visions clashed repeatedly. In 1928, CPP's leader Stjepan Radić was assassinated by a Serb representative in the parliament. The following year, the king abolished the multi-party system and adopted a policy of national assimilation (Djokić 2003, 148–50). The resentment bred by these developments led to the king's assassination at the hands of Croat and Macedonian nationalists in 1934 (2003, 136). While relations between the Serbs and the Croats were not universally antagonistic – Croatia won autonomy in 1939, for instance – the political conflict surrounding the constitutional question stoked tension between members of the two nations. This would have fateful implications for the course of the Second World War in Yugoslavia.

Having reneged on a non-aggression pact with Nazi Germany, Yugoslavia was invaded in April 1941. Within two weeks, it had been defeated and dismembered by the Axis powers and their Balkan allies. Much of what is today's Croatia and Bosnia became the Independent State of Croatia, the governance of which was entrusted to the Ustaše, an Italian-backed fascist organization (Tomasevich 2001, 47–61). The rabidly anti-Yugoslav Ustaše considered the Serbs, amounting to one quarter of the new entity's citizenry, as a hostile element. Consequently, they proceeded to eliminate the Serb population through expulsions, forced conversions, and mass killings (Levy 2009).

The genocide against the Serbs produced the conditions that would ultimately destroy the Croat para-state. The Serb population rose up, joining either the Serb royalist Chetniks or, in increasing numbers, the communist-led Partisan guerrilla army. Over the course of the war, ever greater numbers of Croats would join the Partisan struggle, turning the communist army into a multinational force.[2] The Communist Party of Yugoslavia (CPY) used the war to build a broad-ranging coalition, with which it managed to win the war, taking power in 1945. The key element of CPY's success was its dual-track strategy of fomenting social revolution and addressing the nationality question. Indeed, the party vowed to recognize national differences through a federal reorganization of the state (A. Djilas 1991, Ch. 6). This promise of national equality and recognition through federalism, along with the fact that the Partisans were the only non-sectarian force during the war, enhanced the movement's legitimacy (A. Djilas 1991, 153). In 1945, the Yugoslav state was re-created as a federation of six republics, five of which, including Croatia, were conceived of as homelands of the titular nation.[3] As a matter of political practice, however, the system was highly centralized, with all strategic decisions being made by the CPY Politburo (Shoup 1968, 119).

This would begin to change in 1948, when tensions between Yugoslavia and its Soviet patron exploded into open acrimony. The expulsion of the country from the Soviet Bloc resulted in a thorough rethinking of the regime's ideological foundations (Rusinow 1977, 47–61). To distinguish themselves from the Soviets, the country's leadership developed a new model of socialism. The Yugoslav variant was premised on the deliberate weakening of the state in order to avoid the political and economic ossification characteristic of the Soviet Union. Prior to the break with the Soviets, the political and economic affairs of the country were decided and (micro)managed from the centre. Federal state institutions determined and administered the entire economic activity of the country. The republics served as a policy transmission belt, implementing decisions made by the higher authorities (Tuković 2003, 135).

The anti-statist direction charted in the early 1950s stripped the federal government of a number of its administrative functions, transferring them to the republics, municipalities, and enterprises (2003, 137). The reforms of 1950 and 1952 formally converted enterprises into autonomous organizations, established workers' councils, and gave both a modest amount of decision-making authority (Ward 1957). Local governments were placed in charge of personnel decisions in these enterprises, thus acquiring a significant patronage role (Rusinow 1977, 66, 98; Ward 1957, 375). Beginning in the mid-1950s, the republics acquired limited budgetary control, having been granted a say over investment decisions through the establishment of republican investment funds (Flaherty 1982, 110). Yet despite all these changes, the concentration of power in the federal executive, economic regulation through the federal plan, and control over investment through the federal General Investment Fund (established in 1953) ensured the centre's continuing dominance. As late as 1963, 66.8 per cent of all investment was funnelled through GIF, with only 20 per cent accruing to the republican funds (Dubey and World Bank 1975, 213).

In tandem with these institutional changes, the central leadership started to emphasize commonalities among Yugoslavia's nations. The 1953 constitutional reform de-emphasized the formal sovereignty of the republics expressed in the 1946 constitution. Yugoslavia's constitutional architect, Edvard Kardelj, explained that while the new system did not imply "the fusion of the Yugoslav peoples into one Yugoslav nation," nationality became a secondary factor, and federal Yugoslavia "not only a union of nationalities and their states, but ... above all ... a bearer of the social functions of a unified socialist community of Yugoslav working people" (Kardelj 1953, 26–7). This elevation of explicitly socialist Yugoslavism (to distinguish it from the pre-war integral variant) would be reaffirmed at the 7th Congress of the League of Communists of Yugoslavia in 1958.[4] Again emphasizing the equality and recognition of Yugoslavia's nations, the party program endorsed "Yugoslav socialist patriotism," which, rather than negating individual nationhood, was presented as a precondition for its development (Savez komunista Jugoslavije 1965, 181). Both the instrumental and the symbolic changes contributed to the re-emergence of the national question by the late 1950s.

ROUND 1 – SOCIALIST YUGOSLAVISM TO THE CROATIAN SPRING

The Demand

The political climate of the 1950s makes it difficult to discern the character and intensity of republican demands. The principle of democratic centralism meant that open departures from the strategy charted by the party hierarchy were not tolerated. Consequently, there were no *public* claims for greater autonomy on instrumental grounds. Instead, republics exerted pressure through either obstruction or behind-the-scenes appeals. By the early 1960s, these pressures had intensified. Appeals for the recognition of national uniqueness were even less prominent, though it was clear that legal experts in Slovenia and Croatia (and at times in Macedonia) articulated a different vision of the Yugoslav federation than their counterparts in Serbia. In addition, by the early 1960s intellectuals in Croatia and Slovenia proved more willing to voice displeasure about the symbolic organization of the Yugoslav state.

Croat and Slovene representatives made their instrumental demands clear at the expanded session of the Executive of the Central Committee of LCY in March of 1962. They supported a sharp turn to the market mechanism at the state-wide level and were highly critical of how investment had been centralized in the federal GIF. Croatia's premier, Jakov Blažević, criticized what he saw as the overcentralization of investment and the consequent concentration of political power in Belgrade (Savez komunista Jugoslavije 1998, 155–7).[5] The Slovenian premier, Boris Kraigher, staked out a similar position (1998, 237). Kraigher's speech revealed the Slovenian leadership's opposition to the 1961 social plan and its attempt to unilaterally alter its implementation in their republic (1998, 236). Demands by Slovenia and Croatia for greater autonomy over investment decisions in particular, and over resources and economic policy in general, would continue throughout the 1960s ("Round 1 – Demand 1" in Figure 6.1).

Croat and Slovene politicians were far more circumspect about demanding greater recognition of national identity during Round 1. One possible explanation for this reticence was that the regime already did recognize Yugoslavia's multinationality. A more likely reason is that the federal party leadership found open expressions of national particularism highly problematic and was intent on punishing its manifestations. Nonetheless, one can observe attempts to counter socialist Yugoslavism by reinforcing the idea of Yugoslavia as a community of nations and not much more. Influential legal scholars from Slovenia, Croatia, and at times Macedonia interpreted the Yugoslav constitutional order in a multinational key.

In the aftermath of the constitutional changes that had de-emphasized the sovereignty of republics, Croatian jurist Ferdo Čulinović argued that Yugoslavia was "a composite state, representing a system of dual statehood ... primarily for the purpose of the constitutional expression of Yugoslav multinationality" (Čulinović 1955, 127). Ten years later, on the occasion of the promulgation of the new federal and republican constitutions, the head of Slovenia's legislative commission felt it necessary to emphasize that "the Republican Constitution is an original act of the sovereignty of the working people in the republic; *its validity does not arise from the Federal Constitution*, and it does not have the character of a supplementary act or decree governing the enforcement of the provisions of the Federal

Constitution" (Globevnik 1963, 28; emphasis added). Given the centralization of party organs, and their close alignment with the legislative bodies, it is unlikely that this interpretation was voiced without the explicit consent of the Slovenian party leadership. While it cannot be qualified as an open demand for greater recognition, it amounted to an assertion of national sovereignty.

These positions were amplified in the cultural sphere. The most public and explosive expression of Croatian national identity was the Declaration on the Name and Status of the Croatian Literary Language, published in 1967. That declaration was a direct response to a 1954 initiative when a group of authors and linguists signed an agreement on the unity of the Serb and Croat languages. At that time, the so-called Novi Sad Agreement dovetailed with the official ideology concerning the national question. The 1967 declaration, initiated by the central Croatian cultural institution, Matica hrvatska, and signed by high-profile cultural figures, eighteen other cultural organizations, and relevant university departments, essentially reversed the 1954 agreement. It called for the constitutional recognition of a separate Croat language, regardless that language's linguistic identity with another (Serbian) one ("Deklaracija" 1967).

The signatories of the declaration argued that, by being identified with its Serbian counterpart, the Croatian language had effectively been suppressed within federal institutions and reduced to the status of a local dialect. They therefore called for the constitutional entrenchment of the equality of four Yugoslav languages (Slovenian, Macedonian, Serbian, and Croatian). That public documents frequently included reference to Slovenian, Macedonian, and Serbian (in place of Serbian and Croatian, or as equivalent of Croatian) language, was taken by the signatories to mean that "the Croatian people is not represented and that it is placed in an unequal position" ("Deklaracija" 1967). The Croatian League and state authorities reacted swiftly by expelling a number of signatories from the organization, while issuing warnings to others (Dragović-Soso 2002, 34). Even so, the emphasis on national particularity would intensify in the next stage of negotiations between Croatia's leaders and their federal counterparts.

The Response

THE POLITICAL ECONOMY STORY

The response to the instrumental demands of the Croat (and Slovene) leaders for the transfer of investment resources from the central government to the republics and enterprises must be divided into three periods. Prior to 1964, the central leadership still largely supported the dominant role of central institutions in fostering the country's economic development. During this period, Croatia's and Slovenia's demands were not accommodated. When the strategy shifted to a market-based one during the 1964–66 period, a spate of reforms devolved authority to enterprises and the republics. Nevertheless, some important functions remained vested in central institutions – most notably, the investment funds, which were transferred from the GIF to Belgrade-based investment banks, and policy authority over foreign currency. Thus, while the 1964–70 period did see the decentralization of resources and powers, substantial control over investment flows continued to elude the republican governments. It was only when the Croat leadership escalated its demands in 1970, kicking off Round 2, that the remaining federal economic powers were devolved.

Prior to the 1964–65 economic reform, most of the core demands of the Croat and Slovene leaders went unheeded. The reform made wholesale alteration of Yugoslavia's political economy possible. The GIF was abolished in 1964, though its functions were transferred to Yugoslav banks (Rusinow 1977, 160). The tax burden on enterprises was lowered, which met another demand by pro-reform Croatian and Slovenian leaders (Raičević 1977, 65). Republics and municipalities obtained their own resources for public service provision, compensated by federal transfers if those funds were insufficient to meet their needs. However, between 1964 and 1971, while the republics were entitled to "determine and dispose of their revenues," the federal government controlled the most significant sources of revenue, including sales taxes and levies on personal incomes (Raičević 1977, 68).

As the decade wore on, the Croat leadership adjusted their demands to the new realities. The mid-decade reform of the savings and investment system transferred funds and responsibilities to three large Belgrade-based banks. Since this meant that Croatia continued to be denied access to a significant amount of the wealth its enterprises produced, the leadership asked that the banks be divested of this power.[6] Croatia's government also started asking for greater control over foreign currency by the enterprises that earned it. Since these firms were disproportionately concentrated in Slovenia and tourism-oriented Croatia, this in effect would have meant more revenue autonomy, particularly given the importance of foreign currency for the financing of imports necessary for further development (Rusinow 1977, 207–8).[7] These demands were not met during the first stage of negotiations, but they would be addressed in the early 1970s.

In Yugoslavia, as in Canada and Spain, both the nature of minority demands and the centre's response to them were influenced by the alignment in the governance strategies adopted by the central and claimant governments. Croatia's (and Slovenia's) greater wealth relative to the Yugoslav average predisposed their elites to embrace market-based policies to a greater extent than was the case with their counterparts in the less developed republics. As long as the Yugoslav leadership pursued a statist strategy of governance, the demands made by Croatia and Slovenia for greater investment and fiscal autonomy would not be accommodated. The funds needed for more rapid development and provision of public services for the federation's less developed units were disproportionately raised in the two developed republics. Forgoing those through the decentralization of savings and investment would have undermined the centre's ability to fulfill its obligations to the less developed parts of the country. The central elites' shift to a market-based strategy in the mid-1960s is thus crucial in accounting for the subsequent decentralization of investment and resources to republican governments. Once they embraced the market mechanism and the attendant economic and political consequences (including higher unemployment and greater individual and regional inequality), the decentralization of investment and fiscal resources was no longer prohibitive.

The market-oriented strategy of governance that the Croat and Slovene leaderships endorsed was a reflection of their republics' relative wealth.[8] Both territories had been constituent parts of the Austro-Hungarian Empire until 1918, whereas the other four Yugoslav republics had been ruled by the Ottoman Empire until the nineteenth or, in some cases, the early twentieth century.[9] Though lagging behind Western Europe, Austria-Hungary had nevertheless been part of the "single technological community composing [the] European economic miracle" (Good 1984, 238). Some of its economic dynamism had spread to its South Slav borderlands. The railway link between Vienna and Austria's seaport in Trieste had fostered commercialization and small-scale industrialization in Slovenia (Lampe and Jackson 1982, 77). The Hungarian government, competing with its Austrian partner, had built a railway to its own outlet to the sea, the Croatian port city of Rijeka (Fiume). This stimulated limited economic development in Croatia/Slavonia (1982, 299–300).

By contrast, Bosnia, Serbia, Montenegro, and Macedonia had been marginal territories of a polity that was itself far from economically dynamic.[10] The Ottoman government had little control over the rapacious local elites on which it depended for revenue. As a result, the populations in these areas tried to escape the burden those elites imposed on them by opting for a subsistence pastoral economy (Lampe 1989, 189). Independence did help Serbia modernize but not to the point of catching up with the Slovenian and Croat lands (Palairet 1997, 369). The world wars reinforced these patterns. The material losses of the First World War were disproportionately concentrated in Serbia and Montenegro (Tomasevich 1955, 226–9). The Second World War told a similar story, though in this case Bosnia, the site of some of the most significant military operations during the war, was also affected.

Yugoslav communists thus inherited a regionally lopsided political economy. The country was ruled by a centralized communist party; even so, after it broke with Stalinism in the late 1940s, differences in attitudes toward the role of market forces started to emerge along national lines. Two key elements are of importance here. First, because of the longer tradition of industrial production in Slovenia and Croatia and greater enterprise efficiency, managers and policy-makers in those two republics were more accepting of market mechanisms. Moreover, given the statist bent of federal economic policy both before and after the break with Stalin, Slovenia and Croatia tended to subsidize development in other parts of the country.

Ideas about the socialist market economy that emerged in the early 1950s thus had greater resonance in Slovenia and Croatia than in the rest of the country, where it was feared they would exacerbate relative economic backwardness. We see this most clearly in the early 1960s, when Croatian economists, supported by republican politicians, expressed much more open support of the market mechanism than their colleagues from other republics (Milenkovitch 1971, 125, 160; Rusinow 1977, 124). In the aforementioned March 1962 meeting of the Executive Committee of the LCY, Croat and Slovenian leaders almost universally favoured the market mechanism, with their Serb, Bosnian, Macedonian, and Montenegrin counterparts, along with federal officials, remaining more apprehensive about such a course.[11]

The federal centre's strategy of governance shifted decisively between 1964 and 1966. Between 1950 and 1963–64, one could describe that strategy as formally committed to socialist market production, though in practice it tolerated only the most minimal elements of market competition (Milenkovitch 1971, 101–20; Sirc 1979, 58). As noted, Yugoslavia's break with the Soviet Union had prompted the Yugoslav leadership to come up with an alternative model of socialism. The result was an emergent brand of anti-statist socialism – a system formally devised to undermine the capacity of the state bureaucracy to monopolize social power. The chief ideologue of the party, Milovan Djilas, argued that the state was necessary for the achievement of socialism but that its consolidation and bureaucratization threatened the very socialism it was helping bring about (M. Djilas 1950, 9). The solution to the rigidities of statist socialism was to be found in the "ever broader and bolder drawing of the masses into the administration of the state and economy," and the corresponding reduction of the role of the state in those domains (1950, 31).

The political dimension of Yugoslav anti-statism entailed extensive formal decentralization of authority to the municipal level.[12] On the economic side of things, important aspects of decision-making were formally devolved to enterprises and workers. A 1950 law established workers' councils in all socially owned companies. The councils were meant to have a say in wage differentials, labour incentives, and the hiring of chief executives (Horvat 1971, 77, 114). The operations of enterprises were no longer subject to strict quantitative limits. Within the boundaries of the general social plan, they could decide what to produce, how, and in what quantities (Rusinow 1977, 64). They were also subject to the price signals in the consumer goods sector, at least until the mid-1950s (Horvat 1971, 110). Inefficient enterprises could go bankrupt, though few actually did (1971, 105). These reforms notwithstanding, the federal state continued to play a dominant role in investment, while erecting a veritable forest of regulations that in effect reduced enterprise autonomy and the workings of the market mechanism to the bare minimum during the 1950s (Sirc 1979, 20–3).

By early 1960s, the torrid economic growth of the previous decade had evaporated, precipitating a political crisis in the central Yugoslav leadership. In the debate about how to best restore the country's economic dynamism, one side backed continued government intervention, and the other a more radical deployment of the market mechanism. By 1964, the outcome of this conflict resulted in Yugoslavia's leadership taking a decisive turn toward the market (Rusinow 1977, Ch. 5). The reorientation took place in several steps and was driven by the belief – as expressed by its architect, Sergej Kraigher – that

Yugoslavia had "reached a level of development at which the further advancement of the economy necessitates the expansion of the market as one of the fundamental regulators of economic trends" (Flaherty 1982, 117).

The reform rested on five pillars. First, prices of inputs were to be adjusted upward toward international levels. Second, the fiscal burden on enterprises was to be slashed, leaving a higher proportion of revenue – along with the authority to decide on investment and wages – with those who produced it. Third, investment policy was to be transferred from the abolished General Investment Fund to the companies themselves. Fourth, banks were to start playing a much more prominent role in allocating investment, and were to do so according to business criteria. Finally, Yugoslav economy was to become integrated into the international division of labour through international trade, particularly with the more competitive economies of the West (Bićanić 1966, 637–9).

This shift to laissez-faire socialism was more than mere window dressing. The depth of the regime's commitment to "market socialism" can be seen in its willingness to accept the politically damaging consequences of the reform, most notably a significant and regionally differentiated increase in the rate of unemployment (Woodward 1995, 197, 201–3), and a rise in inequality among the republics (Pleština 1992, 136). In this context, the decentralization of economic decision-making and resources to the republics, notably to those that demanded it the most – Slovenia and Croatia – became feasible.

We see this not only in the early abolition of the General Investment Fund in 1964 but in a number of subsequent measures as well. The constitutional amendments of June 1971 significantly enhanced the fiscal autonomy of the republics, which gained full control over enterprise and personal income taxes, including the ability to determine tax bases and rates (Raičević 1977, 74–5). Perhaps more importantly, the federal government's revenues became subject to republican control. Slightly over half of federal revenues came from the federation's own sources, but between 43 and 47 per cent of the remainder were transfers from the republics and provinces, which now collected those revenues themselves (1977, 71, 73). In addition, the overall limit to the federal budget was set by inter-republican agreement, giving the republics the power to cap federal revenues (1977, 71).

In December of 1971, the hard currency system was reformed in line with the Croatian demands. The amount retained by companies was increased from 7 to 20 per cent, and to 45 per cent in the tourist sector that was overwhelmingly concentrated in Croatia (Burg 1983, 160). As part of the same process, the three large Belgrade-based investment banks were wound down. The largest, the Yugoslav Investment Bank, was broken up, its capital distributed among its republican branches, each of which became a free-standing institution (Lampe, Prickett, and Adamović 1990, 91).

Thus, the shift in the federal strategy of governance made the decentralization of economic resources and powers to the republics possible. As long as the central party and state leadership emphasized the alleviation of inter-territorial imbalances through large-scale intervention by the federal centre, forgoing fiscal and investment resources in favour of the republics was a non-starter. Greater fiscal and investment autonomy for the republics meant that Slovenia and Croatia would get to keep more resources for themselves, which by extension meant there would be less for the remaining republics. These fears were expressed openly in the contentious March 1962 meeting of the LCY Executive Committee.[13]

Indeed, even as the centre embraced laissez-faire socialism, the less-developed republics made their acquiescence to this path conditional on the establishment of a mechanism for the alleviation of territorial inequalities. That mechanism was the Fund for the Accelerated Development of the Less Developed Republics and the Autonomous Province of Kosovo, established in 1965 by consensus of all republics, including Slovenia and Croatia. Ultimately, this concession by the developed republics did not reverse the market-oriented thrust of federal policy. It ensured the less-developed republics' support for the market reform favoured by Croatia and Slovenia, and it set limits on – and implied a possible end to – the aid provided by those republics to the rest of the federation (Pleština 1987, 117). In other words, the compromise built a wall around the fiscal autonomy of the two wealthier republics, though that wall would continue to be assailed for the next two decades, with periodic demands for greater territorial redistribution.

THE SYMBOLIC POLITICS STORY

The concessions granted to Croatia and Slovenia during Round 1 did not result in open political backlash and mobilization among the political elites of the largest community, the Serbs. The comparison with the previous two cases suggests that the reason for this absence was the character of the changes: they were largely confined to instrumental matters and therefore did not constitute a manifest challenge to the symbolic order with which many Serbs identified. The story, however, is more complex. The decade did see a gradual drift away from socialist Yugoslavism and toward multinationalism in formal institutional terms. That shift caused unease among a segment of Serbia's political and intellectual elite but did not cause a reaction that the more far-reaching reforms of the 1970s would.

As in Canada and Spain, conflict over instrumental aspects of autonomy was embedded in debates about the symbolic articulation of the state. The difference was that the Yugoslav central leadership was more comfortable acknowledging the multinational character of the polity it governed. Indeed, the institutional recognition of Yugoslavia's multinationality was, along with workers' self-management and international non-alignment, one of the three pillars of the regime's legitimacy. This orientation had been adopted by the Party in the immediate pre-war period and confirmed during the Second World War (A. Djilas 1991). When the Communist Party took power in 1945, it institutionalized national pluralism through a federal system that granted each of the nations a territorial unit of its own.[14]

However, during the 1950s this multinationalism was tempered by the aforementioned ideology of "Yugoslav socialist patriotism." Socialist Yugoslavism was not meant to replace existing national loyalties (Savez komunista Jugoslavije 1965, 181). According to the party leadership, the introduction of self-managed socialism "[made] the community of the Yugoslav *peoples* a community of the Yugoslav working *people* which makes it possible for every one of our working men to call himself with pride a Yugoslav, a member of the Yugoslav socialist community without renouncing his national origin or his love for his national language and culture" (Kardelj 1953, 27; emphasis added). Thus, while the new socialist community was not to be understood as a hybrid nation, national particularism was to take a back seat to socialist Yugoslavism. This formula was implemented through a variety of initiatives that institutionalized cultural collaboration among Yugoslavia's nations (Budding 1998, 59). Unsurprisingly, socialist Yugoslavism found its greatest and most lasting resonance among Serb intellectuals and politicians (1998, 56).

In the early 1960s the balance between Yugoslavism and multinationalism began shifting in favour of the latter. The 1963 constitution reinstated the right of Yugoslavia's nations to self-determination (Yugoslavia 1963). This reference was dropped from the 1953 Constitutional Law, which merely affirmed that Yugoslavia was a "federal state of sovereign peoples" (Yugoslavia 1953). The constitutional amendments of 1967 and 1968 enhanced the status of the republics by converting the moribund Chamber of Nationalities to the most important house of the federal parliament (Cohen 1977, 131–3). A similar change took place within the League of Communists (Burg 1983, 64).

Accompanying these institutional shifts were increasingly frequent expressions of national particularism in Slovenia and Croatia. In 1961, the Slovene poet Dušan Pirjevec confronted the Serb author, and member of the Serbian League's Central Committee, Dobrica Ćosić, over the latter's critique of excessive "republicanism." Pirjevec emphasized the inviolability of republics as "clearly formed national organisms" against Ćosić's insistence on the threat of inter-republican (and thus national) antagonisms toward the Yugoslav idea (Budding 1998, 72). As prominent was the 1967 Declaration on the Name and Status of the Croatian Literary Language, in which Croat intellectuals conspicuously denounced the spirit of socialist Yugoslavism. In 1969, a Slovenian proposal for a World Bank infrastructure grant was ignored by the federal government. The episode provoked unprecedented political mobilization on the basis of republican and national grievance (Burg 1983, 89).

This gradual shift in the Yugoslav symbolic order and the associated events did not elicit a political reaction from the country's largest community, the Serbs, for several reasons. First, the enumerated changes did not constitute a wholesale transformation of the Yugoslav state. The confederalizing reforms of 1967–68, for instance, were highly technical and likely of little importance to the everyday lives of the general population. Moreover, they had been initiated by Bosnia and Herzegovina, the only republic without a titular nation. They could thus not be framed as an instance of nationalist excess. Second, even if there were pressures on the Serb leadership to push back against the current of events, doing so on the basis of Serb nationalism or integral Yugoslavism was unpalatable since both positions were anathemized by the LCY. Third, the short-lived "liberal" leadership of Serbia, headed by Marko Nikezić and Latinka Perović, itself advocated a kind of symmetric "republicanization" of Yugoslavia between 1968 and 1972.[15]

Finally, regime type mattered. Open departure from policy set by the federal Central Committee was considered the most grievous breach of political norms. Consequently, and given both the league's emphasis on the danger of Yugoslav unitarism and the official turn to greater recognition of national specificity since the 1964 LCY Congress, articulating a pan-Yugoslav position was fraught with dangers for anybody, but particularly for the Serbs (Shoup 1968, 212–26). For all these reasons, despite the gradual drift away from Yugoslavism, there was no comprehensive political mobilization among the Serbs, either among the elites or at the societal level.

Yet resentment among the Serbs did grow. The Association of Writers of Serbia one-upped the Croatian Declaration of 1967 by arguing for separate cultural and educational institutions for Serbs in Croatia and Croats in Serbia, a veiled warning that Croatia's territorial integrity should not be taken for granted (Budding 1998, 140–1). Between 1967 and 1969 the Belgrade literary journal *Književne novine* condemned what it perceived as the rising anti-Yugoslavism in intellectual, economic, and political spheres (1998, 159). Finally, during a contentious session of the League of Communists of Serbia in 1968, two members of the Central Committee, the aforementioned Ćosić, and Jovan Marjanović, criticized the federal league's abandonment of Yugoslavism in favour of national and republican particularism (1998, 170–6; Rusinow 1977, 246). In classic integrationist manner, Ćosić argued that group-based institutional measures should give way to functional (economic or social) issues relevant to individual citizens. Serbia's Central Committee distanced itself from both individuals' statements and then revoked their membership in the body (1998, 175–6).

The only sustained effort to arrest the gradual drift toward national affirmation during the 1960s took place behind the scenes. The head of the federal secret service and one of the most prominent members of Tito's inner circle, Aleksandar Ranković, and his allies in the federal and Serbian security apparatus, obstructed the decentralizing economic reform of the mid-1960s (Rusinow 1977, 179–83). Ranković was charged with abusing the power of his office and stripped of all his functions in 1966 (1977, 183–91). The Serbian League of Communists would accuse him of Serb nationalism, integral Yugoslavism, and centralism. Key figures of the Serb national revival over the next two decades would flag this event a major symbolic turning point. At the same time, however, Ranković's obstructionism was aimed at the reform, rather than accommodation of the national aspirations of non-Serb nations.

Both the halting pace of reforms and the limits to the expression of national particularity contributed to nationalist mobilization in Croatia ("Round 1 – Mobilization" in Figure 6.1). By 1968 the Croatian leadership felt that it could not extract further instrumental concessions through established party procedures. While the General Investment Fund had been dissolved and greater fiscal resources had been transferred to the republics, major economic decisions continued to be made in federal institutions. Croatia's leaders thus felt that their autonomy was still constrained despite the reforms and that this would *continue to be so* as a result of the opposition mounted by the less-developed republics and the federal apparatus (Klasić 2018, 286). It thus decided to change its strategy by mobilizing mass support behind its program. At the same time, the more permissive political climate following Ranković's ouster resulted in mobilization among the Croatian intelligentsia and insistence on greater attention to the Croat national question. The most obvious manifestation of this was the 1967 declaration, but this was only the most dramatic example of the increasing readiness of intellectuals, students, and the media to articulate national grievances more openly (Batović 2017, 99–100; Čuvalo 1987, 91–102).

ROUND 2 – CROATIAN SPRING TO THE FIRST MULTI-PARTY ELECTIONS

The Demand

Croatia's leadership escalated its demands in early January 1970, at the 10th session of the republic's Central Committee. On this occasion, the league's leader, Savka Dabčević-Kučar, reinforced Croatia's demands for the transfer of authority from the federation to the republics, municipalities, and enterprises (notably with respect to investment decisions, foreign trade companies, and foreign currency) with a more vigorous defence of institutionalized multinationalism ("Round 2 – Demand 2" in Figure 6.1). She dismissed the danger of Croat nationalism, foregrounding instead the threat of Yugoslav unitarism to the country and the regime. She denounced the very idea of a "single Yugoslav people" and insisted that only full recognition of multinationality guaranteed a strong Yugoslavia (Savez komunista

Hrvatske 1970, 8). Nations of Yugoslavia "are not bound by some mystical ties, some abstract feeling of Yugoslavism. What binds us are existing and future economic, social, and political *interests*, and political progress we achieved, each nation of Yugoslavia and us all together, through self-managed socialism, under these very social conditions" (1970, 14; emphasis added). For Dabčević-Kučar it was the refusal to acknowledge national sentiments, rather than their excess, that threatened to bolster nationalism among the country's smaller nations (1970, 9). Yugoslavia could prosper only if it continued to decentralize in the political *and* economic spheres and if the country's elites abandoned Yugoslavism.

In addition, Dabčević-Kučar announced a change in political strategy. She argued that the league should accept what she argued was reasonable criticism with respect to pressing social problems even if it contradicted its own policy (1970, 7). This passage must be read in conjunction with her evaluation of the activities of Matica hrvatska, Croatia's foremost cultural association, increasingly assailed by the Belgrade press as the hotbed of Croat nationalism. While acknowledging that some of the organization's activities overstepped the bounds of what the league could consider acceptable, she argued against the complete rejection of Matica's activities in light of that group's positive contributions to public debate (1970, 17).

The session signalled a more permissive environment for the expression of Croat national claims. This would contribute to an outbidding dynamic between the Croat League and the Matica on matters of Croat national interest. The Matica had already been promoting a Croat national program; during 1970 and 1971 it become a *de facto* opposition party, pushing the Croat leadership toward more extreme positions in its negotiations with the centre. During those two years, the organization increased its membership from 2,000 to 41,000, expanded its territorial reach, and articulated increasingly radical nationalist demands (Savez komunista Hrvatske 1972, 151–69). In addition to advocating improved material conditions for Croatia, Matica's publications proposed that the republic be recognized as "a sovereign national state of the Croatian people" (1972, 202).

The Croat leadership used this mobilization as leverage in its negotiations with the centre. As they found themselves increasingly isolated on a number of economic and political issues, Croat elites insisted on the institutionalization of a republican veto in federal league and state institutions, as well as on republican parity in the staffing of all major federal institutions (Burg 1983, 104, 110). These demands reflected the multinational vision of the Yugoslav state announced in Dabčević-Kučar's speech of January 1970. This escalation of Croatia's demands mirrored events in Quebec in 1976–80, with the rise of the Parti Québécois and the 1980 referendum, and the victory of the Tripartit coalition in Catalonia in 2003 and the initiation of statute reform there. The three processes shared several characteristics. They all came after the initial expansion of autonomy, dissatisfaction with the pace of that expansion, and the perception of the centre's failure or refusal to acknowledge the multinational character of the state at the expense of the overarching state-wide identity.

The Response

As noted in the previous section, most of Croatia's demands for greater fiscal and investment autonomy were met in the first half of the 1970s. This included the transfer of fiscal and investment resources to the republics and the increase in foreign currency retention quotas. More importantly, the constitutional changes in 1971 and 1974 continued the symbolic reorganization of the Yugoslav state. The 1967–68 amendments converted the Chamber of Nationalities, previously a subordinate part of the lower parliamentary chamber, into a separate body of republican delegates that would dominate federal legislation. The change signalled that the state drew its legitimacy from the republics as national homelands.

The 1971 amendments reinforced this principle by granting each republic veto power over federal policy, thus satisfying a key Croat demand (Burg 1983, 110). The 1974 constitution would go a step further. Article 1 characterized Yugoslavia as "a federal state *having the form of a state union* of voluntarily united nations and their socialist republics" (Yugoslavia 1974, emphasis added). This contrasts with the same article in the 1963 constitution, in which the country was defined as "a federal state of voluntarily united and equal nations" (Yugoslavia 1963). The 1974 reform thus converted Yugoslavia from a federal state into a federal–confederal hybrid.

Another critical symbolic change was a cumulative result of past institutional adaptations. Serbia was the only republic with autonomous provinces – Vojvodina, with a Serb majority, and Kosovo, with an Albanian one. The constitutional changes between 1967 and 1974 granted these provinces far-reaching formal autonomy. Perhaps as importantly, all elements of this shift in institutional symbolism had come as a result of an unprecedented and well-publicized mass mobilization in Croatia. It became clear that a significant part of the Croatian population, along with their leaders, opposed the idea of a Yugoslavia that was certainly multinational, but in which there was room for an integrative – though not assimilationist – Yugoslavism.

This symbolic reconstitution of the state was doubly distasteful to many Serbs. First, it repudiated Yugoslavia as an institutional fact that *transcended the mere interests of its constituent peoples*. Serb intellectuals of Yugoslav orientation saw the Yugoslav state as inherently valuable. Part of the reason for this was the cost the Serbs were seen as having paid for the creation of both Yugoslavias: in the First World War by winning against overwhelming odds and then ensuring that Austrian and Italian troops did not usurp swathes of Slovene and Croat territory; and in the Second World War by their disproportionate early participation in the Partisan forces. As importantly, in this understanding, the Serbs had been willing to forgo their narrow national interests in the name of South Slavic fraternity.[16]

Because of the paucity of research addressing public attitudes toward the state, we do not know with certainty whether the Serb population shared this attachment to Yugoslavia.[17] Still, a survey conducted in the early 1990s suggests that even after a decade of souring on "brotherhood and unity," the overwhelming majority of Serbs identified with Yugoslavia. Serbs were more likely to list the common state as important for their territorial affiliation (71%) than were either the Croats (48%) or the Slovenes (26%) (Perunovic 2016, 10). Yugoslav nostalgia reveals a similar pattern. A 2017 Gallup poll found that a higher proportion of Serbia's residents (82%) saw the breakup of Yugoslavia as "harmful" than either those in Slovenia (45%) or Croatia (23%).[18] In light of the available evidence from Yugoslavia, and the general tendency of majorities to identify with the state,[19] it is safe to assume that the attitudes toward the Yugoslav state captured by Serb intellectuals were likely held by a significant proportion of the Serb population.

The second reason the new symbolic order fostered Serb resentment was the perception that it was unfair even on its own terms of presumptive equality of nations. The constitutional change of the late 1960s and early 1970s had replaced socialist Yugoslavism in official institutions with pronounced multinationalism. However, this conspicuous multinationalism was asymmetric, since Serbia was the only republic with autonomous provinces. This was quickly seized on by Serb intellectuals, who pointed out that other republics exhibited diversity that warranted their own internal federalization. The uneven application of the multinational principle meant, as Serb intellectuals would end up claiming, that Serbs were the only Yugoslav nation without their own national state. Both strands would inform the gradual mobilization among Serb political and intellectual elites over the coming decade.

Political Consequences

Despite the growing resentment, Serb political campaign against the new symbolic order would be slow in coming. Apart from Ćosić and Marjanović's opposition in 1968, open resistance first came from the legal profession. In March 1971 the Law Faculty at the University of Belgrade hosted a debate about that year's constitutional amendments. All speakers opposed the shift they were witnessing. Two major arguments stood out, reflecting the dual character of Serb resentment articulated earlier. The first was that, by approving the amendments, the Yugoslav leadership "had given up on Yugoslavism" (Budding 1998, 186–7). The second was that the multinationalism expressed through the amendments was unjust: "if Albanians in Serbia had a province, so should Albanians in Macedonia and Serbs in Croatia" (1998, 184).

Some of these arguments would be taken up by the Serb political leadership several years later. After the passing of the 1974 constitution, the Serbian League came up with the so-called Blue Book – an unpublished critique of the position in which Serbia had found itself as the consequence of constitutional changes. Most of the document details the republic's division into three territorial jurisdictions (inner Serbia, Vojvodina, and Kosovo) (Ðekić 1990, 123–74). While the text outlines numerous ways in which the fragmentation either did or *could* lead to inefficiencies in policy-making, and details how it undermined Serbia's power in federal institutions, it locates the gravest affront in the symbolic domain: "In our constitutional system, the Socialist Republic of Serbia [is also] the national state of the Serb people. In light of the pronounced weakening of the unity of the Republic as a single entity, and its increasing differentiation into three separate ... domains, the question emerges *whether or not the Serb people is, in a manner equal to other nations of Yugoslavia, realizing the historic right to its own national state* within a Yugoslav federation that rests on the principle of national self-determination" (1990, 172; emphasis added). In other words, despite a litany of instrumental arguments preceding this passage, the ultimate point was that internal fragmentation was unacceptable because it applied only to Serbia and not any other republic. In the event, the Blue Book would remain out of the public eye in the late 1970s, and Serb politicians would remain largely quiescent for another half decade.[20]

It was the intellectuals, rather than Serbia's politicians, who started developing a public critique of Yugoslavia's new symbolic order ("Round 2 – Majority backlash" in Figure 6.1). The basic premise, voiced by numerous literary figures, philosophers, economists, and historians, was that Yugoslavia had been a costly mistake for the Serb nation. While the list of grievances included the safety and status of Serbs in Kosovo, the inefficiency of the federal state, and various other instrumental issues, the unifying theme was the opposition to the 1974 constitution (Budding 1998, 211–12). The constitution was simultaneously a repudiation of Yugoslavism and the embodiment of the unfair treatment of the Serb nation. The principle of multinationalism that it established was, according to this view, advantageous to all but the Serbs. They were divided in Serbia and dispersed across other Yugoslav republics with no political autonomy (Dragović-Soso 2002, 84–5, 99, 137).

The 1986 Memorandum of the Serb Academy of Sciences and Arts, frequently referenced as the "blueprint" for the later policies of Slobodan Milošević, merely restated grievances that were already well-established by that point: "The Constitution of 1974 in effect split up Serbia into three parts. ... A nation which after a long and bloody struggle regained its own state, which fought for and achieved a civil democracy, and which in the last two wars lost 2.5 million of its members, has lived to see the day when a Party committee of apparatchiks decrees that after four decades in the new Yugoslavia *it alone is not allowed to have its own state*. A worse historical defeat in peacetime cannot be imagined" (Srpska akademija nauka i umetnosti 1995, 133).

While instrumental issues were certainly important in mobilizing the intelligentsia, the political elites, and the general population behind a revisionist Serb national program, the central element was symbolic. Had the main concern of the critics of the 1974 constitution been the protection of political, economic, or social interests of the Serb nation, formal symmetrization would not have facilitated that goal. Granting autonomy to Serbs in other republics on the same grounds presumably would have done little to help their co-nationals in Kosovo, who increasingly protested the pressures by the Albanian majority. By extension, reducing or eliminating Kosovo and Vojvodina's autonomy would have done nothing to improve the political position of Serbs in other republics. The focal political issue, instead, was the abandonment of Yugoslavism and the perception of the unfair treatment of the Serb nation under the multinational framework established in the first half of the 1970s.

These grievances would find their champion in the person of Slobodan Milošević, who took the reins of power in Serbia in 1987. Milošević was stood out from his predecessors in two ways. First, he proved more willing to challenge the institutional status quo established by the 1974 constitution and to ride the wave of mass mobilization in doing so. Second, he was willing to break with the institutional norms of the Yugoslav socialist regime by acting unilaterally. He reduced the autonomy of Serbia's two provinces, Vojvodina and Kosovo, through a combination of constitutional amendments, the use of mass unrest against the government of Vojvodina, and military and police repression in Kosovo (Jović 2003, 415). Ultimately, though, it was his willingness to reach beyond the boundaries of Serbia that provoked a reaction in other republics, most notably in Slovenia and Croatia. Leaders in these republics believed that Milošević influenced the protests that ultimately brought down the leadership of Montenegro in early 1989 (2003, 424).[21] Indeed, in April of that year Milošević would announce that Serbia's real goal was to change the constitutional order and "strengthen" Yugoslavia (2003, 416–17).

The Slovenian leadership was the first to respond to the changes initiated by Serbia with legislative action. Most importantly, the Slovene parliament amended the republican basic law, in effect proclaiming its supremacy over the federal constitution and preparing the legal foundation for independence (Hayden 1992; Huszka 2014, Ch. 2).[22] Croatia's communist leadership would be more cautious, but by the first multi-party elections in May of 1990, it had been displaced by a much more radical option, the nationalist Croatian Democratic Union. Serbia's turn against the institutional status quo of the 1970s facilitated, and was in turn facilitated by, the increasingly secessionist reaction in Slovenia and Croatia. Ultimately, neither international diplomatic intervention, nor the danger of impending war, prevented the two wealthy republics from holding referendums on independence ("Round 2 – Secessionist crisis"). In December 1990, 95.7 per cent of Slovenians voted for independence, and in May of the following year, 93 per cent of Croatia's population opted for the same (2014, 54, 94).[23] War, and the country's dissolution, followed a few short months later.

CONCLUSION

Yugoslavia largely aligns with the expectations of the model developed in Chapter 3. In the early 1960s, Croatian and Slovenian leaders began pressing for greater economic autonomy for their republics. These demands were reinforced by increasingly vocal expressions of national particularism, though the latter initially tended to be voiced by intellectuals rather than political leaders. As long as the centre relied on the federal state apparatus to foster growth in the less developed parts of the country, economic decentralization demanded by the two wealthier republics remained untenable. Such decentralization would have deprived the federal institutions of resources required to fulfill their redistributive mandate.

By the mid-1960s, however, Yugoslavia's leadership had abandoned statism in favour of a market-based strategy of governance. Once the federal government turned its back on the territorial redistribution of resources, decentralization and the accompanying surrender of control over investment and revenues to the republics (particularly the wealthier ones) became more acceptable. Between 1964 and 1971, most of Croatia's economic demands were met, though not at the pace desired by the republic's leadership. The institutional changes made in response to Croat and Slovene demands did not provoke sustained political backlash from the most numerous national community, the Serbs. While official state policy departed from the socialist Yugoslavism of the 1950s, the reforms of the 1960s did not amount to a sudden and wholesale symbolic reconfiguration of the Yugoslav state. Though these developments displeased some members of the Serb political and intellectual elite, they did not mobilize against them openly.

In the late 1960s, the halting pace of reforms frustrated the Croat political leadership, which decided to escalate its demands for reform. At the same time, the regime's tendency to suppress the more vociferous expressions of Croat national identity encouraged nationalist mobilization among the intelligentsia and the students. The cultural society Matica hrvatska became the organizational epicentre of Croat nationalist activity, providing the Croat leadership with an additional reason to radicalize its claims against the Yugoslav state. This mobilization would eventually result in a more far-reaching set of demands by the Croat leadership in 1970, ones that included both instrumental and symbolic elements, including institutional reform along *de facto* confederal lines. The centre acceded on both scores. The constitutional changes of 1967 to 1974 converted Yugoslavia from a federal multinational state into a *de facto* confederation of nation-states.

For many Serbs, this symbolic reconfiguration presented two problems. First, it dispensed with the idea of Yugoslavism as a value in itself, above and beyond a mere community of self-interested nations. Second, even as it established the dominance of the principle of national autonomy and equality, it did so asymmetrically. The constitutional settlement of 1974 left Serbia as the only internally fragmented republic. Both elements would fuel Serb resentment, though open political mobilization took longer to materialize than in Spain and Canada. Serb mobilization was an iterative process initially led by intellectuals in the first half of the 1980s, and only picked up by the political elite with the rise of Slobodan Milošević in 1987. Once Milošević started to dismantle the institutional legacy of the 1974 constitution, his actions fed into a counter-mobilization, first among the Slovene politicians and later among the Croat elites. In both cases, the result was a secessionist crisis in 1990–91, one that would break the country apart.

7

Czechoslovakia from the Velvet Revolution to the Velvet Divorce

In April 1968, Czechoslovakia's leaders attempted to liberalize the country's communist regime and build "socialism with a human face." As part of the package of political and economic reforms that would become known as the Prague Spring, Slovakia won formal recognition and wide-ranging political autonomy. The hardline crackdown and recentralization that ensued froze Slovak self-government until 1989.[1] In terms of the model developed in Chapter 3, the 1968–89 period represented an aborted Round 2 (see Figure 7.1). The end of communism coincided with the re-emergence of demands for greater recognition and autonomy for Slovakia. This chapter explains how federal elites and their counterparts in the Czech Republic responded to those demands, and why and with what political consequences.

Slovakia's post-communist leaders demanded extensive economic and fiscal autonomy (instrumental claim), as well as formal recognition of their republic as the state of the Slovak nation (symbolic claim). The political economy configuration prevented agreement on matters of political economy. The federal and Czech elites pursued radical market reform, whereas their Slovak counterparts endorsed a more interventionist strategy of governance. Since accommodating Slovak demands implied diluting the reform, Czechs negotiators refused comprehensive fiscal and economic autonomy for Slovakia.

Conflict over the symbolic concessions had a more ambiguous outcome. On the one hand, the Czech side continued to acknowledge the binational character of the state and to recognize Slovakia as the state of its titular nation. This was in keeping with the tradition established in 1968. Yet Slovak representatives pushed beyond the existing level of recognition, asking that the country's post-communist

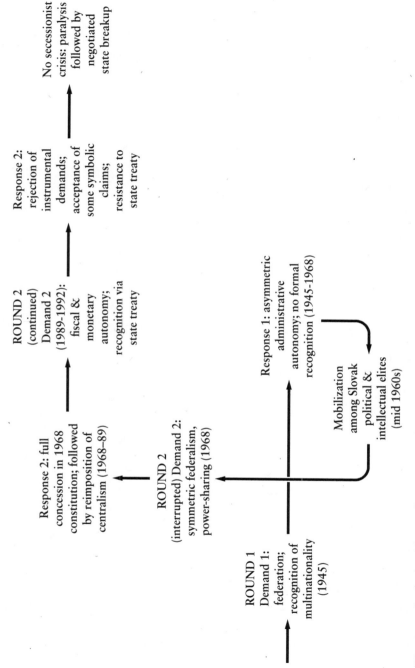

Figure 7.1 Czechoslovakia causal process summary (emphasis on 1989–1992 period)

constitution be based on a "state treaty." That treaty would have
formally created sovereign Czech and Slovak states at the very moment
that it joined them to form the democratic Czech and Slovak Republic.
In contrast to the Canadian, Spanish, and Yugoslav cases, the central
elites did not accept this demand. Consequently, there was no majority
political mobilization against the Slovak national project. As expected
from the model, the absence of majority backlash meant no rise in
support for secession in Slovakia. Independence was the choice of a
mere fifth of the population, and almost none of the republic's relevant
parties pursued it.

Czechoslovakia's break-up, then, was not a consequence of a secessionist crisis. Rather, it was a result of the political impasse just
described and the institutional framework inherited from the communist period. The veto power that both republics wielded according
to the 1968 constitution meant that the Czechs, despite their numeric
preponderance, were unable to impose their institutional preferences.
Faced with the possibility that the federal economic program would
be diluted and the country re-created on confederal foundations, the
Czechs pulled the plug on the common project. The case therefore
largely corroborates the expectations set out in the model developed
in Chapter 3.[2]

THE BACKGROUND: SLOVAK NATIONALISM
AND THE CZECHOSLOVAK STATE

Czechoslovakia was created in the waning weeks of the First World
War (Kirschbaum 1993, 71).[3] While the break-up of Austria-Hungary
and the involvement of the Great Powers were necessary in producing
that outcome, they were not sufficient. A vital ingredient was the
willingness of the Czech and Slovak political elites to create a common state. Each side had good strategic reasons for doing so. The
Slovaks were short on the political infrastructure needed to run their
own affairs, so they hoped that joining the Czechs would further their
political and social development (Kirschbaum 1993, 72). The Czechs,
having developed their own political and administrative elite through
participation in Habsburg politics, were far better equipped to run a
state of their own. Because that state would have included three million potentially restive Germans, adding two million Slovaks would
ensure Slavic political preponderance (Krejčí 1996, 8; Kirschbaum
1993, 72).

Despite overlapping interests, the two sides did not share a common vision either of the state they were entering into or the political community the state would encompass. Czech elites considered the two peoples as the same political nation, with the Slovaks a culturally, politically, and economically inferior appendage. In the ideology of Czechoslovakism, the unification returned the Slovaks to the Czech national fold from which history had hived them off (Bakke 2004, 28, 34–5). Czech elites, along with a substantial proportion of the Czech population, thus did not acknowledge the Slovaks as a nation with the right to recognition and self-government.[4]

These attitudes shaped the institutions and policies of the new state. The 1920 constitution established a unitary system without autonomy for the Slovak part of the country, in breach of the 1918 Pittsburgh Agreement.[5] In fact, the Czechoslovak parliament refused autonomy to the Slovaks on three occasions during the inter-war period (Kirschbaum 1993, 84).[6] This was in keeping with the constitutional preamble, which stipulated a single Czechoslovak nation (Bakke 2004, 26). Furthermore, there was no possibility of declaring oneself to be a Slovak (or a Czech) in the census, and the Slovak language was constitutionally subsumed under the hybrid Czechoslovak category (2004, 26). History books for Czech students tended to relegate Slovak history to a footnote, and those for the Slovak students did not emphasize their identity either (2004, 27–8).

Such developments antagonized an important segment of the Slovak society. The Slovaks were more or less evenly divided between those committed to the Czechoslovak national project and those who viewed that project as dangerously assimilationist (2004, 35). The latter, largely supporting the Slovak People's Party, continued to press for recognition and autonomy throughout the inter-war period (2004, 41). However, as the autonomist parties were largely kept out of power, their demands remained unheeded, contributing to festering dissatisfaction among Slovak nationalists (Krejčí 1996, 11). In 1938, in the aftermath of the Munich Agreement, Slovak nationalist politicians would exploit Hitler's pressure on Czechoslovakia and secure autonomy (Bystrický 2011, 160). The Slovak People's Party subsequently accepted Hitler's offer of independence. The Slovak declaration of independence would provide the pretext for the Nazi occupation of the Czech lands in March 1939 (2011, 174).

Illusory though it was, Slovakia's independence from 1939 to 1945 had a profound effect on postwar Czech–Slovak relations.[7] First, it provided the Slovaks with experience in self-government, thus demonstrating that they were capable of running their own affairs. Second, statehood reinforced Slovak national sentiment among the population, making the return to the unitary state of the inter-war period untenable (Barnovský 2011, 232; Leff 1988, 90). Third, the war led to the ethnic cleansing of Czechoslovakia's Germans, which simplified the country's demography and brought the Czech–Slovak conflict into full view (Frommer 2005).

After the war, anti-fascist Slovak elites – the inheritors of the 1944 Slovak uprising against Nazi rule – demanded that Czechoslovakia be organized on *de facto* federal lines (Barnovský 2011, 233). The Košice Program of 1945 recognized Slovak nationhood and equality among the country's nations, thus abandoning the assimilationism of the 1920 constitution. The wartime Slovak National Council was recognized as the locus of Slovak national sovereignty (2011, 234). The communist takeover in 1948 reversed these gains. The communists doubted the Slovaks' loyalty to the regime (Krejčí 1996, 30) and correspondingly reduced Slovakia's autonomy to an empty shell. The Slovak National Council was retained, but only to administer legislation passed down from Prague.

The country's institutional shape would be revisited during the Prague Spring. A combination of the post-Stalin thaw, liberalizing tendencies among Czechoslovak politicians, and the problems of the planned economy contributed to a shift in the direction of the Czechoslovak Communist Party (Dubček 1993; Kusin 1971; Williams 1997). The new leadership under Alexander Dubček sought to liberalize the country's politics and economy. An important element of that effort was federal reform. Dissatisfaction with the institutional status quo had been mounting among the Slovak elites throughout the 1960s. The most obvious problem was the concentration of political power in Prague, which meant that the Slovaks could not govern their own affairs without Czech tutelage (Brown 2008, 1788). As important was the meaning of the prevailing institutional asymmetry: the Slovaks had their own autonomous institutions while the Czechs did not. For the Slovaks, this meant that the Czechoslovak state was in reality a Czech state, which was in a substantive and formal sense superior to the Slovak autonomous institutions (2008, 1787).

The solution to both issues was to create two federal units with equal political power and status. Slovak demands for extensive substate competencies were not fully met: the federal government retained control over economic matters, an area of particular disagreement between the two sides (Skilling 1976, 868–9). However, the federal legislature was to be organized along near-confederal lines. It would be constituted as a bicameral body, with the two chambers wielding equal power. The lower chamber reflected the majority principle, with the two nations represented proportionally; however, the two republics had parity of representation in the upper chamber, the House of Nations. Important legislation could not pass unless it was endorsed by the absolute majority of each national delegation.

In effect, the Slovaks had obtained veto power over federal policy (1976, 869). Moreover, in legal terms, sovereignty issued from the two republics (Brown 2008, 1791). While the liberalizing political and economic reforms were reversed after the Soviet invasion of Czechoslovakia in 1968, the federal aspects of the reform were retained for the remainder of the communist period. Real power, of course, was vested in the federal communist party (Kirschbaum 1993, 75). It was within this institutional framework that the struggle over the shape of the state would resume once communism fell in 1989.

"HYPHEN WAR" TO DISSOLUTION

The Demand

Tensions between the Slovak elites and their Czech and federal counterparts escalated soon after the communists surrendered power in November 1989. The force of Slovak demands surprised the Czech politicians and created an atmosphere of mistrust. While Slovak elites were far from homogeneous – the Public Against Violence coalition soon gave way to the Christian Democrats and the Movement for Slovakia – they converged on key instrumental and symbolic demands for their republic. They called for broad policy autonomy, including control over their own assets, revenues, and expenditures, as well as a decisive say over the federal government's fiscal policy. They also insisted on the institutional recognition of Czechoslovakia's multinationality and the equality of the two constitutive nations.

The first signs of conflict emerged in an unexpected domain. The end of communism called for a change in state symbols – the flag, the coat of arms, and the removal of the adjective "socialist" from the country's name. President Václav Havel, at whose initiative the change was set in motion, expected an easy task. He proposed that the country be called Czecho-Slovak Republic, inserting a hyphen where previously there was none (Stein 1997, 57). The issue may seem trivial, but it resonated deeply among both the Czech representatives and the public (many of whom opposed it) and among the Slovaks (who were enthusiastic). As the president of the Slovak parliament put it in March of 1990, "we are convinced that the name of the republic expresses and determines the form that the state takes, and the way in which our two nations coexist. Therefore, the name of our country, as a federation of two sovereign republics, must unambiguously reflect this fact" (Bratislava Domestic Service 1990a). The federal parliament eventually agreed on a new name, though not without acrimony and opposition. Until its break-up, the state would be known as the Czech and Slovak Federal Republic (Stein 1997, 59).

By the spring of 1990, debates had turned to instrumental issues, including the division of powers between the federal and republican governments. The months between April and December 1990 saw intense negotiations over the issue of "power-sharing". Slovak demands came to settle on two key points. The first was the devolution of power and resources to the republics. This would entail decentralization of both fiscal resources and productive assets (Národná obroda 1990). The second was a demand for what amounted to fiscal confederalism. The Slovak government insisted that the federal budget be subject to republican agreement (Národná obroda 1990). Slovak leaders would subsequently demand control of monetary policy in Slovakia (Prague ČSTK 1991a).

The symbolic demands were as far-reaching. Even during the 1990 power-sharing talks, the Slovak prime minister Vladimír Mečiar embedded his instrumental claims in principles of multinationalism. The talks were meant to lead to "a complete reassessment of the relation of the Slovak Republic to the Czech Republic and to the common Federation. We do not see this *solely as a struggle for jurisdiction*, but also as an *expression of implementing the nation's right to self-determination*. ... All aspects of decision making by the Federal bodies must be carried out on the basis of law and consensus of the two republics" (Bratislava Domestic Service 1990b, emphasis added). This demand for the recognition of Czechoslovakia's multinationality, and Slovakia's separate identity within it, would come to dominate the negotiations on the shape of the new constitution, which would commence in 1991. The *manner* in which the new constitution was to be passed became a far more contentious issue than its content. Slovak representatives insisted that the constitution be a product of a "state treaty" between the two republics rather than a document based on the sovereignty of the entire people of Czechoslovakia (Stein 1997, 105). The treaty was to express the multinational reality of the state.

The Response

THE POLITICAL ECONOMY STORY

Political economy considerations played a critical role in the way in which the federal elites and their colleagues in the Czech Republic responded to Slovak claims for economic and fiscal autonomy. After the initial devolution of power to the republics in mid-1990, reflecting the drive to divest the previously overbearing federal government of its powers, federal and Czech elites resisted full fiscal autonomy for Slovakia. The power-sharing law of December 1990 retained guiding federal influence over fiscal and economic policy. While the republics were consulted on the federal budget, both revenues and expenditures were subject to federal legislation (Stein 1997, 76). Contrary to the April 1990 agreement between the Czech and Slovak leaderships, the federation was to have its own autonomous source of direct taxation, instead of depending on the decisions of the two republics (Pehe 1990, 7). The Slovak proposal for separate central banks was snubbed in favour of a single bank with separate republican branches (Stein 1997, 77).

This same pattern would hold during the upcoming constitutional negotiations. The constitutional agreement at Milovy in February 1992 would have reinforced the powers of the federal government over the economy, though it also would have solidified republic autonomy in policy implementation and granted residual powers to the republics. In accordance with federal and Czech preferences, the Milovy agreement granted both legislative and executive control over monetary policy, the federal budget, special funds, and the *uniform principles* of budgetary policy *for the entire state* (though the latter in agreement with the republics) to the federal government. It also conferred on the federal government the legislative (though not executive) power over taxation, including those taxes "important for the unity of the market," and over minimum tax rates and exemptions. Finally, the Slovak demand for separate central banks was spurned in favour of a single bank of issue (Hospodářské noviny 1992a). In the end, the Czech elites and the media endorsed the text, whereas the Slovak Presidium rejected it, in effect thwarting the last chance for a constitutional compromise before the 1992 elections, and, as it would prove to be, the last chance to save the common state (Stein 1997, 172).

Driving the federal and Czech intransigence was the misalignment of the strategies of governance between Slovakia on the one hand and the Czech and federal governments on the other. Slovak demands for economic and fiscal autonomy were combined with calls for the softening of the federal government's economic "shock therapy" under the leadership of the finance minister Václav Klaus. The conjunction of these demands signalled that Slovak autonomy would slow down the pace, and dilute the character, of the economic reforms in Slovakia and thus potentially in the country as a whole. Federal politicians publicly expressed their concern about the effects that Slovak autonomy would have on the federation's strategy of governance. In sum, the cautiously statist strategy of Slovakia was clashing with the radically market-oriented strategy of the centre and the Czech Republic.

Slovakia's incrementalist approach to economic reform was a direct consequence of its relative economic underdevelopment. The Slovak lands had developed much later and at a different pace than did the Czech territories. Indeed, the Czech lands had been, along with Austria, the earliest and fastest industrializers in East Central Europe (Berend 1974, 112; Gunst 1989). By the First World War, most of the manufacturing capacity of the Habsburg Monarchy was in the Bohemian Crown Lands (Berend 1974, 117; Good 1984). Slovakia's industry, by contrast, started to develop only after the establishment of the Dual Monarchy in 1867 (Good 1984, Ch. 5). The per capita GDP of what is today Slovakia was only around 56 per cent of the Czech average in 1870, increasing to around 63 per cent of the Czech figure by 1910.[8] The creation of Czechoslovakia in 1918 thus united two regions at drastically different stages of economic development. Slovakia's share of the new state's population was approximately 23 per cent, yet its contribution to the national income was only 12 per cent, and to industrial input only 8 per cent (Capek and Sazama 1993, 212). What industry did exist in Slovakia was quickly weakened by competition with Czech companies (Pryor 1973, 211). Though some branches of Slovak industry prospered, and living conditions improved, socio-economic differences between the country's west and east did not diminish appreciably (1973, 214).

Inter-war Czechoslovak governments had paid little attention to regional development, but their communist successors developed a comprehensive program of territorial redistribution. Per capita industrial and social investment during the communist era was consistently higher in Slovakia than in the Czech Republic. This investment policy had two goals. The first was to "solve" the Slovak national question by addressing the economic disparities between the two halves of the country (Pavlínek 1995, 355). The second was to locate strategically important industries, including armaments factories, as far as possible from the borders with NATO states (1995, 355). As a result, Slovakia was transformed from a largely agricultural region into an industrial one in a single generation.[9] Industrialization was accompanied by a gradual convergence in levels of income and productivity between the Slovak and Czech Republics. For instance, Slovakia's per capita income reached approximately 88 per cent of Czech levels by 1989 (Capek and Sazama 1993, 215).

The trend toward convergence did not survive the shift to the market economy. Slovakia's enterprises were less export-competitive than those of the Czech Republic as well as more reliant on the former Soviet markets. The demise of state socialism therefore hit Slovakia harder than it did the Czech Republic. The gap in per capita GDP between the two parts of the federation more than doubled between 1989 and 1992 (Table A11 in the Appendix). Whereas the Czech economy shed relatively few jobs, the Slovak labour market underwent a profound and rapid transformation. The number of registered unemployed in 1990 was 39,603; a year later it had soared to 301,951 (Štatistický úrad Slovenskej republiky 1995, 37). By mid-1992, the unemployment rate was 11.3 per cent in Slovakia but a mere 2.6 per cent in the Czech republic (Wolchik 1994, 165).

These circumstances prompted the Slovak leaders to push back against the rapid marketization of the economy. While they did accept the need to transform the state-owned command economy into a private, market-based one, they preferred that this happen more gradually and that it be guided by the state. In the first half of 1991, Slovak prime minister Mečiar argued that differences in economic conditions between the Czech and Slovak lands required policies more sensitive to local conditions:

We are told that Klaus has conceived a reform, and now we are to shut up and implement it. We say: O.K., but Slovakia is different! We have the conversion [of the armament industry] in Slovakia to cope with ... our energy situation is different, and so is our unemployment. ... If there are to be structural changes in the economy, someone must introduce them, someone must supervise them. ... Yes, many people will have to leave factories ... but they must be able to find work [elsewhere]; however, somebody must organize all this, it must be financed and supervised by someone. *If the government does not do it satisfactorily*, what am I to tell my own deputies? (Bratislava Verejnost 1991a)

We see here both the identification of the problem (a one-size-fits-all economic policy dictated from the federal centre) and the implicit prescription to it – greater government involvement to soften the blow of the reform.

Indeed, when pressed by a journalist about the meaning of his critique of the federal strategy of governance, Mečiar explicitly endorsed "temporary" state involvement in the economy and a gradualist strategy of governance (Mladá fronta Dnes 1991). Mečiar's successor between 1991 and 1992, Ján Čarnogurský, was initially less confrontational on economic policy. However, his government soon started to implement measures to soften the blow of Prague's shock therapy, ultimately calling, in Slovakia at least, for a replacement of "the indiscriminately restrictive economic policy with an expansive policy aimed at development" (Bratislava Česko-slovenský rozhlas Radio Network 1991).

While Slovakia's strategy of governance was shaped by the republic's structural position, the origins of the federal strategy were more contingent. The radically laissez-faire approach implemented by the federal government at the start of 1991 arose from the convergence of three trends. The first was the perception of the adverse consequences of communism on the Czech economy. Slovakia owed its development to socialist economic policies; those same policies were behind the Czech republic's decline. The Czechoslovak economy had been on a par with the economies of industrialized Belgium and Austria in the inter-war period. By 1989 its per capita income was less than half that of capitalist European countries (Brada 1991, 172). This experience had delegitimized the role of the state for the Czechs. A 1991 poll found that only 35 per cent of Czechs – against 58 per cent of Slovaks – preferred a government-controlled economy (Olson 1993, 306).

The second source of the federal government's market radicalism related to the personal biographies of the architects of the reform. Václav Klaus, the federal finance minister and future prime minister of the Czech Republic, had participated in the attempts to reform the Czechoslovak economy in the 1960s and had seen his career prospects decline during the post-1968 crackdown. The combination of the hardline communist reaction and the neoclassical economic thinking to which he was subsequently exposed turned Klaus and those who would join him in the federal finance ministry into free market radicals. They opposed "third way" approaches to economic management, embracing instead a radical reduction of the state's role in the economy (Eyal 2003; Orenstein 2001, Ch. 3).

Once in office, Klaus and his team advocated a "market economy without adjectives" (Klaus 1991, 149). Their primary concern was the control of inflation, to be achieved through restrictive fiscal and monetary policy (Klaus 1991, 153, 160). They emphasized the need to accept the dictates of the market and noted that trying to employ targeted public policy in order to soften the blow of the transition would be counterproductive (Klaus 1993, 2). Klaus's radical approach to market reform was further bolstered by the neoliberal zeitgeist, the third factor that shaped the federal strategy of governance. By the time socialist regimes started collapsing in Central and Eastern Europe, free market ideas were approaching hegemonic status in the West. The notion that markets were superior to policy-makers at addressing economic problems was institutionalized in international financial institutions, including the World Bank and the International Monetary Fund (Wade 2002). Both organizations provided economic expertise and training to post-communist governments (Aligică and Evans 2009, 70).

Klaus's free market zeal was initially tempered by the political realities on the ground. Far-reaching plans to cut government spending in the 1990 budget were limited to defence and security, while health spending and investment subsidies remained (Myant 1993, 173). As these measures failed to contain the rapid expansion of credit in the economy, political pressure was building for more drastic policy steps (1993, 173). Ultimately, a more comprehensive market reform was adopted by the federal parliament on 17 September 1990. Its central goal was macroeconomic stability through tight fiscal and monetary policies, combined with the liberalization of foreign trade and the "improvement" of social policy. Economic growth, full employment, and balanced payments all took a back seat to halting inflation (Martin 1990, 5–6). Budgetary subsidies were to be cut from 16 to about 7 per cent of GDP, and overall public spending was to be reduced from 60 to 47.4 per cent of GDP within a single year (Aghevli 1992, 4, 8; Table 1). The least severe cuts were applied to social programs in order to ensure popular adherence to the reform (Orenstein 2001, 73).

Slovakia's moderate strategy of governance was fundamentally incompatible with the market radicalism of the federal government. Granting far-reaching autonomy to the Slovak republic meant that federal policy priorities could be undermined by the more expansionist fiscal and monetary policies that would have been deployed in Slovakia. These concerns were voiced on numerous occasions by both federal and Czech political leaders. As early as September 1990, the federal premier Marián Čalfa warned that "the economic disintegration of the Czech and Slovak Federative Republic would seriously endanger, if not prevent totally, the implementation of the economic reform. Macroeconomic policies spawning an anti-inflationary climate of a dissimilar quality, markedly different ways of carrying out privatization, a different pace of the liberalization of prices and imports, or differently conceived tax systems could hardly function side by side" (Prague Domestic Service 1990b). Note that it was not the existence of parallel fiscal or economic policies in a procedural or institutional sense that was the problem here, but rather the fact that the two republics might diverge from one another in policy substance.

Indeed, in a later interview, Čalfa would say that if one were to accept a differential pace of reform for Slovakia, then the Czech leaders should make compromises and accept the same (Bratislava Verejnost 1991b). However, the federal government was concerned about the contagion effects of expansionist fiscal and monetary policy in the Slovak republic, as seen in the following statement by the federal minister for strategic planning, Pavel Hoffmann: "[Applying divergent policies for different regions is] fraught with considerable danger. This danger resides in the fact that, even with changed budget rules, the consequences of disparate basic methods can pass over from one part of our economy to the other. This means that, with a single currency, a different budget policy in Slovakia, for example, can bring about a different rate of inflation there, the negative concomitant effects of which can then be transferred to the other part of the state as well" (Hospodářské noviny 1991). Statements like these demonstrate the awareness of the link between Slovak fiscal autonomy and the fate of the federal strategy of governance. It is thus not surprising that the more far-reaching Slovak demands remained unfulfilled throughout the 1990–92 period.

THE SYMBOLIC POLITICS STORY

The reaction to Slovak symbolic demands was more ambiguous. On the one hand, the federal and Czech elites willingly acknowledged the multinational character of the common state in public pronouncements, in policy, and during the constitutional negotiations throughout the period. On the other hand, they recoiled from the idea of a state treaty between the Czech and Slovak republics as the basis of the new constitution. One way to make sense of this pattern is to note that the acknowledgment of Czechoslovakia's multinationalism did not represent a major departure from previous constitutional norms. After all, the 1968 constitution already established the precedent on this score. The intervening period allowed the Czechs to internalize the multinational view of the state, even if they were not as enthusiastic about it as the Slovaks. However, the demand for a state treaty was a major symbolic departure from prevailing norms and a step too far in the direction of confederalism. It therefore did not meet the same sympathetic reception among Czech representatives.

In keeping with the way in which majorities generally tend to view minority demands, the Czech elites (as well as the general population) were at first mystified and later exasperated by the Slovak insistence on symbolic concessions (Stein 1997, 109–10, 151). Nevertheless, Czech representatives accepted and acknowledged Czechoslovakia's multinationality. This was first evidenced in their willingness to change the country's name to the Czech and Slovak Federal Republic. In April 1990, Czech prime minister Pithart openly acknowledged "the primary nature, specific identity, and integrity of the national republics" (Prague Domestic Service 1990a). Later in the year, the federal president Havel stressed the need to inform the outside world of the fact that Czechoslovakia was "formed by two equal nations" (Stein 1997, 64). The power-sharing law of 1990 also included reference to "the "inalienable right" of the two republics to self-determination "up to separation" and no fewer than eight references to their sovereignty and right to self-determination (1997, 73).

The right of self-determination made it into the Milovy agreement, the last-ditch effort to salvage the constitutional talks in February

1992. According to Article 1 of the agreement, "the foundation of the Czech and Slovak Federal Republic is the voluntary bond between the national states of the Czech and Slovak nations, based on the right of self-determination of each of them. ... The two republics respect each other's sovereignty and the sovereignty of the common state. Each of the two republics can secede from the common state or divide it by way of consent" (Hospodářské noviny 1992a). On the one hand, this was evidence of a far greater willingness by central elites to recognize both the multinational character of the state, and the equal place of the minority nation in it, than was the case in either Spain or Canada. Yet these concessions appear less remarkable in light of the preceding experience, including the constitution of 1968. Viewed in context, they constitute the functional equivalent of the 2006 Canadian parliamentary declaration on Quebec's nationhood – a dispensation not meant to depart substantively from previous practice.

The demand for a state treaty between the two republics, however, introduced a new symbolic element into the debate. Slovak political parties argued that the new constitution would have to issue from the agreement of the two republics as national states of the Czechs and the Slovaks. According to Mečiar, the arrangement would formally signify that it was the republics that had created the Czech and Slovak Federal Republic and delegated it some of their powers, rather than the federation (and its assembly) devolving power to the republics (Bratislava Domestic Service 1990c). Mečiar's idea of a state treaty would be picked up by his successor Ján Čarnogurský of the Slovak Christian Democrats in February 1991 (Stein 1997, 105). Indeed, all relevant Slovak political parties, driven by mutual nationalist outbidding, adopted the state treaty as their credo (Stein 1997, 109).

This demand encountered tenacious opposition among the Czech actors, in particular Václav Klaus's Civic Democratic Party. Each round of negotiations consequently fell short of accommodating the Slovak proposal for a state treaty. The Kroměříž agreement in June 1991, for instance, stipulated an internal rather than an international treaty among the republics, as well as no requisite constitutional law to empower republics to arrive at a treaty (Stein 1997, 117). President Havel's proposal to make a treaty between the two republics subject to legally binding international law was blocked by the Czechs (1997, 134). The aforementioned Milovy agreement in February 1992 also fell short of accommodating the Slovak position. The final text eliminated republics as parties to any agreement and did not make the treaty among them legally binding (1997, 159). Unsurprisingly, especially given the intensifying competition among the Slovak parties on who would best protect national interests, the Slovak parliamentary presidium refused to ratify the agreement. Slovak representatives were explicit: they rejected the agreement because republics – as national states – were not parties to the proposed treaty (1997, 173).

In public debates among Slovak representatives, the idea of a state treaty and the ill-defined confederal arrangement assumed totemic status. Indeed, by April 1992 the Slovak public was almost as interested in a confederation (28% according to one poll) as they were in a federation (33%). Only a minority of 19 per cent supported independence (Prague čsTK 1992). Slovak interest in symbolic recognition was more than mere window dressing for power games. Slovak representatives continued to oppose anything short of state treaty, even when, in the aftermath of the 1992 election, Václav Klaus offered a "Marshall plan" for Slovakia as sweetener in exchange for a more integrated federal arrangement. The Slovaks rebuffed Klaus's offer because it ran "counter to the immutable aspirations for "visibility" on the international scene" (Stein 1997, 202).

Czech inflexibility with respect to the state treaty was similarly rooted in symbolic considerations. Czech leaders frequently argued that the state treaty would create a "dysfunctional" political arrangement, thus suggesting that their opposition was rooted in instrumental considerations.[10] However, as Stein notes, making republics parties to the state treaty had few implications for the division of powers that had already been agreed upon or for the functionality of the state (1997, 160). While it is difficult to find a conclusive rationale behind this, it stands to reason that Czech political parties, and particularly Klaus's Civic Democratic Party, understood that accommodating Slovak demands for a quasi-confederal state treaty might antagonize the Czech electorate.

Indeed, prior to the 1992 election, Klaus had cautioned against using the constitutional issue in political battles in the Czech Republic (Hospodářské noviny 1992b). Czech politicians willing to accept the state treaty as the basis for the new constitution were immediately assailed in the Czech press as "hopelessly pro-Slovak"' (Stein 1997, 136), so it stands to reason that Klaus understood the political danger of going too far in meeting Slovak symbolic demands. This speculation is borne out by the fact that opinion polls at the time demonstrated that most Czechs wanted an integrated federation rather than a confederal arrangement. In April 1992, only 5 per cent of the residents of the Czech Republic were in favour of a confederation. More than one third (37%) wanted a unitary state, and 48 per cent favoured a federal arrangement (Prague čsTK 1992).

Political Consequences

The Czechoslovak case presents a unique test for the hypotheses developed in Chapter 3. This is the only case among the four considered in this book in which the strategies of governance adopted by the central and claimant governments did not eventually align.[11] Consequently, the centre refused to yield more resources and fiscal control. The response to the symbolic claims was more ambiguous, combining accommodation with refusal. Yet, the unwillingness of the Czech negotiators to concede on the more far-reaching claims for fiscal and monetary autonomy and on the constitutional "state treaty" did not push the Slovak population or the largest of the political parties toward secessionism. After all, fewer than 20 per cent of Slovaks supported independence throughout this period, and only the Slovak National Party, which came a distant third with 9.4 per cent of the vote in the 1992 election, was openly secessionist (Innes 2001, 274).

A crucial part of this story is the absence of open political backlash against the Slovak demands. According to the hypotheses developed in Chapter 3, accommodation of minority *symbolic* demands increases the likelihood of majority mobilization against those demands. While Czech and federal leaders acknowledged the multinational character of the state, their doing so failed to provoke the expected backlash. One plausible explanation for this outcome is that the acceptance of multinationality did not depart from previous political practice. After all, multinationality had been inscribed in state institutions since the 1968 federal reform. Indeed, foreign legal experts advising Czechoslovakia's leaders on constitutional reform were taken aback by the willingness of the Czech Civic Forum to include the right to secession in all constitutional proposals (Stein 1997, 42). Resentment at the Slovak demands, including notably the pressure to change the country's name in 1990, did grow, but no Czech political party mobilized against them in the ways this happened in the other three cases.

While we have no way of knowing whether circumstances would have been different had the Czechs yielded to the Slovak demand for a state treaty, their unwillingness to do so certainly removed one issue around which Czech resentment could have been mobilized politically. Instead of anti-Slovak mobilization, the only notable majority manifestation took place in November 1991, in defence of Czechoslovakia and in repudiation of both the Czech and Slovak elites. Sensing the potentially disintegrative consequences of the political impasse between Czech and Slovak negotiators, President Havel developed a series of proposals the goal of which was to preserve the common state. Among them was a call for integrative institutional solutions such as a unicameral parliament and broader presidential powers to guard against political deadlock. The wave of support for his proposals was concentrated in the Czech Republic. His ultimately unsuccessful campaign culminated in a massive demonstration in Prague in November 1991, when 40,000 people gathered in support of Czechoslovak unity (Stein 1997, 139–40).

The negotiations between the Czechs and the Slovaks did not result in a secessionist crisis, but they did lead to the country's dissolution. The Slovaks did not favour independence, but they were clearly not content with the institutional status quo. Their grievances ranged from the economic conditions attributed to the policies developed in Prague, to the organization of the common state.[12] Mečiar's uncompromising defence of Slovak interests ensured that his Movement for Slovakia would win power in the 1992 elections. At the same time, Václav Klaus's equally uncompromising pursuit of radical market reforms and "functional federalism" ensured the victory of the Civic Democratic Party in the Czech Republic. Under different institutional arrangements, the more numerous Czech representatives would have been able to outvote their Slovak counterparts and impose a compromise solution of sorts. However, the blocking power of Slovak representatives in the upper house of parliament meant a potentially extended stalemate. In light of this, following the 1992 election, the two leaders initiated the process of state dissolution. Over the coming months, they agreed to a break-up without a referendum. On 1 January 1993, Czechoslovakia ceased to exist (Innes 1997, ch. 6).

CONCLUSION

The Czechoslovak case is unique compared to the other countries covered in this book. It covers a far shorter period of time and thus does not capture the complete causal process outlined in Figure 3.1. By contrast to the other three cases, the central and claimant government strategies never aligned with each other during this time period. Despite these differences, the case offers valuable insights into the process of accommodation and largely corroborates expectations of the model developed in Chapter 3.

As stipulated by the theory, the clashing strategies of governance between the federal government on the one hand, and the government of Slovakia on the other, precluded the accommodation of Slovak demands for greater fiscal and monetary autonomy. The post-communist federal government adopted a far-reaching set of market-oriented measures, with emphasis on macroeconomic stability. The Slovak government objected to the disproportionate harm these measures would cause in Slovakia and increasingly called for the continued role of the state in guiding the market reforms and softening their impact. The Czech and federal leaders understood that the fiscal, policy, and monetary autonomy the Slovak leaders called for would be used to counter the effects of the federal reforms in the eastern half of the country. Consequently, they resisted accommodating those demands throughout the period under consideration.

The federal government's response to Slovak symbolic demands was more complex. On the one hand, the Slovaks' insistence on the recognition of the multinational character of the Czechoslovak state was greeted with understanding and accommodation. The country's name was changed in line with Slovak preferences, major political actors emphasized the multinational character of the country, and all key documents during the constitutional negotiations acknowledged the Slovaks as a nation and Slovakia as their state. On the other hand, the demand that the post-communist constitution be the product of a "state treaty" between the two republics was roundly rejected.

The political outcome of this part of the process does not offer a clear corroboration of the hypotheses in Chapter 3. The theoretical expectation is that accommodating minority nations' symbolic demands will increase the likelihood of majority political backlash. This, however, did not happen. No major political party in the Czech Republic mobilized in opposition to the fairly extensive accommodation of minority symbolic demands – in stark contrast to the open majority backlash in Canada, Spain, and Yugoslavia. Nonetheless, I do not consider this outcome to be an outright falsification of the hypothesis. At the core of that hypothesis is the notion that accommodating minority symbolic demands introduces a qualitatively new understanding of the state, forcing members of the majority to reconsider their own political identity and their understanding of the common state. The acknowledgment of Czechoslovakia's multinationalism was hardly an institutional novelty. Instead, it confirmed the long-accepted view of Czechoslovakia as a binational state. By contrast, the Czech elites were steadfast in their rejection of the new symbolic element pursued by the Slovak negotiators – the state treaty.

Perhaps more important were the political consequences of the absence of majority backlash: the corresponding lack of any rise in support for independence among the Slovak population and the region's largest political parties. This outcome fully corroborates the theoretical expectations set out in Chapter 3. Indeed, one could go a step further. The absence of secessionist crisis in Slovakia despite the stubborn refusal of Prague to budge on core *instrumental* demands further cements the book's central argument: system-threatening conflict in multinational states is more likely to emerge in the realm of symbolic politics than in the instrumental domain. If majority push-back undermines the very self-understanding of members of the minority nation, if it, in other words, jeopardizes their ontological security, it is far more likely to provoke a massive response than if it undermines the instrumental levers of minority power.

8

The Multinational State
and the Analytic Imagination

In the fall of 2007, I was in Prague running interviews for this project. One interviewee proved a particularly vexing conversation partner, stubbornly pushing against my questions about the political economy of the Czech–Slovak discord. Economics did matter, he acknowledged, but it was not central to the conflict; in essence, it had been about clashing visions of statehood. At the time, I did nothing with this information. In fact, I chose to ignore it as background noise to the "real stuff" of politics – resources and interests. My resistance to this interviewee's insights derived from my understanding of the institutions I was interested in – the federal arrangements over which the conflict in early-1990s Czechoslovakia unfolded. Institutions, as the mainstream of my discipline had taught me, were *instruments* with which politicians protected their own and their constituents' interests.

In the ensuing years, my commitment to the instrumental view of institutions eroded with each wave of "uncomfortable" evidence that cropped up in new interviews, documents, and political developments. My analytic blinders, derived from the dominant traditions in comparative politics – rational choice and historical institutionalism – eventually fell off. Ultimately, I came around to the sociological institutionalist position, one that values the meaning of institutions as much as their instrumental function. This, as the book shows, has profound implications for how we understand the politics of multinational states.

MONEY, SYMBOLS, AND SECESSIONIST CRISES: THEORY AND FINDINGS

The defining characteristic of multinational statehood is the absence of consensus over formal institutional arrangements, over whether or not they are a valid manifestation of the character of the state and the community or communities they encompass. Majorities tend to prefer that formal institutions express the idea that the state's entire citizenry belongs to a single political community, even if that community is culturally, linguistically, or otherwise plural.[1] Minorities, by contrast, tend to prefer that the formal organization of the state express the idea of multiple political communities, each with the right to decide its own political affairs. The relevant collective *selves* (note the plural) are decidedly *not* coterminous with the entire citizenry of the state.

This incongruity of institutional visions is *the* moving force behind identity conflict in multinational states. The majority's self-understanding is a potential threat to the ontological security of minority nations, just as the minority self-understanding is a potential threat to the ontological security of majorities. Institutionalizing either vision requires that those subscribing to the contrary view alter – or abandon altogether – the way they understand the political community to which they themselves belong, and what they consider to be that community's appropriate institutional manifestation. At its worst, conflict in multinational states takes the form of mutually assured misrecognition. Neither community is likely to yield easily to the expectations of adjustment. In fact, those expectations merely retrench identities on either side. The fact that people are socialized into their communities' narratives since childhood, combined with communities' tendencies to police their identity narratives, contributes to the intractable character of conflicts in multinational states.

The Political Economy Story Revisited

While the analytical locus of this study is the symbolic dimension of institutions, its starting point is their instrumental function. The original question behind this project was why some central governments are more willing than others to accommodate demands by minority regions for more fiscal autonomy. I argue that the central government response depends on the degree to which such accommodation compromises the centre's ability to meet commitments to its state-wide constituents. This, in turn, hinges on the congruence between the policy priorities adopted by the central and claimant governments.

For the sake of parsimony, I distinguish between statist and market-oriented strategies. The former entails an interventionist state using its regulatory, organizational, and fiscal capacity to guide economic and social development. The latter privileges macroeconomic stability in order to let the private sector and the market mechanism coordinate the creation and distribution of wealth. As I note in Chapter 3, I understand these to be tendencies rather than absolutes. Clearly, no government adopts one of these policy strategies to the complete exclusion of the other. As importantly, I do not claim that these strategies are unchanging. I do demonstrate that they endure for extended periods of time.

Where both governments pursue similar strategies of governance, the centre is likely to accommodate minority demands for enhanced fiscal autonomy. If, on the other hand, the claimant government pursues an approach that diverges from the policy priorities of the central state, central elites will resist demands for expanded autonomy. The logic is that a minority government will deploy expanded powers and resources to, in effect, undermine the centre's agenda. These hypotheses drove the book's case selection (see Table 3.2). Each case approximated one of the configurations of centre/claimant government strategies. Empirical chapters largely confirm the above hypotheses. Where both governments adopted a statist approach, the centre accommodated the minority region's demands for more resources. We see this outcome in Quebec and Canada during the 1960s. Likewise, where the two orders of government pursued a pro-market strategy, a similar result obtained, as in Spain during the 1980s and 1990s and in Yugoslavia after 1964.

On the other hand, where the two levels of government pursued conflicting policy strategies, the centre resisted accommodation. This was the result in Yugoslavia prior to 1964–66, when the federal government deployed an expansionist, territorially redistributive strategy, while the claimant region(s) favoured a market-oriented approach. A similar result occurred in Czechoslovakia between 1989 and 1992. Here, the federal government implemented a program of radical market reform, resisting the greater fiscal and monetary autonomy advocated by the more interventionist Slovak government. This, then, is the instrumental institutionalist story. Greater fiscal autonomy can harm or protect the interests of different constituencies and along with these the political fortunes of those who claim to represent them. Those interests facilitate or hinder the accommodation of minority claims for greater control over fiscal resources and economic policy.

This narrative, however, provides a narrow and ultimately misleading understanding of the politics of the multinational state. First, it overstates the importance of the instrumental aspect of the institutions about which conflict plays out. In all four cases explored in this book, minority nationalists combined instrumental with symbolic claims. They sought not only more resources and power but also formal institutional recognition of the state's multinationality or, barring that, of the national status of their community. The political economy story tells us little about how central governments respond to these symbolic claims. Second, that story cannot account for some of the most interesting and important political outcomes in multinational states – notably the secessionist crises that broke out in three of the four cases covered in this book.

The Symbolic Politics Story Revisited

To make sense of those issues, I needed to first dismantle the "analytical scaffolds" of instrumental institutionalism that were constraining my theoretical field of vision (James 2012, 563). The necessary shift, simple though it was, required recognizing that the institutions of state were *symbols* that expressed and enacted – or, alternatively, suppressed and erased – collective identities. They were thus far more than mere instruments for the promotion of economic, social, or security interests. Once I made this analytical choice, a more comprehensive causal narrative began to emerge. I remind the reader of the stylized version of that narrative in Figure 3.1.

While minority governments do demand greater control over their fiscal affairs (for reasons outlined above[2]), they accompany those demands with claims for the institutional recognition of the national specificity of their own group, and – implicitly or explicitly – the multinational character of the state. In the early going ("Round 1 – Response 1" in Figure 3.1), central governments tend to address the former but normally disregard the latter. If the political economy configuration lends itself to accommodation, the result is partial satisfaction of minority demands. This ambiguous result can provide political material to both the moderate and radical actors in the minority region. The outbidding logic between the two, though, leads to the escalation of minority demands ("Round 2 – Demand 2" in Figure 3.1).[3]

In Round 2, minority elites make more sweeping claims, normally following a period of radicalization in the minority region (the rise of the Parti Québécois in Quebec and the first referendum [1976–1980];

the Croatian Spring [1970–71]; the escalation of demands by the non-secessionist parties in Catalonia [2003–5]).⁴ The result in these three cases (I address the Czechoslovak exception below) was the more comprehensive accommodation of minority demands to include both instrumental and symbolic concessions: Quebec as distinct society in Meech Lake and Charlottetown negotiations; the recognition of Catalonia as a nation in the 2006 Statute of Autonomy; and the confederalization and recognition of republican sovereignty in the 1971–74 constitutional reforms in Yugoslavia.

These concessions amounted to a reconstitution of the symbolic order of the state. They were not only a step toward institutionalizing the *minority's* view of the polity. They also necessitated a shift in the way in which *majorities* thought of that polity and, by extension, of the character of the political community to which they themselves belonged. Since the institutional status quo was the expression of the majority's collective selfhood, its reform was not just a change in political rules. It was a strike against the very identity of a significant part of the majority population. Jeffrey Ayers's summary of the implications of the Meech Lake and Charlottetown accords in Canada makes for a vivid illustration of this point:

> Both accords threatened to undermine core, primordial collective representations that had nourished and anchored English Canadian national identity. The liberal bent of the Charter of Rights and Freedoms, the ethic of individual rights, of ten equal provinces, of one, unhyphenated Canada – such symbols collectively came to represent the English Canadian national community over the past decade. To tinker with this symbolic-cultural edifice – as the state twice attempted to do – risked an unfavorable response. (1995, 193–4)

This logic was reproduced in Spain and Yugoslavia as well. For many among the majorities, the symbolic institutional change was *an act of misrecognition* of their own vision of the state and the political community, a threat to their ontological security.⁵

The result was open political mobilization against the symbolic concessions in all three cases ("Round 2 – Majority backlash" in Figure 3.1). This mobilization had several interconnected consequences. First, it provided clear evidence that a substantial segment of the majority population was opposed to the minority's vision of the common state. Prior to the mobilization against Meech Lake or the 2005 Statute Draft in Catalonia, Quebeckers and Catalans would have been able to *guess* how the average Canadian or Spaniard felt about their vision of the country. Now they had tangible and recurring evidence. Second, this opposition facilitated either the rescinding or the reversal of the concessions extended to minorities. In Canada, it resulted in the failure of Meech Lake and Charlottetown accords; in Spain, in the narrowing of the scope of the 2006 Statute of Autonomy as a result of the 2010 Constitutional Court decision; and in Yugoslavia in the Serbian leadership's attempt to recentralize the country in the late 1980s.

These were all highly visible instances of repudiation of the minority vision of the state. In all three cases, they weakened the moderates and strengthened the radicals among minority political elites. The Liberal Party of Quebec, the Socialist Party of Catalonia,[6] and the reformed communists in Croatia, all moderate on the issue of independence, were marginalized by the events, fighting an uphill battle against the independentists. In each instance, the upshot was a secessionist crisis ("Round 2 – Secessionist crisis" in Figure 3.1).[7] Thus, the mere existence of autonomy did not bring these countries to the brink of break-up – or beyond. Nor was the key bone of contention the degree of autonomy, or the division of powers or resources between governments. These issues are at any rate too opaque, cognitively inaccessible, and emotionally "flat" to provoke massive swings in public opinion. Instead, the adoption of the minority nation's symbolic vision produced a majority overreaction, which in turn turbocharged secessionist politics.

These conclusions are reinforced by the contrasting case of Czechoslovakia. In the aftermath of the Velvet Revolution, the Slovak political elites pursued greater fiscal and monetary autonomy, along with institutional recognition of the state's multinational character. The federal elites did not budge on instrumental matters but were more accommodating of symbolic claims, acknowledging Czechoslovakia's multinationalism on numerous occasions. This did not provoke a reaction among the Czechs in part because it was not a major departure from previous political practice, institutionalized as far back as 1968.

The federal and Czech leaders were unyielding when faced with a new symbolic demand: a state treaty that the Slovaks stipulated as the foundation for the country's post-communist constitution. The treaty was a step too far for the Czech and federal leaders. It was a new and potentially destabilizing concession in a context in which an overwhelming majority of Czechs favoured a more integrated political system. In the event, the Czechs' rejection of the treaty precluded the kind of majority reaction that emerged in Canada, Spain, and Yugoslavia. While there was palpable resentment and frustration among Czechs at many of the Slovaks' demands, it did not result in open, politicized majority backlash.

The outcome corroborates the model summarized in Figure 3.1, if only in the negative. In the absence of majority backlash to minority national projects, it is far more difficult to obtain sufficient minority support for secession. During the 1990–92 period, independence was never favoured by more than 20 per cent of Slovaks, and no major political party included it in its platform. While the country did break apart, its dissolution was a result of an elite agreement between two republican leaders: Slovakia's Vladimír Mečiar and the Czech Republic's Václav Klaus. The two were far apart on both the instrumental and symbolic issues. Where Mečiar supported more gradual and state-assisted economic reform and a confederal state arrangement, Klaus favoured market radicalism and would not countenance anything short of an integrated and "functional" federation. The veto-laden political rules inherited from the socialist period left no way out of the impasse, leading the two leaders to dissolve the state.

RETHINKING THE MULTINATIONAL STATE: CONTRIBUTIONS TO A FIELD

Multinational State as a Sui Generis Phenomenon

This book shows that we cannot grasp the politics of multinational states with the analytical tools developed to make sense of nation-states. What is needed is a separate field expressly dedicated to theorizing multinational systems. The cornerstone of that field ought to be the recognition of the fundamental difference between the two kinds of polity. The legitimacy of the nation-state is practically unlimited among its citizenry. No conflict, no matter how explosive, will put the nation-state's territorial/political order in question. By contrast, the legitimacy of the multinational state is chronically contingent. Its territorial integrity is not in constant jeopardy, but it is *in play*. The state's territorial reconfiguration is not inconceivable and is often the subject of open and serious speculation in public debates.

The political implications of this difference between the two institutional formations are profound. The margin of error that elites in the former have is vastly greater than what is available to their counterparts in the latter. In multinational systems, the most mundane issue can bring the entire political edifice into question. This is not the case in nationally homogeneous polities. Regime change, party politics, federalism, political economy, public policy, and the politics of nationalism play out according to an entirely different script. If we proceed from this distinction, it becomes clear that theories developed for the nation-state are a poor guide to the multinational state.

Consider the now widespread concept of banal nationalism. This is the notion that the national idea is at its most powerful when it is reproduced in daily rituals that go unnoticed, when it becomes the imperceptible background against which life happens (Billig 1995, 8). This kind of taken-for-grantedness simply cannot obtain in a multinational state (Rosie et al. 2006; Skey 2009). Here, a commonplace symbol of collective identity for the majority may be objectionable and thus decisively *not* banal to the minority. The minorities' negative reaction to these symbols, in turn, makes it difficult for the majorities to take those symbols for granted. Rather than being invisible and banal, they assume outsized prominence.

The most important symbol in multinational polities is the state itself. What is for one community the correct way to organize and designate the state's institutions – say, for instance, its federal arrangements and the way these are inscribed and expressed in the constitution – may produce collective anxiety in another. I do not mean to suggest that the meanings attaching to these arrangements are fixed or homogeneous within the communities, but the evidence in the empirical chapters suggests a significant difference in the way in which majority and minority communities perceive specific institutional arrangements. I am also not implying that residents of multinational states go to their beds contemplating state institutions. However, such concerns *are* present in multinational states in ways in which they are not in nationally homogeneous ones.

Institutional Symbolism as the Locus of Political Conflict

In addition to calling for a new branch of scholarly inquiry, the book makes several concrete contributions to it. It does so by challenging and extending the insights of existing literature on multinational states, the primary focus of which is the institutional management of difference. Most importantly, *against the largely instrumental understanding of institutions* in extant scholarship (e.g., various federal, power-sharing, and power-dividing arrangements), the book *foregrounds the significance of institutions as symbols*. Mainstream political science operates with the notion of institutions as rules of the political game. Those rules can privilege specific political projects by enhancing the influence of certain actors over others (as in historical institutionalism), or facilitate or hinder cooperation in the face of collective action problems (as in rational choice institutionalism).

Institutions *are*, of course, political tools. Federal arrangements may protect a vulnerable population's safety, foster an underdeveloped community's economic advancement, or preserve a language that might otherwise disappear. But institutions are also expressions of particular visions of the political community. This sociological institutionalist insight is important for two reasons. First, there is no one-for-one correspondence between the instrumental and symbolic dimensions of institutions. A particular arrangement can protect a community's purported interests *without* expressing its identity. By having access to autonomous political institutions, Quebeckers can protect their cultural and material interests even if their identity is not recognized through federal asymmetry or constitutional language. By the same token, the ability of Canadians outside of Quebec to protect *their* safety or prosperity would not have been compromised either by formal federal asymmetry or by the constitutional recognition of Quebec as a distinct society.

Second, because of the lack of necessary connection between the instrumental and symbolic aspects of institutions, secessionist crises can flare up in contexts in which the material circumstances, including the physical security of a specific community, are in no meaningful way compromised. What this points to, and what this book demonstrates, is that systemic political crises in multinational states are often a function not of instrumental issues (such as the degree of autonomy, access to power, or "inclusiveness," as stipulated in much of the existing literature), but rather of conflicts over the symbolic aspects of state institutions. It is these issues – ones that go to the heart of collective identity, and thus are both emotionally evocative and cognitively accessible – that are crucial for political mobilization. This is also what explains the durability of these conflicts – they are less about "who gets what, when, and how" than about *whose story gets institutionalized.* Because these stories are difficult to reconcile, such conflicts tend to endure over time.

This understanding of the politics of nationalism turns the conventional approaches to ideational explanations on their head. Henry Hale argues, for instance, that ethnopolitics is only apparently about non-material (or, in the language of this book, symbolic) factors. When individuals take up the cause of secession in defence of symbols and at the expense of their immediate material well-being – including their safety – they do so, Hale contends, for at least two reasons. First, they are considering not only the immediate cost–benefit calculus but also the future stream of material gains. Second, whatever symbols are being fought over are not inherently valuable – they are mere standins for the future material circumstances and prosperity of a community and its individual members (Hale 2008, 53–4).

This book casts doubt on that view of nationalist contestation – at least in the four cases considered here. It demonstrates that instrumental factors may not have the same mobilizational power as symbolic ones. Policy shifts with long-term material implications did not cause quite the same response among either majority or minority communities as did symbolic reversals. Indeed, in at least two of the cases under consideration (Spain and Canada), surveys show that the clear material implications of instrumental policy choices were not considered to be as important by majorities as were the symbolic issues. While it is true, as Roeder asserts, that secessionist "entrepreneurs" try to appeal to the material concerns of their constituents (Roeder 2018, 8, 83), it may be worth entertaining the possibility that symbolic claims are not window dressing for the more prosaic material interests, but that the reverse may be the case. Individuals may be using the language of interests to rationalize their more deepseated and far less "rational" commitments to particular institutional visions (Kaufman 2015, 34–5). After all, who would want to publicly express that they favour a political outcome just because "it feels right"? The authority of Enlightenment rationality weighs heavy on our political imagination.

The Role of Institutional Dynamics and Time in Explaining Crises

The standard narrative about the role of institutions in multinational states is that the presence or absence of a particular arrangement either mitigates or facilitates conflict. This is the focal point of the accommodation/integration debate that has unfolded over the past half century or so (McGarry, O'Leary, and Simeon 2008). Recent work has introduced greater nuance into the discussion, pointing to the contextual conditions under which institutions might or might not "work" to manage conflict. These accounts tend to view institutions in a largely static manner. Two major methodological problems emerge as a result.

The first problem is that similar institutional contexts (for instance, regions with "objectively" similar levels of autonomy) exhibit a wide variety of outcomes across space *and time*. Explanations based on static snapshots of institutional conditions provide not only a limiting but also an inaccurate understanding of politics. The second, and related, problem emerges from the mostly implicit premise that institutions help or hinder stability irrespective of the manner in which they are implemented. In other words, the question of institutional development has been considered separately from the question of institutional impact. This book addresses both issues.

By contrast to cross-sectional analyses that compare fixed institutional states (e.g., the presence/absence of autonomy or its "degree"), this book compares processes. Each multi-year process is treated as a single, integrated case. This allowed me to demonstrate how institutional development influenced the political stability of the countries under examination. The causal narrative and the evidence it provides demonstrate that it is impossible to divorce the issue of institutional impact from the question of institutional development. Institutions are not prefabricated pillars that can simply be inserted into any political soil and expected to support the edifice of the state.

As the book shows, institutional change is a contentious process that infuses institutions with specific, contingent *meaning*. An identical institution will not have the same impact from one place to another, not only because of contextual circumstances but also because of the process of institutional implementation – which is endogenous to the institutions themselves. It also means that the same institution will not have the same impact in the same place *at different times*. As Chapters 4 through 7 show, what might dampen minority nationalism at one point (say, an instrumental concession without much of a symbolic one), may not do so years later, once the ensuing political events have shifted expectations. To sum up, institutions influence political outcomes not only by virtue of their objective features, but also because of what they come to mean to relevant political actors, in large part as a consequence of their implementation.

How the Interaction between Minority and Majority (and within each camp) Matters

Another problem characterizing existing literature on the multinational state concerns the enduring overemphasis on the political demands and actions of minority nationalists. Most scholarship on the management of difference explores how institutional accommodation facilitates *minority* acceptance of the common state, or provides *minorities* with incentives and tools to secede. This book demonstrates that the political dynamics of multinational states, from institutional development, to institutional impact, including secessionist crises, cannot be understood without an analytical perspective that integrates the demands and actions of both claimant *and respondent* communities and actors.

The political preferences and actions of minority nationalists are not independent of what happens among majority elites and populations. Rather, the politics of minority nationalism feed into, and are in turn influenced by, the politics of majority nationalism. The empirical chapters show that minority demands do not destabilize the common state as long as their satisfaction does not undermine the symbolic order that underpins the majority's political identity. When it does, political entrepreneurs among the latter will find it tempting to politicize majority resentment. If they can successfully galvanize a significant segment of the majority population in opposition to the concessions granted to minorities, their reaction will strengthen the radicals among the minority nationalists and help garner support for secessionist alternatives.

Thus, the actor landscape is much richer than the one suggested by existing scholarship in which it is minority nationalists who carry the responsibility for the politics of the multinational state. Majority nationalism also matters, even if majorities themselves often try to escape that designation. This is not to say that minority nationalists have no role to play in the escalation of political tensions. Minority radicals can explicitly seek to provoke a majority reaction, in a variant of political *kuzushi* – unbalancing the opponent by using their inertia. But even where this *is* the case, any account of the political dynamic emerging from it is incomplete unless we understand why and how majorities react to those minority moves.

As important is the attention that, in this context, we must give to intra-communal dynamics. This is not a new insight. Scholars have been pointing to intra-communal outbidding as an integral driver of inter-communal conflict for decades.[8] The more important point from the perspective of this work is that national communities are themselves internally heterogeneous, including notably with respect to institutional visions they endorse (Lluch 2014). It is these differences, along with struggles for political power, that give rise to internal conflicts. In these conflicts, the side that can marshal sufficient evidence in support of its program has the upper hand. For minority moderates, majority escalation against their national project is the kiss of death. In fact, in nearly all of the cases covered in the book, I have encountered frequent and explicit claims by minority moderates suggesting that hardline responses from majority actors are likely to weaken their hand. In those circumstances, it is the radicals who benefit, since their arguments about the futility of attempting to negotiate greater autonomy and recognition start to gain strength among moderate minority nationalists.

By the same token, key symbolic concessions to minority nations can play into the hands of majority radicals and weaken the hand of majority moderates.[9] This majority radicalization can lead to open mobilization against concessions to minority concerns, which can in turn help secessionist mobilization among minorities. This book thus provides a corrective to the standard analytical perspective according to which the presence or absence of particular institutions makes minorities more or less accepting of the common state. I demonstrate that the dynamic is far more complex and multifaceted. In doing so, I offer a more precise understanding of the conditions under which we might expect to see a spike in support for secession.

FUTURE DIRECTIONS AND A CAUTIONARY NOTE

Toward a New Subfield

In Chapter 2, I laid out a list of themes relevant to understanding the politics of multinational states. I see that list as a preliminary map – one I expect will be revised and amended – that scholars may consider in their efforts to produce synthetic knowledge about the multinational state. Understanding *why and how some states become multinational in the first place* – that is, why and how multiple institutional visions emerge and endure in some places, whereas in others a hegemonic idea of the state and nation takes hold – ought to be an important background concern. While there is some work on this by Stein Rokkan, that work is both too rudimentary and far too Eurocentric. More recent contributions may, by contrast, be too sweeping in their claims. Related to this is the possibility of political integration or even merger between previously mobilized national communities. This has a bearing on the possibility of the management of nationalist conflict, particularly in the aftermath of violent episodes or wars. One possibility is suggested by works that imply the possibility of conflict alleviation not through integration but through mutual national indifference (Zahra 2010).

As important is the question of *institutional development*. This issue has attracted academic interest in recent years but is still inadequately understood. By contrast, institutional *impact* continues to receive outsized attention. As I noted in Chapter 2, this is understandable – institutions offer a shortcut solution to some of the most pressing problems that multinational states face. Nevertheless, as this book shows, neglecting the question of institutional development undermines our ability to understand institutional impact as well. Future research ought to pay far more attention to modalities of institutional evolution and to the influence those modalities have on the ability of institutions to channel and contain conflict. This book suggests only some of the possible ways forward on this score.

The *meaning of institutions* is an issue that is both well under the radar and absolutely critical to understanding multinational state dynamics. This volume's conclusions about the role of institutional symbolism are far from a definitive statement. All of the claims I make here need to be further tested, refined, revised, or rejected – as necessary. Where and how this happens is up to other scholars, but I do see several potential areas of inquiry. The first has to do with the genesis of particular ideas of the state. Where do those ideas come from? Are they embedded in the structural features of the minority and majority condition? Some of the consistencies across the cases identified here seem to suggest so. But perhaps there is a degree of ideational cross-pollination between contexts that must be taken into account. Perhaps ideas developed in one setting travel to another where they may, but need not, find receptive ground.

The case-based, macrohistorical approach I deploy here also means that the book does not offer fine-grained evidence about how ideas about the state are developed and received by the population on the ground. Engaging with this lacuna will require a multidimensional methodological approach that might combine case work in the ethnographic vein with surveys and focus groups. The former could provide insights into the genealogy of ideas and narratives about the state. The latter might be very useful in ascertaining the pattern, spread, and intensity of attachment to those ideas. This might be complemented by a more complete and systematic mapping of the discourses of statehood among minorities and majorities, along the lines of the Making Identity Count project in international relations (Hopf and Allan 2016).

While *secession* motivated – mostly implicitly – much of the integration/accommodation debate, it has been under-studied as an issue in its own right until very recently. This emerging subfield continues to be isolated from the study of other aspects of multinational state politics. Yet as this volume demonstrates, secessionist crises are intimately linked to the politics of institutional change in multinational states. Moreover, extant work – including on the structural factors increasing the likelihood of secession, on secession referendums (including the public opinion research focusing on them), and on the international relations of secession – tends to focus on fairly static issues related to the politics of independence.[10] Moreover (again), the emphasis on identifying structural factors that channel secessionism leaves the question of political creativity and agency aside. Future work must address this omission. Another issue is the role of actors we do not normally consider to be central to secessionist politics – including bond rating agencies, labour unions, religious organizations, informal networks, and – an issue I have started to examine recently – private and public business organizations (Basta 2020b).

Finally, there is the set of meta-issues that intersect with all of the foregoing themes. Among the most important is the resilience and "viscosity" of narratives of nationhood and statehood, discourses that constitute and nourish identities (Oklopcic 2018, 164). In some cases, these narratives are remarkably consistent over decades, but in others they simply disappear or shift rapidly. While some scholars suggest that this is due to the extent to which institutions foster such narratives, that claim seems to be fully contradicted by the persistence of specific discourses in unfavourable circumstances. One need think only of the way in which Catalan narratives of identity managed to thrive during the Franco era. This returns us to the importance of the ways in which ideas survive even when they do not have formal institutional support (state autonomy – something flagged by integrationist critics of multinational federalism).

On the Limits and Possibilities of Generalization

Scholars of the multinational state – particularly those interested in theory-building through comparative analysis – will have to contend with the expectation that their theories ought to be as general as possible. According to John Gerring, one of the most widely cited methodologists in comparative politics, "a proposition informing us about many events is, by virtue of this fact, more useful than a proposition applicable to only a few" (Gerring 2005, 173). This maxim is rooted in the dominant, if implicit, understanding of causality in political science, one that owes much to Hume's notion of constant conjunction. This is the expectation that a particular set of variables should, *ceteris paribus*, produce similar outcomes of similar magnitude (Desrosiers and Vucetic 2018, 486). The premise, borrowed from natural sciences, carries with it the understanding that the political world is subject to forces akin to natural laws – that is, laws that hold across social systems.

In line with these expectations, a book like this one, based on a qualitative comparison of a handful of cases, would be expected to – at a minimum – conclude with a cursory extension of the argument to a larger number of cases. Ideally, it would combine qualitative case work with a statistical analysis of a larger dataset (Ahmed and Sil 2012). If the book's theory proved to be a poor fit when applied to the broader universe of cases, the conclusion would be that this is because the theory is faulty, rather than because there is no theory that *can* apply to all cases. I suggest that we should proceed from the opposite assumption. Until we are certain that there are theories that *can* apply to the entire universe of cases (e.g., *all* multinational states), we should not assume that there *is* a theory that can apply to them all.

When I refer to theory in the context of this discussion, I have in mind the covering-law model that mainstream political scientists work with. This is a statement of law-like relationship between two or more sets of phenomena along the lines sketched by Hempel, where one phenomenon covaries in a predictable pattern with the other (Hempel 1962, 103). Indeed, the model anchoring this book, especially as articulated in Table 3.4, resembles this logic. As I have noted on several occasions, however, I am not claiming that this model applies to all multinational states, nor, more to the point, do I *believe* that it does. Rather than developing a universal model to understand *all* multinational states, the goal of the book was to leverage a set of highly comparable cases in order to demonstrate the causal importance of institutional symbolism – the meaning that people attach to the rules of political organization.[11]

The applicability of the model developed here is thus limited by the meaning of statehood prevailing in the cases I have chosen to study.[12] Yet to say that a *specific* set of causal statements is not fully transposable to other contexts does not amount to suggesting that the core theoretical insight that informs those statements – in this case, the centrality of institutional meaning – cannot help illuminate the politics of other settings. The meaning of the state and its institutions is far more variable than in the four instances compared in Chapters 4 through 7. If we contemplate the theoretical implications of those differences, we can see how institutional meaning may nevertheless remain a relevant factor in understanding multinational states beyond the four covered in this book. A few speculative examples should suffice to illustrate this point.

Consider, to begin with, the United Kingdom of Great Britain and Northern Ireland. While the UK is a self-consciously – indeed, etymologically – multinational state, its political dynamics differ markedly from those covered in this work. Over the past two centuries, the country's elites have combined explicit recognition of their state's multinationality (in its symbols, name, and legitimizing ideology: unionism) with little formal territorial autonomy until late in the twentieth century (Keating 2009, 18).[13] Once devolved parliaments for Wales and Scotland were introduced in 1999, there was no majority backlash, despite predictions to the contrary (Condor 2010; Jeffery et al. 2016, 335–6). Moreover, there was little English (or British) mobilization against devolution even in the aftermath of the 2014 Scottish independence referendum. While English resentment at the perceived advantages enjoyed by the minority nations – notably the higher per capita public spending and the devolved jurisdiction MPs' ability to legislate on laws that apply to England only – has grown, it remains more a sport than a political program (2016, 338).

There is arguably a qualitative difference between the state idea as it developed in the UK and, say, continental Europe, an argument Dyson makes in his underappreciated contribution to state formation debates (Dyson 1980). Whatever the reasons behind this distinction, it has had a bearing on the political feasibility and direction of institutional reform in the UK. The implications are visible not only in the relative ease of the initial devolution in 1999 but also in the subsequent episodes of constitutional change with respect to Scotland in particular. The UK government was willing to accept a legally binding referendum on independence, and it subsequently enhanced Scottish devolution through the Scotland Acts of 2012 and 2016. No majority backlash followed. The English (perhaps more than the British, at the risk of drawing too sharp and perhaps too obviously facetious a line between the two) seem to be *indifferent* to the state as such and to the UK state in particular.

The meaning of statehood is also the starting point of Vujačić's attempts to explain why the Soviet Union and Yugoslavia broke up in such different ways (Vujačić 1996, 2004, 2015). In both cases, state dissolution meant that many members of the most numerous nation – the Russians and the Serbs, respectively – would become minorities in several of the newly created states. While the Russian elites did not attempt to "retrieve" their co-ethnics by redrawing inter-republican boundaries, the Serb leadership did, with well-known consequences. Vujačić explains this divergence by arguing that the state *as such* had a different meaning in the Russian and Serb national imaginaries. Briefly, while the Serbs identified with Yugoslavia, Russians were not so much indifferent as *hostile* to the Soviet state.

Understanding the symbolic dimension of state institutions can help make sense of post-conflict multinational settings as well. Efforts to reunify Cyprus stumbled as much on the symbolic aspects of the institutional question as on the more instrumental concerns (McGarry 2015, 278). The dispute over the appearance of *what* the reunification was creating and *in what manner* mirrors the Czechoslovak state treaty debate of the early 1990s. For the Greek Cypriot leadership, the new federal polity was to be a result of top-down devolution – implying the existence of a previously unified polity and a single political community, and precluding the legitimation of the Turkish partition of the island (McGarry 2015, 279). Their Turkish Cypriot partners preferred to view united Cyprus as a new polity, a merger of two pre-existing entities and peoples. Their preferences in terms of the organization of the state were similarly geared toward expressing this national duality, in terms of both territorial arrangements (by insisting on a single Turkish federal unit) and the design of central state institutions (by endorsing a co-presidency) (2015, 281–2).

While some of this logic reflected both sides' fears of the political consequences of their choices (notably the Greek Cypriot worry that confederal institutions would facilitate secession or amplify Turkey's influence in the country's domestic affairs; or the Turkish Cypriot apprehension about being dominated by the Greek community), several episodes during the negotiations demonstrate that the symbolic aspects of various proposals frequently outweighed the instrumental. Greek Cypriot negotiators, for instance, were willing to accept far-reaching decentralization across a range of policy areas but not the symbolic elements hinting at a binational state. Similarly, the Turkish Cypriot delegation rejected an integrated electoral system even though their total vote share under said system would have amounted to 50 per cent (2015, 282).

Clashing institutional meanings stood in the way of the federal solution to the Sri Lankan conflict, too. Here, the Sinhalese Buddhist religious and political establishment managed to weld religion, nationhood, and the state – indeed, an expressly *unitary* state – into a single discursive package (DeVotta 2007). This vision of the polity did not admit any institutional recognition of the country's ethnic or national diversity. Majority intransigence on this issue had manifested itself as opposition to claims for self-government by the Tamil minority since the early years of Sri Lanka's independence (Oberst 1988). When, after decades of suffering second-class status and periodic bouts of violence, a segment of the Tamil population took up arms in pursuit of independence, a generation-long civil war broke out (Ganguly 2018).

The international effort to resolve the conflict centred on a federal arrangement that was supposed to provide the Tamils with territorial self-government while preserving the integrity of the Sri Lankan state. However, in the Sinhalese Buddhist nationalist narrative, the very notion of federalism was *a priori* illegitimate, constituting as it did the symbolic negation of a single political/religious community as expressed through a unitary state. The politically influential Buddhist clergy were notionally willing to accept devolution as a way out of the impasse but were explicitly opposed to federalism. One monk explained the difference thus: "We do not want a federal system, but devolution of power. It is crucial to understand the difference between 'united,' which is when different states get into one state, and 'unitary,' one state. For example, the United States were separate states later united. In Sri Lanka, we never had separate states – we only have had Sri Lanka. Therefore, the state has to be unitary" (Frydenlund 2005, 21). As in Czechoslovakia and Cyprus, the elites claiming to represent the numerically dominant community were loath to accept any institutional framework implying that the state was a composite of pre-existing units. Instead they saw Sri Lanka as a polity of long standing that was *reforming itself*, rather than *being brought into existence by* antecedent political entities and communities.[14]

Elsewhere, the state may be viewed through a largely instrumental prism rather than represent a potent political symbol with either positive or negative valence. According to Paul Brass, "Indian politics have been characterized by an all-pervasive instrumentalism which washes away party manifestoes, rhetoric, and effective implementation of policies in an unending competition for power, status, and profit" (Brass 1994, 19). The obvious riposte to this characterization is that such instrumentalism marks institutional change not directly implicated with religious affairs.[15] Yet as soon as institutional reform takes on confessional connotations, matters change. For instance, while Indian elites have accepted the linguistic principle in the creation of new federal units, they have been outright hostile to state-making on religious grounds (Lacina 2020; Tillin 2013).

To sum up, the *idea of the state* – the way in which it is understood by the political elites and the general population – can take on a range of meanings.[16] The state can be seen as the expression of a political community (as in the cases covered in this volume and in several of the countries mentioned in this section); or as an entity inherently inimical to such expression (in which case we may be talking about communities that are not necessarily national);[17] or it may be viewed through an instrumental lens. In some cases, it may leave people indifferent and not signify much of anything.[18] Different perceptions of the state may then shape distinctive emotional dispositions toward it (Gupta 2015, 275–6). The validity of this admittedly crude and preliminary typology of state meaning is less important than the very plausible notion that the meaning of statehood *does* in fact vary. That possibility has far-reaching theoretical and methodological implications.

If the meaning of a particular institution is more or less constant across contexts, then we would expect that institution's causal effects to be constant as well. In other words, institutions could be treated as a standard causal variable – a "fixed entity with variable attributes" (Hirschman and Reed 2014, 262). We could then measure a state's inclusiveness (Wimmer, Cederman, and Min 2009), its degree of regionalization (Eaton et al. 2019; Marks, Hooghe, and Schakel 2008), a community's loss of autonomy (Germann and Sambanis 2020; Siroky and Cuffe 2015), or any other institutional characteristic. Variation in those features should produce different outcomes, but cases with similar scores on a particular variable should see similar political consequences. For instance, an equally low level of group autonomy should, *ceteris paribus*, produce similar levels of dis/satisfaction with the political status among members of said group. Under these assumptions, specific causal statements ought to be broadly generalizable and, consequently, testable against large datasets.

If, however, institutional meaning varies, so that instead of a homogenous population of cases we have discrete case clusters, the potential theoretical reach of specific causal statements will be much more limited. Measures of *objectivized* institutional traits such as "levels of autonomy" or "degree of inclusion" would no longer offer the same causal leverage: symbolically divergent cases with the same value on a particular variable could yield very different outcomes. Our "variables" would no longer be "fixed entities with variable attributes." Instead they would capture, or rather *fail* to capture, qualitatively different phenomena. In this section, I have offered some suggestive evidence that this set of assumptions might be more closely aligned with the actual texture of politics than the postulates underpinning comparative work based on large datasets, work that is increasingly the norm in comparative political science (Schedler and Mudde 2010).

I am far from alone in making this point. A veritable army of scholars, albeit perhaps a guerrilla army as far as mainstream political science is concerned, has been warning for half a century that we cannot treat social categories as if their meaning among actors on the ground does not matter, or as if that meaning could be assumed (Almond and Genco 1977; Bevir and Kedar 2008; Emirbayer 1997; Farr 1985; Hacking 1995; Hirschman and Reed 2014; MacIntyre 1972; Steinmetz 2004; Wolin 1969). The causal efficacy of any *social* fact – and institutions are social phenomena par excellence – hinges on the way it is perceived by the relevant populations, rather than on its objectivized attributes as understood by expert coders.[19] If those perceptions vary to the extent to which I am arguing they might, any methodological exercise that does not take account of this is bound to produce problematic outcomes.

What is the implication of this for future theorizing about multinational states? As I have already noted, a specific theory of the multinational state would only be generalizable in those cases where a similar idea of the state prevailed – for instance, as is the case in this book, in a subset of countries in Europe and North America during the second half of the twentieth and early twenty-first centuries. If I were to apply the theoretical insights developed here to other multinational states, characterized by a different understanding of statehood, and if I were to find that they did not hold, what would the conclusion be? If one adopts the mainstream view, then the theory at the heart of this book would have been falsified. If, by contrast, one were to adopt the "concept-dependent" view of causality (Steinmetz 2004, 378), then the conclusion might be that a different theory is required for each subset of cases.

This ontological stance implies the need to calibrate comparative causal analysis to carefully delineated clusters of cases, instead of privileging transgeographic and transtemporal insights for the sake of maximum generalizability. On the theoretical side, it points to the illusory character of any potential quest for a unifying theory of the multinational state, and toward the acceptance of theoretical multiplicity within the same thematic domain. In methodological terms, it means that large-n studies based on sprawling datasets are not inherently superior to small-n theorizing. In fact, to the extent to which the former disregard the causal relevance of the political meaning of the concepts they use in order to broaden the empirical base of their conclusions, we should treat their theoretical claims with a generous dose of skepticism. None of this means we should not compare widely. But we should be far more open-minded in terms of our understanding of causality, with all the attendant implications for what constitutes rigorous methods and, ultimately, good social science.

Appendix

Table A 1
Share of population by province
(as % of Canada's total)

	1971
Alberta	7.55
British Columbia	10.13
Manitoba	4.58
New Brunswick	2.94
Newfoundland	2.42
Nova Scotia	3.66
Ontario	35.71
Prince Edward Island	0.52
Quebec	**27.95**
Saskatchewan	4.29

Source: Own calculations, based on
Statistics Canada, *Canada Year Book*
(1975).

Table A 2
Share of GDP by province (as % of Canada's total)

	1961	1970	1980
Alberta	7.94	8.03	13.93
British Columbia	9.95	10.55	12.35
Manitoba	4.55	4.17	3.61
New Brunswick	1.97	1.89	1.62
Newfoundland	1.26	1.36	1.32
Nova Scotia	2.64	2.51	2.03
Ontario	41.08	42.03	37.13
Prince Edward Island	0.28	0.27	0.27
Quebec	**26.14**	**25.45**	**23.32**
Saskatchewan	3.95	3.44	4.00

Source: Own calculations, based on data from Statistics Canada,
Canadian Economic Observer: Historical Statistical Supplement
(1986).

Table A 3
Per capita GDP by province (as % of Canada's average)

	1961	1971	1981
Alberta	108.74	107.00	152.74
British Columbia	111.44	105.96	111.46
Manitoba	90.05	89.11	87.78
New Brunswick	60.20	64.26	58.51
Newfoundland	50.25	55.95	55.98
Nova Scotia	65.30	67.65	59.33
Ontario	120.15	117.82	104.62
Prince Edward Island	49.39	51.49	56.38
Quebec	**90.64**	**90.07**	**86.66**
Saskatchewan	77.96	83.32	101.36

Source: Own calculations, based on data from Statistics Canada,
Canadian Economic Observer: Historical Statistical Supplement
(1986).

Table A 4
Share of population by autonomous
community (as % of Spanish total)

Autonomous community	1991
Andalusia	17.8
Aragon	3.1
Asturias	2.8
Balearics	1.9
Basque Country	5.3
Canaries	4.2
Cantabria	**1.3**
Castille and León	6.5
Castille la Mancha	4.2
Catalonia	15.5
Extremadura	2.7
Galicia	6.9
La Rioja	0.7
Madrid	12.8
Murcia	2.7
Navarre	1.3
Valencia	9.9

Source: Instituto Nacional de Estadística,
Statistical Yearbook of Spain (various
years); http://www.ine.es/prodyser/
pubweb/anuarios_mnu.htm.

Table A 5
Share of G D P by autonomous community
(as % of Spanish total)

Autonomous community	1980	1990	2000
Andalusia	13.04	13.54	13.73
Aragon	3.31	3.47	3.14
Asturias	2.71	2.59	2.26
Balearics	1.99	2.38	2.29
Basque Country	7.45	6.48	6.41
Canaries	3.58	3.52	3.87
Cantabria	**1.41**	**1.35**	**1.25**
Castille and León	6.37	6.10	5.77
Castille la Mancha	3.66	3.78	3.50
Catalonia	19.12	18.90	18.38
Extremadura	1.69	1.88	1.77
Galicia	7.45	6.48	6.41
La Rioja	0.77	0.87	0.76
Madrid	14.14	15.15	17.21
Murcia	2.55	2.53	2.41
Navarre	1.69	1.70	1.72
Valencia	9.89	9.90	9.73

Source: Instituto Nacional de Estadística, *Statistical Yearbook of Spain* (various years); accessed at http://www.ine.es/prodyser/pubweb/anuarios_mnu.htm.

Table A 6
Per capita GDP by autonomous community
(as % of Spanish average)

	1981	1991	2000
Andalusia	75.32	76.08	73.25
Aragon	102.03	112.76	104.46
Asturias	91.73	91.93	83.44
Balearics	119.00	131.91	122.93
Basque Country	133.19	119.12	122.29
Canaries	99.83	90.53	94.27
Cantabria	**105.49**	**97.03**	**92.99**
Castille and León	88.04	91.00	90.45
Castille la Mancha	80.75	88.28	78.34
Catalonia	119.90	122.22	121.66
Extremadura	58.24	69.84	63.69
Galicia	85.26	78.09	77.71
La Rioja	118.19	128.27	113.38
Madrid	114.74	120.20	135.67
Murcia	101.90	89.57	83.44
Navarre	129.65	123.74	126.75
Valencia	105.25	100.87	96.18

Source: Own calculations, based on Instituto Nacional de Estadística, *Statistical Yearbook of Spain* (various years), http://www.ine.es/prodyser/pubweb/anuarios_mnu.htm; and Eurostat, Gross Domestic Product at current market prices at NUTS level 2, http://appsso.eurostat.ec.europa.eu/nui/show.do?dataset=nama_r_e2gdp&lang=en.

Table A 7
Industrial production by autonomous community
(share of the Spanish total)

	1993	1995	2000
Andalusia	7.8	8.3	8.8
Aragon	4.8	5.4	4.5
Asturias	2.5	2.5	2.2
Balearics	0.5	0.5	0.4
Basque Country	9	9.2	10
Canaries	1	0.9	1.4
Cantabria	1.5	1.6	1.3
Castille and León	7	7.4	6.8
Castille la Mancha	3.3	3.2	3.6
Catalonia	**28.4**	**27.2**	**26.6**
Extremadura	0.4	0.5	0.6
Galicia	5.8	5.2	6.1
La Rioja	1.1	.1.2	1.2
Madrid	11.1	10.6	9.5
Murcia	1.7	1.7	2.3
Navarre	3.6	3.8	3.6
Valencia	10.3	10.7	11

Source: Instituto Nacional de Estadística, *Statistical
Yearbook of Spain* (various years); http://www.ine.es/
prodyser/pubweb/anuarios_mnu.htm.

Table A8
Net central government spending by select autonomous community (as % of AC GDP)

	Andalucia	Basque Country	Castilla-La Mancha	Castilla y Leon	Catalonia	Extremadura	Madrid	Valencia
1991	15.16	4.3	16.02	9.56	-6	26.13	-10.18	1.66
1992	15.99	6.38	15.01	9.88	-6.29	25.73	-11.11	2.07
1993	20	8.17	18.97	12.39	-2.44	29.9	-8.14	5.21
1994	18.21	9.07	16.88	11.81	-3.29	26.89	-7.94	4.83
1995	18.81	8.77	18.42	12.25	-3.08	27.97	-6.21	4.08
1996	16.79	9.58	13.89	9.16	-4.97	25.33	-8.78	1.61
1997	11.83	3.21	10.42	7.78	-4.15	20.32	-9.24	0.7
1998	13.16	1.71	11.34	8.66	-4.6	21.51	-9.72	0.48
1999	10.54	1.24	9.91	8.64	-6.33	19.45	-10.02	-1.73
2000	8.74	1.54	9.6	7.95	-6.21	18.24	-10.69	-2.23
2001	7.9	0.35	8.54	7.28	-6.36	17.2	-10.47	-2.96
2002	6.68	1.99	5.55	13.42	-6.72	18.67	-12.54	-2.56
2003	5.87	2.1	8.25	7.23	-5.91	15.99	-12.69	-2.44
2004	8.02	3.14	7.82	7.28	-5.19	16.08	-11.91	-2.08
2005	4.09	3.37	5.99	5.76	-6.46	15.8	-13.06	-3.63

Note: Net central government spending is calculated by subtracting total revenues collected in a particular autonomous community by the central government from total central government spending in that AC.

Source: Ezequiel Uriel Jiménez & Ramón Barbéran Ortí, *Las Balanzas Fiscales de las Comunidades Autónomas con la Administración Pública Central (1991–2005)* (Bilbao: Fundación BBVA, 2007), 302–5.

Table A9
Share of population by republic
(as % of Yugoslav total)

Republic	1971
Bosnia and Herzegovina	18
Croatia	**22**
Macedonia	8
Montenegro	3
Serbia	41
Slovenia	**8**

Source: Own calculations, based on
Statistical Office of Yugoslavia, *Statistical
Yearbook of the Socialist Federative
Republic of Yugoslavia* (various years).

Table A 10
Share of Yugoslavia's gross social product, by republic (%)

	1960	*1970*	*1980*
Bosnia and Herzegovina	13.38	12.29	12.04
Croatia	26.81	26.77	25.86
Macedonia	4.83	5.60	5.63
Montenegro	1.64	1.99	2.07
Serbia	37.86	37.02	38.50
Slovenia	15.49	16.33	16.94

Source: Statistical Office of Yugoslavia, *Statistical Yearbook of the
Socialist Federative Republic of Yugoslavia* (1981), 407.

Table A 11
Per capita G D P in the Czech Republic and Slovakia
(current prices in Czechoslovak Crowns)

	1989	*1990*	*1991*	*1992*
Czech Republic	50627	54742	69532	74775
Slovakia	44383	45972	53264	55098
Slovak per capita G D P as a percentage of Czech	**87.67**	**83.98**	**76.60**	**73.69**

Source: Czech Statistical Office, *Statistical Yearbook of the Czech Republic* (1993),
for all figures except for Slovakia in 1991 and 1992. Figures for Slovakia in 1991 and
1992 based on Štatistický úrad Slovenskej republiky, *Statistical Yearbook of the Slovak
Republic* (1995).

Notes

1 As Murphy observes, "by the 1950s ... most Western social scientists were using the term [nation-state] to refer to any so-called sovereign state, no matter how ethnically or nationally heterogeneous that state might be" (1996, 104). For a similar statement, see Mikesell (1983). Things have changed little since the mid-1990s.

2 The situation is different in the domain of political and legal philosophy, where the multinational state has received more systematic treatment. For only a small sample of relevant writing, see Moore (2015); Norman (2006); and Tierney (2004).

3 See Resnick (2012) for a similar statement.

4 One need only consider Austria-Hungary and Czechoslovakia (one helping trigger the First World War, and the other paving the way for the Second World War), as well as India and Pakistan's on/off conflict over Kashmir, and most recently the chain reaction from Iraq to Syria and the attendant regional and global strategic consequences.

5 Recall the problems with the Soviet Union's nuclear arsenal when that multinational federation broke apart (Allison et al. 1996), the refugee flows resulting from the Yugoslav wars, or population exchanges stemming from the break-up of multinational empires (Brubaker 1995).

6 This is what Siniša Malešević captures with his concept of ideological "grounding" of nationalism (Malešević 2019, 12–14).

7 The extent to which the state does do so is subject to often hotly contested debates within national communities themselves, as well as, naturally, between them.

8 This happens quite frequently and across space, time, and regime type.
  Demands for such internal self-determination normally go unheeded only
  where the majority elites deny the very existence of separate identity for the
  claimant community, as was the case in Turkey for most of the twentieth
  century. Aktürk (2012) refers to these cases as anti-ethnic regimes.

9 This applies certainly to democratic states, where re-election prospects
  are closely linked to policy performance, especially in the economic sphere
  (Duch and Stevenson 2008; Lenz 2012; Lewis-Beck 1988). One might
  argue that government performance is even more important in authoritarian
  regimes, since these rest on fewer pillars of legitimacy than do democracies,
  and because the stakes of losing power are higher. For the link between
  authoritarian breakdown and economic crises, see Geddes (1999) and
  Haggard (1995).

10 While these strategies can fluctuate to a moderate degree across governments, their core principles are resilient to change. Note, for example,
   the durability of the Keynesian paradigm (Hall 1989) and its neoliberal
   successor (Schmidt and Thatcher 2013).

11 Interventionist centre, market-oriented region in Yugoslavia; interventionist
   centre, interventionist region in Canada; market-oriented centre, market-
   oriented region in Spain; and market-oriented centre, interventionist region
   in Czechoslovakia. In the Yugoslav case, the orientation shifted over the
   course of the 1960s, with important implications for institutional change.

12 I cover these issues in greater detail in Chapter 3.

13 The book's focus is on the second-largest community in each state, though
   I periodically address the demands and political actions by other, smaller
   communities such as the Basques in Spain and Slovenes in Yugoslavia.

14 Walzer offers an evocative summary of the symbolic dimension of the
   state: "The state is invisible; it must be personified before it can be seen,
   symbolized before it can be loved, imagined before it can be conceived.
   An image like the body politic, then, is not simply a decorative metaphor …
   Rather, the image is prior to understanding or, at any rate, to theoretic
   understanding, as it is to articulation, and necessary to both" (1967, 194).

15 This point bears emphasizing considering that the literature on recognition
   tends to foreground institutional meaning for excluded or discriminated
   minorities. Taylor's seminal essay emphasizes the importance of recognition
   for minorities and otherwise un(non)-recognized communities (C. Taylor
   1994). To the extent to which he considers the "recognition" of majority
   projects, he notes – rightly – that they often exist at the expense of
   minorities' dignity. This is an understandable point of emphasis given
   the normative thrust of the scholarship on recognition – redressing the

historically cumulated harm to minority communities. However, such lopsidedness is analytically problematic for any attempt to *explain* social outcomes. The fact that institutional imagery associated with majority projects is potentially injurious to minorities hardly negates its symbolic and emotional relevance for at least some members of the majority community.

16 For alternative modes of accommodation, see McEwen and Lecours (2008); and Swenden (2013). Whether or not minority politicians pursue this goal in earnest is an open question. My research in Catalonia suggests that at least one segment of the Catalan political elite advocated such recognition as a goal in itself. Those a priori committed to independence advocated symbolic recognition as a wager that it would be turned down by the Spanish elites. Thus, as literature on ethnic conflict has demonstrated repeatedly, this policy is also subject to contestation internal to the "group."

17 Literature on ethnic outbidding has a long lineage. See Chandra (2005); Horowitz (1985); Rabushka and Shepsle (1972); and Rothschild (1981).

18 A cursory overview of these pathways will suffice to illustrate the point. Territorially accommodative institutions can result from one or more of the following processes: democratization (Spain), gradual decentralization in stable democracies (UK, Belgium, Italy), decolonization (India, Nigeria), civil wars (Nigeria, Bosnia, Soviet Union, Yugoslavia), low-level insurgency (Philippines, Indonesia), external intervention (Bosnia, Iraq), colonial intervention and consolidation (Canada), and social(ist) revolution (Soviet Union, Yugoslavia). For a more optimistic view on the possibility of a comprehensive theory, see Cunningham (2014).

19 This critique is informed by William Sewell Jr's observation that "the experimental conception of temporality ... is inseparable from conventional comparative method, and it can be imposed only by what Burawoy aptly dubs 'freezing history' – and ... by fracturing the congealed block of historical time into artificially interchangeable units" (Sewell Jr 1996, 257–8).

20 For a schematic representation, see Table 3.2 in Chapter 3.

21 In each case, the largest minority nation comprised between 15 and 30 per cent of the overall population. I note this while cognizant of the problems with pinning down the "size" of minority nations in such environments (Stojanović 2011; Brubaker 1996).

22 While this study considers the process of accommodation in Czechoslovakia during the brief period between 1989 and 1992, the state has been formally federalized since 1969.

23 In pioneering the term, Vertovec (2007) refers primarily to diversity driven by immigration, but one could distinguish between multinational states

such as the ones studied here, and those in which the sheer number of possible ethnic and national categories is an order of magnitude greater, as in India, Nigeria, or Indonesia.

24 By this I mean both the constitutional tradition of stateness and the manner in which the state features in the social discourses and the collective self-understanding. While there are certainly differences between, say, the Canadian and the Spanish "culture of statehood," the differences are less pronounced than those between either of the two and cases in, for instance, South Asia or Sub-Saharan Africa. For underrated discussions on the cultures of statehood, see Nettl (1968); and Dyson (1980).

25 For example, scholarship on the impact of consociational institutions forms part of this literature, but it is far from exhaustive, in part because it tends to focus on institutional impact to the exclusion of institutional formation and development. Moreover, not all works on consociational democracy relate to multinational states – Lijphart's original contribution was developed in reference to the Dutch system, where political tensions took a different form. The literature on ethnofederalism is limited in similar ways – a point I make in Chapter 2. It can be categorized as a subset of the broader literature on federal systems, but as I argue in the next chapter, the very purpose, meaning, and functioning of federal institutions are fundamentally different in multinational states than they are in the nationally homogeneous ones. The lack of disciplinary backbone has thus far meant that we too often lose sight of the specific characteristics, and thus the specific institutional and political dynamics, of multinational states.

26 The specific implications of this will differ from case to case. I do wish to emphasize that I am not saying accommodation should not be tried at all. Rather, and particularly as it concerns symbolically salient issues, it should be done in such a way as to obtain the broadest possible majority buy-in in order to reduce the likelihood of future reversals.

CHAPTER TWO

1 While resilience and intensity are fairly self-explanatory, "viscosity" refers to the extent to which a particular political identity is capable of exerting gravitational pull on its purported constituents.

2 By which I mean that they have not been pursued by theoretically inclined scholars seeking to explain (or conceptualize for theoretical purposes) the related phenomena. Of course, there are many individual country studies that deal with one or more of these phenomena.

3　Such design often takes the form of constitutional or quasi-constitutional change. One can see this across a wide swathe of countries in Europe, Africa, and Asia (Arato 2009; Aybet and Bieber 2011; Belloni 2009; Bertrand 2004; Horowitz 1991; Lecours 2013; McGarry and O'Leary 2007).

4　This is true even of some of the key works in the study of post-colonial states (Herbst 2000; C. Young 1997).

5　Consider, for example, the conscription crises in Canada during the two world wars (Granatstein 1977), or the conflict in inter-war Czechoslovakia over how to deal with the German threat.

6　One method of addressing this problem is fiscal equalization that shores up the infrastructural capacity of the less developed federal units.

7　Thus, even as early Yugoslav federalism was largely window-dressing superimposed on a highly centralized communist regime, each republic was furnished with its own institutions of state (legislatures, executives) and its own communist party structures.

8　Rodden does make allowances for multinational states, as secession may complicate the picture, but this is not central to his hypotheses. The problem is that this insight only helps distinguish between national and multinational federations, not *among* the latter.

9　The argument is significantly more complex. For one, like Wibbels, Beramendi pays attention to both inter- and intra-regional inequality patterns.

10　Beramendi's work is particularly attentive to this issue, though he openly notes that the nexus of identity politics and fiscal architecture of federations will have to wait for a future study (2012, 246).

11　Lluch demonstrates that even these parties are effectively nationalist (Lluch 2014).

12　Quebec Liberals severed formal links with their federal counterparts in 1964 (Hepburn 2010, 534). The Catalan Socialist Party is not formally a branch of the Spanish PSOE but is affiliated with it through a formal agreement (Roller and Houten 2003, 10).

13　Filippov et al. (2004) argue simultaneously that an integrated party system may be possible even in multinational states (235), *and* that it may be difficult for it to emerge at all in such polities (263). One may foster integrated party systems in plural states by implementing centripetal electoral rules that incentivize politicians to appeal to voters across different communities. One of the most obvious examples of this is Nigeria (Bogaards 2010). However, this would be difficult to achieve without top-down imposition, as "ethnic" politicians are keenly aware of the power-distributive consequences of different institutional rules. Filippov and his co-authors recognize this explicitly (2004, 267–8).

14 For a succinct commentary on institutionalist varieties, see Hay (2006).

15 I develop the concept of institutional symbolism in greater detail in Chapter 3.

16 For an updated treatment of everyday nationalism, see Bonikowski (2016); and Skey and Antonsich (2017).

17 For more on symbols and nationalism, see Butz (2009); Hassin et al. (2007); and Kemmelmeier and Winter (2008). On symbolic politics and ethnic conflict, see Desrosiers (2011) and Kaufman (2001). Again, none of these treat institutions as symbols, or to the extent to which they do, that observation does not make it to the centre of analysis. Donald Horowitz also pointed to the importance of symbolism in his seminal study of ethnic conflict (1985, 216–26). He did not, however, pay much attention to the symbolic importance of formal institutions.

18 As importantly, few of these works combine explanatory theorizing with systematic empirical research. In most instances we see conceptual overviews of single case studies, broader conceptual exercises informed by illustrations from multiple cases, or systematic documentation of institutional options but without attempts to provide explanatory or analytical leverage.

19 Michael Keating is a notable exception, given his frequent discussion of UK unionism and the way in which it shapes that country's politics (e.g., Keating 2012). Philip Resnick's contribution stands out as well in that he joins the analysis of institutional meaning for both minority and majority nations (Resnick 2012).

20 See, among many others, Adeney (2007); Basta et al. (2015); Bermeo (2002); Cederman et al. (2015); Gurr (2000); McGarry and O'Leary (2005); Norris (2008); Stepan (1999); Stepan et al. (2011); and Wimmer (2013).

21 See Bunce (1999); Ciepley (2013); Cornell (2002); Jenne (2009); Nordlinger (1972); Roeder (2005; 2007); Simonsen (2005); and Snyder (2000).

22 See Anderson (2012); Bakke (2015); Brancati (2009); Hale (2004); and McCulloch (2014).

23 For an important recent exception, see Cunningham et al. (2017; 2020).

24 Again, Beissinger's work comes closest.

25 Hechter noted the absence of systematic study of secession in his 1992 article (Hechter 1992). Little would change for another decade and a half.

26 A similar principle was endorsed by King, Keohane, and Verba (1994), and even by Rueschemeyer in his contribution to the study of comparative historical analysis (2003).

27 Pepinsky, however, notes that the single case study has been staging a comeback (Pepinsky 2019).

28 To say this does not mean that there has been no work on the multinational state or that there has been little work applicable to it. Indeed, the theoretical framework developed in the following section builds on the insights of a wide range of scholars working on different aspects of multinational statehood. Nevertheless, it is accurate to say that the multinational state lacks its own dedicated subfield of study, in large part because of the paucity of links between various works that do address some of the issues I flag in this chapter. Note, for instance, the lone contribution on the multinational state in the *Oxford Handbook of Transformations of the State*, published in 2015 (Keating 2015).

CHAPTER THREE

1 I reduce the discussion to majority/minority distinction for the sake of simplicity in exposition and because in all four of the cases in this book, the main claimants for greater autonomy and recognition were the putative representatives of demographic minorities. I am aware that this is not the case in all multinational states. In some, the claimant community may be a demographic majority. However, accurate designation would require that I call the claimants "purported representatives of communities most of whose members feel themselves to constitute a national community apart from the entire citizenry of the state." I trust the reader needs no further justification for my choice of terminology.

2 Autonomy also provides minority elites with political goods (patronage, resources) enabling them to enhance their power. This benefit tends not to get advertised by the claimants and is overemphasized by their opponents.

3 Of course, national federations can also implement regional development policies, but the purpose of those policies is substantively different.

4 As was the case in the UK prior to devolution. Both Wales and Scotland benefited from administrative decentralization prior to this point, and Scotland had retained its civil institutions since the union in 1707.

5 This pattern holds across regime types, levels of development, and geographic areas. Territorial autonomy was thus realized in democratic (Canada, Spain, UK) and authoritarian (Soviet Union, Yugoslavia, Czechoslovakia, Ethiopia) states; in highly developed ones (Belgium) as well as those significantly less wealthy (Philippines or Nepal); and in post-conflict (Iraq, Bosnia) and peaceful ones.

6 I have only been able to identify the awareness of these cross-pressures in the work of Eaton and Dickovick (2004, 91), though their observation relates to national federations of Latin America rather than to multi-national federal systems.

7 Krause and Bowman make a similar argument about the patterns of authority decentralization in the United States. Though their argument relates to party congruence at the two levels of governance, they argue that the central government will be more likely to delegate authority "when its policy interests are more apt to be faithfully represented at the subnational level" (2005, 361).

8 Alfred Marshall's pioneering work paved the way for the study of economic clustering (Marshall 1890).

9 See, *inter alia*, Horowitz (1985) and Sambanis and Milanović (2014).

10 For a recent study of redistributive preferences and the impact of one's region's position on those preferences see Balcells, Fernández-Albertos, and Kuo (2015). It is of course possible that a government in a minority region might endorse one strategy for the region and another for the country as a whole. The inconsistency between those two strategies may weaken either or both – and does not normally occur. Even when pro-market minority politicians argue in favour of public spending, as they do in Catalonia, the goal is to boost the supply-side factors and thus further enhance the market mechanism.

11 Note that greater autonomy for regions with lower fiscal capacity may mean less government spending without redistributive mechanisms. This is why demands for fiscal autonomy are normally accompanied by parallel demands for continuing redistribution. In Scotland there was fear that greater revenue autonomy might undermine the benefits derived from the redistributive Barnett Formula (McLean 2013, 66).

12 This is not always the case, of course. Albertans in particular have traditionally been much more resentful of the redistribution facilitated by Ottawa than have Ontarians. But then, there *are* Ontarians.

13 By extension, a wealthy region, but one that accounts for a very small percentage of the overall tax revenue, is much more likely to be accommodated under this scenario.

14 This focus on power-distributional aspects of institutions remains the central feature of historical institutionalism three decades after these lines have been written. As Mahoney and Thelen put it, "most historical institutionalists embrace a power-political view of institutions that emphasizes their distributional effects, and many of them explain institutional persistence in terms of increasing returns to power" (2010, 7). The same

emphasis can be found in the introductory chapter to the *Oxford Handbook of Historical Institutionalism*, where the editors note that "structural power often resides in institutions that produce policy biases and that give political groups mobilizational advantages in seeing their preferred policies enacted" (Fioretos, Falleti, and Sheingate 2016, 19). This is not to say that historical institutionalists have not extended their insights to new areas of inquiry and that their theorizing has stagnated. To the contrary, they have paid much greater attention to institutional change and have been far more willing to incorporate ideational factors into their models (Blyth, Helgadottir, and Kring 2016). As Hall argues, some historical institutionalists admit into their analyses the possibility that institutions, apart from being rules, are "constituted by ... accompanying rituals and symbols" (2010, 217). Still, even in this formulation, institutions are not themselves symbols – though they may be "constituted" by them. I know of few instances of historical institutionalist work that view institutionalized policies and institutions as symbolic expressions of identity. Béland and Lecours come closest in their work on social policy in multinational states (Béland and Lecours 2010). Scholarship on race in American political development is not quite as explicit about the expressive dimension of institutions, but it does resonate with the ideas of sociological institutionalism (King and Smith 2005).

15 Roeder's work (2007) reflects some of this logic, but for the clearest examples, see Hoddie and Hartzell (2005); and Martin (2013).

16 An aspect of social reality is a symbol if it represents something other than itself. For the coverage of the way in which both classical and contemporary scholars conceive of symbols, see Janssen and Verheggen (1997); Klatch (1988); and Wagner (1974).

17 For example, a community might be subdivided into several territorial units in each of which it constitutes a majority. The arrangement may be expressly designed to deny that community recognition, but the institutions of self-government may simultaneously allow its members to run their own affairs and protect their material and cultural interests.

18 To suggest that meaning bifurcates is not to say that national communities are internally homogeneous. The point is that much of the conflict around institutions tends to produce opposing understandings of state institutions among members of majority and minority communities. This need not mean that the entire putative population of either community lines up neatly behind a single idea, or that there may not be variants of political claims, however similar, or that those political claims are impervious to change over time. I demonstrate this intra-group diversity in Bosnia

(Basta 2016); Lluch makes a similar claim for Spain and Canada (Lluch 2014).

19 Students of nationalism have been increasingly attentive to the role of majority or state nationalism and dominant ethnies in the construction of nationhood and statehood. Anthony Smith's contribution on core ethnies established conceptual foundations for this work (Smith 1986). Subsequently, a number of other scholars have addressed the conceptual and theoretical issues arising from this nexus. See Cetrà and Swan (2020); Gagnon, Nootens, and Lecours (2011); E. Kaufmann (2004); Kaufmann and Haklai (2008); Lecours and Nootens (2009); and Loizides (2015).

20 We see that pattern in all four of the cases here. Members of the largest nation tend to welcome the members of the minority nation into their own fold (be that fold Canadian, Spanish, or composite Yugoslav or Czechoslovak community). While system justification theory has not been applied to multinational states, it is highly relevant to those settings.

21 The politics of federalism is by definition "complex," with voters finding it difficult to assign responsibility for policy performance to the appropriate level of government in federal systems (Cutler 2004; Wlezien and Soroka 2011).

22 I discuss the differences between Yugoslavia on the one hand, and Spain and Canada on the other, and the limits to this generalization, in Chapter 6.

23 Note, however, that this recognition was tempered by moving the reference to Catalan nationhood from the body to the preamble of the statute's text.

24 See Sorens (2012, 63). Short-lived or non-mass movements may not provide as strong an incentive for the central government to tackle constitutional reconstruction.

25 Fragile State Index, for example, demonstrates that both Spain and Canada, as well as all of the successor states of the former Yugoslavia and Czechoslovakia, rank higher in state strength than a number of multi-national states in Africa and Asia. This pattern holds even for those post-Yugoslav states that experienced war. See www.fragilestatesindex.org.

26 German-speakers in South Tyrol, Corsicans, Tibetans, Acehnese, and Kashmiri Muslims are all a much smaller proportion of the population in their respective states. For measures of group strength as it relates to group size and territorial concentration, see Cunningham (2011).

27 Conflict tends to be greater at a moderate degree of ethnic fractionalization than when the fragmentation of a polity is significantly higher (Collier and Hoeffler 1998, 569–70).

28 This distinguishes them from the Soviet Union, Russia, or China, for example.

29 Bracketing Canada's First Nations, whose claims are qualitatively different from that of Quebec and less threatening to the integrity of the state. This is not meant to suggest a normative hierarchy of movements, nor that First Nations self-government claims are *a priori* less important than those made in the name of the Québécois nation. However, the size of the respective communities, their degree of territorial concentration, their political power, and their capacity to put in question the territorial integrity of the Canadian state is very different. At the same time, the First Nations' claims in response to the 1995 Quebec referendum, notably the possibility of recursive secession by the James Bay Cree, made an already fraught process more complicated still (Jenson and Papillon 2000).

30 Central governments are more likely to accommodate demands for secession where there aren't additional self-determination movements that might be influenced by such decisions (Walter 2006).

31 Not under any circumstances, of course. A noticeable increase in support for Scottish independence in the polls from about the mid-30 per cent range to about 50 per cent in the second half of 2014 was clearly a consequence of that year's independence referendum campaign, which did not come on the wave of secessionist mobilization in response to a major institutional shift. The support for independence prior to mid-2014 was remarkably consistent. See https://yougov.co.uk/topics/politics/articles-reports/2020/08/12/scottish-independence-yes-leads-53-47.

CHAPTER FOUR

1 This reality emerged in the 1930s and 1940s. Prior to the Great Depression and the Second World War, Canada was more decentralized, albeit in a context in which the state played a much more limited role (Banting 1987, Ch. 5; Guest 1980).

2 On asymmetries, see Brock (2008).

3 Québécois nationalists tend to view the Conquest as the foundational moment in English–French relations (Cook 1986, 50–1).

4 For a succinct overview and literature review, see A. Greer (1995).

5 Some scholars have challenged this interpretation of life in Quebec under Duplessis. Coleman, for instance, argues that postwar Duplessis governments had not been as anti-statist as is usually suggested (Coleman 1984, 11).

6 According to the Canadian constitution, provinces have a right to levy direct taxes. However, this right was surrendered by all of the provincial leaders, on a temporary basis, in 1941 for purposes of fighting the war. For the next two decades, the provinces "rented out" their tax bases to the

federal government, which in turn patriated a portion of these proceeds to fund provincial programs (Government of Canada 1975, 2).

7 Indeed, Lesage presented the Quebec Pension Plan as a recognition of Quebec's "special status" in the Confederation (Simeon 2006, 59).

8 For the relevant documents, see https://www.sqrc.gouv.qc.ca/relations-canadiennes/positions-historiques/positions-quebec-1936-2001-en.asp.

9 The source is a document compiled by the Quebec Secretariat for Canadian Relations, https://www.sqrc.gouv.qc.ca/documents/positions-historiques/positions-du-qc/part1/1960JeanLessage_en.pdf.

10 By mid-nineteenth century, Montreal dominated British North America; its commercial and industrial influence would extend into the twentieth century (Norrie and Owram 1991, 152).

11 Between 1938 and 1944, of all the provinces, Ontario saw the largest increase in its share of gross value of production, whereas Quebec experienced the second largest drop (Norrie and Owram 1991, 527).

12 For an overview, see D. Thomson (1984, Chs. 7, 9–12).

13 The basis of Canada's social welfare policy until 1996.

14 See Tables A1 through A3 in the Appendix.

15 The governments of Lesage, Bourassa, and even Lévesque demanded a greater share of revenues but not complete fiscal control. See the relevant documents at https://www.sqrc.gouv.qc.ca/relations-canadiennes/positions-historiques/positions-quebec-1936-2001-en.asp. Only the Johnson government claimed "100% use of the three major direct taxes." However, while it called for the federal government to only raise funds for federal matters, it allowed for "unconditional grants [to] be paid to provinces, either according to a general equalization formula, or to stabilize their finances." See arts. 102 and 87 respectively at https://www.sqrc.gouv.qc.ca/documents/positions-historiques/positions-du-qc/part1/1966DanielJohnsonPere_en.pdf.

16 The government of Quebec could have demanded that the federal government recuse itself from taxing Quebec residents altogether. Ottawa would have had the constitutional mandate to resist those demands, since it has the unlimited right to raise revenues.

17 In this respect, Ontario's elites follow provincial public opinion. Ontarians identify with Canada far more than residents of any other Canadian province. See Mendelsohn and Matthews (2010, fig. 5).

18 The formal symmetrization principle was retained in 1962 when the tax rental framework was replaced by a generalized system of tax-sharing (Boadway and Hobson 1993, 38).

19 Canadian Broadcasting Corporation, "1968 Leaders' Debate - CBC Archives," https://www.cbc.ca/archives/entry/1968-leaders-debate.

20 Federal elites did use policy and legislative mechanisms to preclude the appearance of special status for Quebec. For numerous instances, see Simeon (2006).

21 The Victoria Charter, for instance, granted Quebec constitutional veto (Robinson and Simeon 1990, 208).

22 This is very much in line with Behiels's interpretation of the Meech Lake Accord and its implications (Behiels 2007, 264).

23 Readers familiar with Canadian politics may point out that in 2006 the Canadian House of Commons passed a parliamentary motion recognizing Quebeckers as a nation, without ensuing backlash. This move hardly compares in prominence and purpose to either the Meech Lake or Charlottetown accords. The then prime minister Stephen Harper emphasized that the motion was "not a constitutional amendment [or] a legal text. It is simply a declaration of recognition and a gesture of reconciliation" (MacDonald 2006). Other federal leaders, including Bob Rae and Stéphane Dion, wanted to ensure that the resolution lacked legal force (Delacourt 2006). Finally, the English-language wording of the motion (it recognizes the Québécois, an "ethnic" category, rather than Quebec, a political category) was meant to convey a "sociological" fact, not a legal/constitutional one, and was thus not intended to constitute an institutional endorsement of binationality (Flanagan 2006).

24 Prospect theory posits that we value a loss of something more than a gain of equal magnitude (Mercer 1995). Thus, a withdrawn promise of concession should be more antagonizing than no concession.

CHAPTER FIVE

1 The Basque Country and Navarra are subject to a separate fiscal arrangement.

2 In 1950, the population of Catalonia was approximately 3.2 million.

3 The initial decentralization framework was highly asymmetric, but it would become more coordinated over time (Aja 2014; Colomer 1998; Moreno 2001). Here I am referring to the powers the Catalan government acquired over this period, without discussing in detail the extent of decentralization in other ACs. This choice serves to focus the discussion, not to ignore important processes taking place elsewhere.

4 For details of relative regional contribution to the central budget, see Table A8 in the Appendix.

5 Both Article 1 and Article 2 of the constitution in effect express a monist understanding of the Spanish political community. Article 1, Section 2,

states: "National sovereignty belongs to the Spanish people, from whom all state powers emanate." Article 2 simultaneously asserts: "The Constitution is based on the indissoluble unity of the Spanish nation, the common and indivisible homeland [*sic*!] of all Spaniards." Also, "it recognizes and guarantees the right to self-government of the nationalities and regions [*sic*!] of which it is composed."

6 The amendment was, of course, defeated.

7 Catalonia's economy contributed a disproportionate share of Spain's total GDP (relative to its population), regularly had a higher GDP per capita than the country average, and also contributed a share of Spain's industrial production out of proportion to its population size. See Appendix, Tables A4 through A7.

8 In 1979 it also abandoned the Marxist rhetoric that underpinned some of those policies (Share 1988, 423).

9 Agranoff and Gallarin make this point explicitly, though without specifying the exact mechanism. They merely note that the centrism of the Catalan (and Basque) governing parties facilitated cooperation with Madrid (Agranoff and Gallarín 1997, 15).

10 I am grateful to Xavier Arbós Marín for pointing this distinction out to me.

11 This is not to say that there was no opposition to minority nationalism in Spain. Indeed, the right-wing media had been highly critical of Catalanism since the early 1990s. However, even the more nationalist PP of Aznar's second term was not openly opposed to autonomy, but instead dedicated to a kind of symmetric expression thereof (Balfour and Quiroga 2007, 109, 110).

12 Indeed, the term "nationalities" was not UCD's preference. Arias-Salgado saw it as necessary to enhance the democratic legitimacy of the constitution among a large segment of the Catalan and Basque populations, and because he believed that denying this term would eventually result in the rise of nationalism (Cortes Generales 1978b, 2267).

13 CiU, the Basque Nationalist Party, and the Galician Nationalist Bloc.

14 For details of the process, see Colino (2009); and Keating and Wilson (2009).

15 The entire document, including an English version, can be found at https://www.parlament.cat/document/cataleg/48104.pdf.

16 By contrast, 53.1 per cent of Catalonia's residents supported the expression of Catalan nationhood, with 39 per cent rejecting it. Also, 70.2 per cent were in favour of a separate fiscal arrangement, with 19.7 per cent against.

17 Interview, Elisenda Paluzie, Barcelona, 30 May 2014.

18 Interview, Miquel Strubell, Barcelona, 19 July 2018.

19 There was no marked shift in public opinion (see Figure 5.2), nor did the largest nationalist parties move decisively to secessionist positions. Instead, support for independence continued to grow at the same pace it did prior to the Court's decision. In the regional elections held four months after that decision, the main axis of the campaign was the economic crisis that had started in 2008. Neither the victorious CIU (including Artur Mas's CDC), nor ERC advocated a secessionist turn in response to the downgrading of the statute. The only openly independentist party, Catalan Solidarity for Independence (SI), obtained 3.3 per cent of the vote (Basta 2018, 1261).

20 As told to the author by Elizabeth Castro, a member of ANC's national secretariat. Interview, Elizabeth Castro, Barcelona, 26 April 2017.

21 Interview, Artur Mas, Barcelona, 24 October 2018. Mr Mas told me that despite being cautioned by the Catalan business community not to engage in the shift toward a secessionist position, he was unable to ignore what was happening in the streets and, particularly, what was happening in the polls.

CHAPTER SIX

1 Originally the Kingdom of Serbs, Croats, and Slovenes, it was renamed the Kingdom of Yugoslavia in 1929.

2 By the end of the war, the Partisan army was nationally diverse. At the outset, however, it was largely a Serb outfit (Hoare 2002; Irvine 1993, 115).

3 Slovenia, Croatia, Serbia, Montenegro, and Macedonia. Bosnia and Herzegovina was the only republic without a titular nation.

4 The CPY was renamed the League of Communists in order to symbolize its transformed, less interventionist role in the new ideological constellation.

5 This critique was already circulating among the Croat republican leaders some years prior. The Croatian Central Committee expressed concern over the concentration of investment resources at a meeting with Kardelj in late 1959 (Vojnović, Šarić, and Jukić 2008, 80). A year later, the CCC discussed the possibility of escalating Croatia's demands for decentralization of investment resources (Vojnović, Šarić, and Jukić 2008, 230–66).

6 In a 1967 meeting of LCY's top body, Croatia's premier Dabčević-Kučar argued that the Yugoslav Investment Bank alone accounted for 44 per cent of the investments of the entire country. Archives of Yugoslavia, Belgrade, Record Group CK SKJ 507, file III/129, Appendix 2: Minutes of the 6th meeting of the Presidency of the Executive Committee of the Central Committee of the League of Communists of Yugoslavia, 19 October 1967, 12.

7 I was able to find the earliest reference to this issue in 1966, when a discussion of the Croat Central Committee pointed to the centralizing implications of enterprises not having access to their own foreign currency. Croatian State Archive, Zagreb, Record Group 1220D SKH, Box 7.17 (2536), Minutes of the discussion about foreign currency regime, 23 February, Central Committee of the League of Communists of Croatia, 20–1.

8 With only about 30 per cent of Yugoslavia's population, the two republics produced over 40 per cent of the country's gross social product between 1960 and 1980 (See Tables A9 and A10 in the Appendix).

9 Bosnia, part of the Ottoman Empire, was formally annexed by Austria-Hungary in 1908, though it had been occupied by it during the previous three decades.

10 Bosnia was a partial exception, having received significant investment under the Habsburgs (Lampe 1989, 67).

11 Among the former were Miha Marinko (member of the federal and Slovenian EC), arguing in favour of the termination of inefficient firms (Savez komunista Jugoslavije 1998, 94); Edvard Kardelj (then the second most influential politician behind Tito, also a Slovene), for whom the market mechanism was "a law of life" (1998, 198); Slovenia's premier Boris Kraigher, who advocated market incentives for enterprises and integration into the international division of labour (1998, 234–35); Croatia's premier Jakov Blažević, who attacked state control over investment and extolled the rationality of decentralized enterprises operating according to laws of economics (1998, 152); and Vladimir Bakarić, Croatia's top party official, who similarly favoured marketization (1998, 244). On the other side were the Montenegrin premier Filip Bajković, who argued that the market mechanism might work for wealthier republics (1998, 122); Serbian party secretary Jovan Veselinov, who claimed that the "liberalism" of the new economic approach was unsuited to Yugoslav circumstances (1998, 130); and Macedonian premier Aleksandar Grličkov, who suggested that the market mechanism was both given too much emphasis (1998, 141) and inconsistently applied, benefiting the developed and undercutting the underdeveloped (1998, 144). Mijalko Todorović, a member of the federal government, fretted over the market mechanism being presented as "practically an inheritance of socialism" (1998, 54). Serbia's premier Miloš Minić (1998, 212) and the Montenegrin head of the Yugoslav union of syndicates, Svetozar Vukmanović, both supported the market turn (1998, 73).

12 Even this formal level of decentralization increased the power of municipal bodies by letting them appoint enterprise directors, securing their funding

and making it less dependent on central organs, and thus facilitating the capture of enterprise revenues (Rusinow 1977, 70).

13 See, for instance, references to the decentralization of investment policy and its differential implications for more and less developed republics (Savez komunista Jugoslavije 1998, 171, 187–8, 201, 244).

14 Bosnian Muslims only started to gain recognition as a national community in the late 1960s, in the lead-up to the 1971 Yugoslav census (Lučić 2012).

15 Nikezić urged the Serbs to give up on the idea that Yugoslavia was inherently valuable and to accept the confederal understanding of the state increasingly advocated in the northern republics (Budding 1997, 412).

16 Dragović-Soso's book is packed with examples of such claims. For a sample, see Dragović-Soso (2002, 37, n86, 92, 95, 99).

17 Surveys during this era and into the 1980s and beyond largely examined matters of ethnic distance or census "Yugoslavs," rather than attitudes toward the common state or narratives about it. See, among others, Botev (1994); Hodson, Sekulic, and Massey (1994); Sekulic, Massey, and Hodson (1994); and Vušković (1982).

18 See https://news.gallup.com/poll/210866/balkans-harm-yugoslavia-breakup.aspx. These results must be viewed *cum grano salis* in light of the passage of time, intervening events, and subsequent interpretation.

19 See Elkins and Sides (2007); and Staerklé et al. (2010).

20 Serbia's leadership did attempt to reverse some of the features of the new constitutional order, but it did this in line with established league procedures and thus far too timidly for the tastes of the Serb nationalist intelligentsia.

21 Vladisavljević notes that the charges were exaggerated (Vladisavljević 2008, 160–6). In fact, his book constitutes an important corrective to the broadly top-down view of nationalist mobilization in Serbia one finds in most of the literature on this era.

22 In doing this, the Slovene communist leadership continued along the path down which it had already ventured some years earlier, in effect seeking to align itself with the various movements challenging the legitimacy of socialism and Yugoslavia. One segment of those movements focused on the Slovene national question; another emphasized civil freedoms and democracy (Hansen 1996). They came together during 1988. The relatively liberal Slovene leadership understood that they could ill afford to ignore nationalist pressures if they hoped to retain their political relevance (Hafner 1992).

23 The convoluted question posed in Croatia's referendum suggests that it was, in fact, a vote not on independence but on confederation. This,

I believe, makes too much of the formal pronouncements of Croat leadership at the time.

CHAPTER SEVEN

1 With the exception of the lead-up to the Prague Spring in 1968, Czechoslovak political culture was far less amenable to opposition and political friction than was the Yugoslav one during the same era.

2 The major caveat is the willingness of the Czech elites to endorse the multinational framework in repeated negotiations. According to the model, such willingness was supposed to have resulted in majority backlash. I discuss the ambiguity of this situation in other parts of the chapter.

3 While both parts of what would become Czechoslovakia were for centuries ruled by the Habsburg dynasty, they were nevertheless subject to different political systems. The Czech lands had separate status as the Lands of the Bohemian Crown, whereas Slovak territory was ruled directly by the Hungarian Crown, without distinct legal status or separate political and administrative institutions (Evans 1979, Chs. 6 and 7; Taylor 1976).

4 A 1946 survey of the Czech population found that 65 per cent of respondents believed that Czechs and Slovaks were "two branches of the same nation," with only 21 per cent considering them distinct nations (Bakke 2004, 31).

5 This agreement, signed in May of 1918 by Czech and Slovak émigré organizations, established the principles on which the new state was to be based. Slovaks were to have their own administration, parliament, and courts, and Slovak was to be the official language of their unit (Grinnell 2007).

6 The government did reorganize the state's territorial-administrative boundaries in 1927, creating a Slovak administrative unit (Krejčí 1996, 11).

7 Slovakia was a Nazi puppet regime. It sent troops to the Eastern Front and collaborated in the extermination of Slovakia's Jews (Kirschbaum 2005, Ch. 6). Nevertheless, both in instrumental and symbolic terms, the experience was formative.

8 Own calculations, based on the figures supplied in Good (1994, Table 3; 879).

9 For a general overview of the patterns in the political economy of states in the Soviet orbit under state-socialism, see Berend (1996).

10 See, for example, Klaus's statement before the 1992 election (Prague Telegraf 1992).

11 In the Yugoslav case, the strategies began to converge around the mid-1960s. From 1972, the federal strategy was diluted as a consequence of pressures from the disaffected proponents of statism in the federal party, who used the nationalist surge in Croatia to delegitimize the liberalization of the late 1960s and re-establish some degree of political control over the market (Basta 2010, 102–3; Rusinow 1977, Ch. 8).

12 For instance, in an October 1991 poll, 78 per cent of Slovak respondents expressed dissatisfaction with their standard of living, as opposed to 54 per cent of Czechs (Prague čsтк 1991b).

CHAPTER EIGHT

1 Even though both the Serbs and the Czechs had their narrower national identifier (unlike the Anglo-Canadians and Spaniards), many of them were comfortable with the broader (Yugoslav/Czechoslovak) political identity, to the point that they considered the two to be one and the same, or at the very least, that they were willing to subsume their particularist, ethnically informed identity into the broader one. Neither the Croats/Slovenes/Macedonians nor the Slovaks were as comfortable with the overarching state-wide identity.

2 Or, for that matter, simply in order to be able to say that they had won something in a political contest, regardless of the actual instrumental utility of that "win." I am grateful to James Mitchell for this point.

3 The outbidding dynamic can be observed in all four cases, with Liberal Party of Quebec (in the early 1980s), the Socialist Party of Catalonia (early 2000s), the Croatian League of Communists (late 1960s and early 1970s), and the Christian Democrats of Slovakia all moving closer to the demands of the more radical political parties or, in the Croatian case, the equivalent to an opposition party, the cultural society Matica hrvatska.

4 Societal mobilization was widespread in Croatia and Quebec, not so much in Catalonia at this point.

5 The performance of majority identity is particularly noteworthy here. In Canada, the slogan "My Canada includes Quebec" (from the 1995 referendum) captures perfectly the welding of institutional visions and identity. It means, of course, that Quebeckers are themselves Canadians, whether or not all of them feel that way. In Spain, the unionist Ciutadans adopted as their emblem a heart incorporating the flags of the EU, Spain, and Catalonia (the non-independentist variety) to express the idea of unity in diversity, but ultimately under a single, Spanish political community.

The idea that Serbs and Croats are the same people was still alive a decade and a half after Yugoslavia's demise, when the Serbian tennis star Novak Đoković expressed indifference to being called a Croat at an award ceremony in Montreal in 2007. However anecdotal, all these instances are highly relevant for the point at hand.

6 Along with eco-socialists, Christian democrats, and even the more moderate wings of the nationalist CDC and ERC.

7 As I noted in the introductory chapter, this book does not address why these crises had such different outcomes – break-up in the case of Yugoslavia, a legal referendum that came short in Quebec, and an illegal attempt at a referendum in Catalonia. Nevertheless, this is one of the key issues that future work on the multinational state will have to reckon with. I have started to address the question in my project on the role of business in the lead-up to secession referendums (Basta 2020b).

8 For an early statement, see Rabushka and Shepsle (1972).

9 There is clear evidence of this process in Serbia (where the dissident intellectuals accused Serb leaders of effectively betraying first the Yugoslav idea and then the Serb nation itself), Spain (with the PP charging that PSOE surrendered the idea of a united Spanish nation in the 2004–6 period of statutory negotiations with the Catalan government), and Canada (with the Reform Party in particular charging that by conceding to Quebec's demands, both the federal Liberals and Conservatives were yielding to a political program that was foreign to Canadians).

10 For recent exceptions, see Griffiths and Muro (2020); Lecours (2020); and Roeder (2018).

11 This is along the lines of what Farr means by situational analysis, where our capacity to generalize "depends wholly upon our ability to isolate similar or typical actors in similar or typical situations with similar or typical problems" (Farr 1985, 1102).

12 By which I mean that the state *as such* is perceived as a positive entity, and either a potential or actualized expression of a specific national community. For members of a minority nation, the regional state (Quebec, for example) can be the expression of one's community, but so can the sovereign state of which the regional state is a component (Canada), provided it is appropriately organized to express its multinational character. As I show here, that organization may entail constitutional stamping ("distinct society" status) and a level of federal asymmetry to reflect *national* symmetry (McGarry 2007).

13 Scottish civil institutions – law, education, and religion – were all preserved. Northern Ireland is a different matter altogether, having

gained territorial autonomy in 1921 in the aftermath of the Irish War of Independence.

14 The same struggle over the meaning of the state and its "longevity" can be observed in Bosnia and Herzegovina (Basta 2016). In a different vein, in Nepal the most contentious aspect of the new postwar constitution proved to be its federal arrangement, notably the number of units and their names. Variations on both had very different implications for the meaning of federalism – whether it was going to be accommodative or integrative, and what kind of political community it was going to express (Lecours 2013).

15 This is another dimension of identity that has a bearing on how the state is seen. In societies where religion plays a more prominent role than nationalism – unless the two are welded together – the state idea may take a very different shape than in more secular contexts.

16 There is a long sub-current of thought about the state as an idea, rather than as – or in addition to – an organizational-institutional complex. See Abrams (1988); Mitchell (1999); Painter (2006); Gupta (1995; 2015); and Dyson (1980).

17 This is, for instance, the anarchists' view (Bakunin 1990). Wael Hallaq makes the case that the modern state is inherently incompatible with authentically Islamic governance (Hallaq 2013).

18 I am not arguing that systems of ideas about the state are bound by political geography. Specific dispositions toward the state may compete with other, often diametrically opposing ones, within the same space (say, urban or rural areas of a given region or a country), and may be shared by communities that range far beyond the boundaries of a specific sovereign entity. Nor am I suggesting that ideas about statehood are static.

19 Against critique that this is a problem solvable by more sophisticated coding, I offer the following response. Institutional meaning is not only variable across cases – it is plural within them. If we are to code it, we invariably undercut the validity of our observations. How, for instance, would one code the perception of a particular *negative* institutional change among a population whose members cannot agree among themselves either on the severity of the change or the appropriate political response to it? This multiplicity of institutional meaning, its *dynamic* polysemy (Fiske 1986), stands firmly in the way of coding practices pervading contemporary political science.

References

Abrams, Philip. 1988. "Notes on the Difficulty of Studying the State." *Journal of Historical Sociology* 1(1): 58–89.

Adeney, Katharine. 2007. *Federalism and Ethnic Conflict Regulation in India and Pakistan*. New York: Palgrave Macmillan.

Aghevli, Bijan B. 1992. *Stabilization and Structural Reform in the Czech and Slovak Federal Republic: First Stage*. Washington, D.C.: International Monetary Fund.

Agranoff, Robert. 1993. "Inter-Governmental Politics and Policy: Building Federal Arrangements in Spain." *Regional Politics and Policy* 3(2): 1–28.

Agranoff, Robert, and Juan Antonio Ramos Gallarín. 1997. "Toward Federal Democracy in Spain: An Examination of Intergovernmental Relations." *Publius: The Journal of Federalism* 27(4): 1–38.

Ahmed, Amel, and Rudra Sil. 2012. "When Multi-Method Research Subverts Methodological Pluralism – or, Why We Still Need Single-Method Research." *Perspectives on Politics* 10(4): 935–53.

Aja, Eliseo. 2014. *Estado Autonómico y Reforma Federal*. Madrid: Alianza Editorial.

Ajzenstat, Janet, Paul Romney, Ian Gentles, and William D. Gairdner, eds. 2003. *Canada's Founding Debates*. Toronto: University of Toronto Press.

Aktürk, Sener. 2012. *Regimes of Ethnicity and Nationhood in Germany, Russia, and Turkey*. New York: Cambridge University Press.

Aligică, Paul Dragoș, and Anthony John Evans. 2009. *The Neoliberal Revolution in Eastern Europe: Economic Ideas in the Transition from Communism*. Cheltenham: Edward Elgar.

Allison, Graham T., Owen R. Coté Jr., Richard A. Falkenrath, and Steven E. Miller. 1996. "Avoiding Nuclear Anarchy." *Washington Quarterly* 20(3): 185–98.

Almond, Gabriel A., and Stephen J. Genco. 1977. "Clouds, Clocks, and the Study of Politics." *World Politics* 29(4): 489–522.

Álvarez Junco, Jose. 2013. "Spanish National Identity in the Age of Nationalisms." In *State and Nation Making in Latin America and Spain: Republics of the Possible*, edited by Miguel Angel Centeno and Agustín Ferraro. Cambridge: Cambridge University Press.

Andersen, Robert, and Josh Curtis. 2015. "Social Class, Economic Inequality, and the Convergence of Policy Preferences: Evidence from 24 Modern Democracies." *Canadian Review of Sociology/Revue Canadienne de Sociologie* 52(3): 266–88.

Anderson, Liam D. 2012. *Federal Solutions to Ethnic Problems: Accommodating Diversity*. Routledge.

Arato, Andrew. 2009. *Constitution Making under Occupation: The Politics of Imposed Revolution in Iraq*. New York: Columbia University Press.

Aybet, Gülnur, and Florian Bieber. 2011. "From Dayton to Brussels: The Impact of EU and NATO Conditionality on State Building in Bosnia and Hercegovina." *Europe-Asia Studies* 63(10): 1911–37.

Ayers, Jeffrey. 1995. "National No More: Defining English Canada." *American Review of Canadian Studies* 25(2–3): 181–201.

Bakke, Elisabeth. 2004. "The Making of Czechoslovakism in the First Czechoslovak Republic." In *Loyalitäten in der Tschechoslowakischen Republik, 1918–1938: politische, nationale und kulturelle Zugehörigkeiten*, edited by Martin Schulze Wessel. Munich: Oldenbourg.

Bakke, Kristin M. 2015. *Decentralization and Intrastate Struggles: Chechnya, Punjab, and Québec*. New York: Cambridge University Press.

Bakunin, Mikhail Aleksandrovich. [1873]1990. *Statism and Anarchy*. Cambridge: Cambridge University Press.

Balcells, Albert. 1996. *Catalan Nationalism: Past and Present*. New York: St. Martin's Press.

Balcells, Laia. 2013. "Mass Schooling and Catalan Nationalism." *Nationalism and Ethnic Politics* 19(4): 467–86.

Balcells, Laia, José Fernández-Albertos, and Alexander Kuo. 2015. "Preferences for Inter-Regional Redistribution." *Comparative Political Studies* 48(10): 1318–51.

Balfour, Sebastian, and Alejandro Quiroga. 2007. *The Reinvention of Spain: Nation and Identity Since Democracy*. Oxford: Oxford University Press.

Banac, Ivo. 1984. *The National Question in Yugoslavia: Origins, History, Politics*. Ithaca: Cornell University Press.

Banting, Keith G. 1987. *The Welfare State and Canadian Federalism.* 2nd ed. Kingston and Montreal: McGill-Queen's University Press.

Barnovský, Michal. 2011. "The Slovak Question, 1945–1948." In *Slovakia in History,* edited by Mikuláš Teich, Dušan Kováč, and Martin D. Brown. Cambridge: Cambridge University Press.

Barrio, Astrid, Juan Rodríguez Teruel, and Jacques Fontaine. 2014. "Pour quelles raisons les partis politiques en Catalogne se sont-ils radicalisés?" *Pole Sud* 40(1): 99–119.

Basta, Karlo. 2010. "Non-Ethnic Origins of Ethnofederal Institutions: The Case of Yugoslavia." *Nationalism and Ethnic Politics* 16(1): 92–110.

– 2016. "Imagined Institutions: The Symbolic Power of Formal Rules in Bosnia and Herzegovina." *Slavic Review* 75(4): 944–69.

– 2017. "The State between the Minority and Majority Nationalism: Decentralization, Symbolic Recognition, and Secessionist Crises in Spain and Canada." *Publius: The Journal of Federalism* 48(1): 51–75.

– 2018. "The Social Construction of Transformative Political Events." *Comparative Political Studies* 51(10): 1243–78.

– 2020a. "'Time's Up!': Framing Collective Impatience for Radical Political Change." *Political Psychology* 41(4): 755–70.

– 2020b. "Business as a Political Actor: Mapping the Role of the Private Sector in Independence Referenda." In *Strategies of Secession and Counter-Secession,* edited by Ryan D. Griffiths and Diego Muro. Lanham: ECPR Press.

– 2020c. "Performing Canadian State Nationalism through Federal Symmetry." *Nationalism and Ethnic Politics* 26(1): 66–84.

Basta, Karlo, John McGarry, and Richard Simeon, eds. 2015. *Territorial Pluralism: Managing Difference in Multinational States.* Vancouver: UBC Press.

Batović, Ante. 2017. *The Croatian Spring: Nationalism, Repression and Foreign Policy under Tito.* London: I.B. Tauris.

Bednar, Jenna. 2009. *The Robust Federation: Principles of Design. Political Economy of Institutions and Decisions.* Cambridge: Cambridge University Press.

Behiels, Michael D. 1985. *Prelude to Quebec's Quiet Revolution: Liberalism Versus Neo-Nationalism, 1945–1960.* Kingston and Montreal: McGill-Queen's University Press.

– 2007. "Mulroney and a Nationalist Quebec: Key to Political Realignment in Canada?" In *Transforming the Nation: Canada and Brian Mulroney,* edited by Raymond Benjamin Blake. Montreal and Kingston: McGill-Queen's University Press.

Beissinger, Mark R. 2002. *Nationalist Mobilization and the Collapse of the Soviet State*. Cambridge: Cambridge University Press.

Béland, Daniel, and André Lecours. 2010. *Nationalism and Social Policy: The Politics of Territorial Solidarity*. New York: Oxford University Press.

Belloni, Roberto. 2009. "Bosnia: Dayton Is Dead! Long Live Dayton!" *Nationalism and Ethnic Politics* 15(3–4): 355–75.

Bengtsson, Bo, and Hannu Ruonavaara. 2017. "Comparative Process Tracing: Making Historical Comparison Structured and Focused." *Philosophy of the Social Sciences* 47(1): 44–66.

Bennett, Andrew, and Jeffrey T. Checkel. 2015. "Process-Tracing: From Philosophical Roots to Best Practices." In *Process Tracing: From Metaphor to Analytic Tool*, edited by Andrew Bennett and Jeffrey T. Checkel. Cambridge: Cambridge University Press.

Bennett, Andrew, and Jeffrey T. Checkel, eds. 2015. *Process Tracing: From Metaphor to Analytic Tool*. Cambridge: Cambridge University Press.

Beramendi, Pablo. 2012. *The Political Geography of Inequality: Regions and Redistribution*. Cambridge: Cambridge University Press.

Berend, T. Iván. 1974. *Economic Development in East-Central Europe in the 19th and 20th Centuries*. New York: Columbia University Press.

– 1996. *Central and Eastern Europe, 1944–1993: Detour from the Periphery to the Periphery*. Cambridge: Cambridge University Press.

Berger, Peter L., and Thomas Luckmann. 1967. *The Social Construction of Reality: A Treatise in the Sociology of Knowledge*. London: Penguin.

Bermeo, Nancy. 2002. "The Import of Institutions." *Journal of Democracy* 13(2): 96–110.

Bertrand, Jacques. 2004. *Nationalism and Ethnic Conflict in Indonesia*. New York: Cambridge University Press.

Bevir, Mark, and Asaf Kedar. 2008. "Concept Formation in Political Science: An Anti-Naturalist Critique of Qualitative Methodology." *Perspectives on Politics* 6(3): 503–17.

Bićanić, Rudolf. 1966. "Economics of Socialism in a Developed Country." *Foreign Affairs* 44(4): 633–50.

Bickerton, James. 2011. "Janus Faces, Rocks, and Hard Places: Majority Nationalism in Canada." In *Contemporary Majority Nationalism*, edited by Alain Gagnon, André Lecours, and Geneviève Nootens. Montreal and Kingston: McGill-Queen's University Press.

Bilefsky, Dan. 2013. "Protest in Bosnia over IDs Traps Hundreds in Parliament." *New York Times*, 7 June 2013. http://www.nytimes.com/2013/06/08/world/europe/protest-in-bosnia-over-ids-traps-hundreds-in-parliament.html.

Billig, Michael. 1995. *Banal Nationalism*. London and Thousand Oaks: Sage.

Biondich, Mark. 2000. *Stjepan Radić, the Croat Peasant Party, and the Politics of Mass Mobilization, 1904–1928*. Toronto: University of Toronto Press.

Blais, André, and Jean Crête. 1990. "Porquoi l'opinion publique au Canada anglais a-t-elle rejeté L'áccord du Lac Meech?" In *L'Engagement Intellectuel: Mélanges En l'honneur de Léon Dion*, edited by Raymond Hudon and Réjean Pelletier. Sante-Foy: Presses de l'Université Laval.

Blyth, Mark, Oddny Helgadottir, and William Kring. 2016. "Ideas and Historical Institutionalism." In *The Oxford Handbook of Historical Institutionalism*, edited by Karl Orfeo Fioretos, Tulia Gabriela Falleti, and Adam D. Sheingate. Oxford: Oxford University Press.

Boadway, Robin, and Paul A.R. Hobson. 1993. *Intergovernmental Fiscal Relations in Canada*. Canadian Tax Paper, no. 96. Toronto: Canadian Tax Foundation.

Boadway, Robin, and Ronald L. Watts. 2000. "Fiscal Federalism in Canada." Kingston: Institute of Intergovernmental Relations, Queen's University.

Bogaards, Matthijs. 2010. "Ethnic Party Bans and Institutional Engineering in Nigeria." *Democratization* 17(4): 730–49.

Boix, Carles. 1998. *Political Parties, Growth, and Equality: Conservative and Social Democratic Economic Strategies in the World Economy*. Cambridge: Cambridge University Press.

Bonikowski, Bart. 2016. "Nationalism in Settled Times." *Annual Review of Sociology* 42: 427–49.

Botev, Nikolai. 1994. "Where East Meets West: Ethnic Intermarriage in the Former Yugoslavia, 1962 to 1989." *American Sociological Review* 59(3): 461–80.

Bourdieu, Pierre. 1994. "Rethinking the State: Genesis and Structure of the Bureaucratic Field." *Sociological Theory* 12(1): 1–18.

Brada, Josef C. 1991. "The Economic Transition of Czechoslovakia from Plan to Market." *Journal of Economic Perspectives* 5(4): 171–7.

Brancati, Dawn. 2009. *Peace by Design: Managing Intrastate Conflict through Decentralization*. Oxford: Oxford University Press.

Brass, Paul R. 1994. *The Politics of India Since Independence*. 2nd ed. Cambridge: Cambridge University Press.

Bratislava Česko-slovenský rozhlas Radio Network. 1991. "Čarnogursky Addresses Council." FBIS-EEU-91-135, Daily Report. East Europe, 11 July 1991.

Bratislava Domestic Service. 1990a. "SNC's Schuster Protests Federation Name." FBIS-EEU-90-063, Daily Report. East Europe, 30 March 1990.

– 1990b. "Mečiar Delivers Slovak Government Statement." FBIS-EEU-90-127, Daily Report. East Europe, 29 June 1990.

– 1990c. "Mečiar Delivers Speech on Federal Systems." FBIS-EEU-90-225, Daily Report. East Europe, 20 November 1990.

Bratislava Verejnost. 1991a. "Mečiar Appeals to Public for Approval." FBIS-EEU-91-061, Daily Report. East Europe, 25 March 1991.

– 1991b. "Calfa on Slovak Economy, Mečiar's Personality." FBIS-EEU-91-064, Daily Report. East Europe, 29 March 1991.

Breton, Albert. 1964. "The Economics of Nationalism." *Journal of Political Economy* 72(4): 376–86.

Brock, Kathy. 2008. "The Politics of Asymmetrical Federalism: Reconsidering the Role and Responsibilities of Ottawa." *Canadian Public Policy* 34(2): 143–61.

Brooks, Stephen, and A. Brian Tanguay. 1985. "Quebec's Caisse de Dépôt et Placement: Tool of Nationalism." *Canadian Public Administration* 28(1): 99–119.

Broschek, Jörg, Bettina Petersohn, and Simon Toubeau. 2017. "Territorial Politics and Institutional Change: A Comparative-Historical Analysis." *Publius: The Journal of Federalism* 48(1): 1–25.

Broschek, Jörg. 2011. "Historical Institutionalism and the Varieties of Federalism in Germany and Canada." *Publius: The Journal of Federalism* 42(4): 51–76.

Brown, Scott. 2008. "Prelude to a Divorce? The Prague Spring as Dress Rehearsal for Czechoslovakia's 'Velvet Divorce.'" *Europe-Asia Studies* 60(10): 1783–804.

Brubaker, Rogers. 1995. "Aftermaths of Empire and the Unmixing of Peoples: Historical and Comparative Perspectives." *Ethnic and Racial Studies* 18(2): 189–218.

– 1996. "Rethinking Nationhood: Nation as Institutionalized Form, Practical Category, Contingent Event." In *Nationalism Reframed: Nationhood and the National Question in the New Europe.* Cambridge: Cambridge University Press.

Budding, Audrey. 1997. "Yugoslavs into Serbs: Serbian National Identity, 1961–1971." *Nationalities Papers* 25(3): 407–26.

– 1998. "Serb Intellectuals and the National Question, 1961–1991." PhD diss., Harvard University.

Bunce, Valerie. 1999. *Subversive Institutions: The Design and the Destruction of Socialism and the State.* Cambridge: Cambridge University Press.

Burg, Steven L. 1983. *Conflict and Cohesion in Socialist Yugoslavia: Political Decision Making Since 1966*. Princeton: Princeton University Press.

Büthe, Tim. 2002. "Taking Temporality Seriously: Modeling History and the Use of Narratives as Evidence." *American Political Science Review* 96(3): 481–93.

Butz, David A. 2009. "National Symbols as Agents of Psychological and Social Change." *Political Psychology* 30(5): 779–804.

Bystrický, Valerián. 2011. "Slovakia from the Munich Conference to the Declaration of Independence." In *Slovakia in History*, edited by Mikuláš Teich, Dušan Kováč, and Martin D. Brown. Cambridge: Cambridge University Press.

Campbell, Robert Malcolm. 1987. *Grand Illusions: The Politics of the Keynesian Experience in Canada, 1945–1975*. Peterborough: Broadview Press.

Canada. 1945. *Employment and Income with Special Reference to the Initial Period of Reconstruction*. Ottawa: E. Cloutier, printer to the King.

– 1987. *The 1987 Constitutional Accord. Backgrounder*. Ottawa: Library of Parliament, Research Branch.

Canada. Royal Commission on Bilingualism and Biculturalism. 1969. *Report of the Royal Commission on Bilingualism and Biculturalism*, vol. 3A. Ottawa: Queen's Printer.

Canada. Royal Commission on Dominion-Provincial Relations. 1940. *Report of the Royal Commission on Dominion-Provincial Relations*. Ottawa: J.O. Patenaude, I.S.O., printer to the King.

Capek, Ales, and Gerald W. Sazama. 1993. "Czech and Slovak Economic Relations." *Europe–Asia Studies* 45(2): 211–35.

Carmines, Edward G., and James A. Stimson. 1980. "The Two Faces of Issue Voting." *American Political Science Review* 74(1): 78–91.

Carr, Raymond. 1982. *Spain, 1808–1975*. 2nd ed. Oxford: Clarendon Press.

Casanas Adam, Elisenda, and François Rocher. 2014. "(Mis)Recognition in Catalunya and Quebec: The Politics of Judicial Containment." In *Constitutionalism and the Politics of Accommodation in Multinational Democracies*, edited by Jaime Lluch. Houndmills and New York: Palgrave Macmillan.

Cederman, Lars-Erik, Simon Hug, Andreas Schädel, and Julian Wucherpfennig. 2015. "Territorial Autonomy in the Shadow of Conflict: Too Little, Too Late?" *American Political Science Review* 109(2): 354–70.

Centeno, Miguel Angel. 2003. *Blood and Debt: War and the Nation-State in Latin America*. University Park: Pennsylvania State University Press.

Cetrà, Daniel, and Coree Brown Swan. 2020. "State and Majority Nationalism in Plurinational States: Responding to Challenges from Below." *Nationalism and Ethnic Politics* 26(1): 1–7.

Chandra, Kanchan. 2005. "Ethnic Parties and Democratic Stability." *Perspectives on Politics* 3(2): 235–52.

Ciepley, David. 2013. "Dispersed Constituency Democracy Deterritorializing Representation to Reduce Ethnic Conflict." *Politics and Society* 41(1): 135–62.

Clark, Douglas H. 1988. "Canada's Equalization Program: In Principle and in Practice." In *Equalization: Its Contribution to Canada's Economic and Fiscal Progress*, edited by Robin Boadway and Paul Hobson. Kingston: John Deutsch Institute for the Study of Economic Policy, Queen's University.

Clemens, Elisabeth S., and James M. Cook. 1999. "Politics and Institutionalism: Explaining Durability and Change." *Annual Review of Sociology* 25: 441–66.

Coggins, Bridget. 2014. *Power Politics and State Formation in the Twentieth Century: The Dynamics of Recognition.* Cambridge: Cambridge University Press.

Cohen, Lenard J. 1977. "Conflict Management and Political Institutionalization in Socialist Yugoslavia: A Case Study of the Parliamentary System." In *Legislatures in Plural Societies: The Search for Cohesion in National Development*, edited by Albert F. Eldridge. Durham: Duke University Press.

Coleman, William D. 1984. *The Independence Movement in Quebec, 1945–1980.* Toronto: University of Toronto Press.

Colgan, Charles. 1993. "Economic Development Policy in Québec and the Challenges of a Continental Economy." *Quebec Studies* 16: 69–84.

Collier, Paul, and Anke Hoeffler. 1998. "On Economic Causes of Civil War." *Oxford Economic Papers* 50(4): 563–73.

Colino, César. 2009. "Constitutional Change without Constitutional Reform: Spanish Federalism and the Revision of Catalonia's Statute of Autonomy." *Publius: The Journal of Federalism* 39(2): 262–88.

Colomer, Josep M. 1998. "The Spanish 'State of Autonomies': Non–Institutional Federalism." *West European Politics* 21(4): 40–52.

Condor, Susan. 2010. "Devolution and National Identity: The Rules of English (Dis)Engagement." *Nations and Nationalism* 16(3): 525–43.

Convergència i Unió. 1988. "La Majoria Pel Progrés de Tots."

– 1992. "Resum Programa 1992-1996."

- 1995. "Portem Catalunya Més Lluny: Un Programa per a La Catalunya Del Segle XXI."
- 1999. "Catalunya, Primer: Programa Electoral Eleccions al Parlament de Catalunya."

Conversi, Daniele. 1997. *The Basques, the Catalans, and Spain: Alternative Routes to Nationalist Mobilization.* Reno: University of Nevada Press.

Conway, Kyle. 2011. *Everyone Says No: Public Service Broadcasting and the Failure of Translation.* Montreal and Kingston: McGill-Queen's University Press.

Cook, Ramsay. 1986. *Canada, Quebec, and the Uses of Nationalism.* Toronto: McClelland and Stewart.

Cornell, Svante E. 2002. "Autonomy as a Source of Conflict: Caucasian Conflicts in Theoretical Perspective." *World Politics* 54(2): 245–76.

Cortes Generales. 1978a. "Diario de Sesiones Del Congreso de Los Diputados: Comisión de Asuntos Constitucionales y Libertades Públicas." 64, session #4, 11 May 1978.
- 1978b. "Diario de Sesiones Del Congreso de Los Diputados: Comisión de Asuntos Constitucionales y Libertades Públicas." 66, Session #5, 12 May 1978.

Coyne, Deborah. 1992. *Roll of the Dice: Working with Clyde Wells during the Meech Lake Negotiations.* Toronto: James Lorimer.

Cuadras-Morató, Xavier, and Toni Rodon. 2018. "The Dog That Didn't Bark: On the Effect of the Great Recession on the Surge of Secessionism." *Ethnic and Racial Studies* 42(12): 2189–208.

Čulinović, Ferdo. 1955. "Problem o višedržavnosti jugoslavenske federacije." *Zbornik pravnog fakulteta u Zagrebu* 5(3–4): 119–33.

Cunningham, Kathleen Gallagher. 2011. "Divide and Conquer or Divide and Concede: How Do States Respond to Internally Divided Separatists?" *American Political Science Review* 105(2): 275–97.
- 2014. *Inside the Politics of Self-Determination.* New York: Oxford University Press.

Cunningham, Kathleen Gallagher, Marianne Dahl, and Anne Frugé. 2017. "Strategies of Resistance: Diversification and Diffusion." *American Journal of Political Science* 61(3): 591–605.
- 2020. "Introducing the Strategies of Resistance Data Project." *Journal of Peace Research* 57(3): 482–91.

Cutler, Fred. 2004. "Government Responsibility and Electoral Accountability in Federations." *Publius: The wJournal of Federalism* 34(2): 19–38.

Čuvalo, Ante. 1987. "The Croatian National Movement, 1966–1972." PhD diss., Ohio State University.

Darden, Keith, and Harris Mylonas. 2016. "Threats to Territorial Integrity, National Mass Schooling, and Linguistic Commonality." *Comparative Political Studies* 49(11): 1446–79.

Deiwiks, Christa, Lars-Erik Cederman, and Kristian Skrede Gleditsch. 2012. "Inequality and Conflict in Federations." *Journal of Peace Research* 49(2): 289–304.

Đekić, Mirko. 1990. *Upotreba Srbije: Optužbe i Priznanja Draže Markovića.* Beograd: Besede.

"Deklaracija o Nazivu i Položaju Hrvatskog Književnog Jezika." 1967. *Telegram* 359 (March).

Delacourt, Susan. 2006. "Rae Seeks Assurance from PM; Quebec Motion Can't Change Constitution via 'Back Door.'" *Toronto Star,* 24 November 2006.

Delledonne, Giacomo. 2011. "Speaking in the Name of the Constituent Power: The Spanish Constitutional Court and the New Catalan Estatut." *Perspectives on Federalism* 3(1): 1–14.

Desrosiers, Marie-Eve. 2011. "Reframing Frame Analysis: Key Contributions to Conflict Studies." *Ethnopolitics* 11(1): 1–23.

Desrosiers, Marie-Eve, and Srdjan Vucetic. 2018. "Causal Claims and the Study of Ethnic Conflict." *Journal of Global Security Studies* 3(4): 483–97.

DeVotta, Neil. 2007. "Sinhalese Buddhist Nationalist Ideology: Implications for Politics and Conflict Resolution in Sri Lanka." Policy Studies #40. Washington, D.C.: East-West Center.

Di Matteo, Livio. 2017. *A Federal Fiscal History: Canada, 1867–2017.* Vancouver: Fraser Institute.

Díaz Cayeros, Alberto. 2006. *Federalism, Fiscal Authority, and Centralization in Latin America.* Cambridge: Cambridge University Press.

Dickovick, James Tyler. 2011. *Decentralization and Recentralization in the Developing World: Comparative Studies from Africa and Latin America.* University Park: Pennsylvania State University Press.

Dieckhoff, Alain. 2016. *Nationalism and the Multination State.* London: C. Hurst.

Djilas, Aleksa. 1991. *The Contested Country: Yugoslav Unity and Communist Revolution, 1919–1953.* Cambridge, MA: Harvard University Press.

Djilas, Milovan. 1950. *On New Roads of Socialism; Address Delivered at the Preelection Rally of Belgrade Students, 18 March 1950.* Belgrade: Jugoslovenska knjiga.

Djokić, Dejan, ed. 2003. "(Dis)Integrating Yugoslavia: King Alexander and Interwar Yugoslavism." In *Yugoslavism: Histories of a Failed Idea, 1918–1992*. London: C. Hurst.

– 2012. "Nationalism, Myth, and Reinterpretation of History: The Neglected Case of Interwar Yugoslavia." *European History Quarterly* 42(1): 71–95.

Dovidio, John F., Samuel L. Gaertner, Elze G. Ufkes, Tamar Saguy, and Adam R. Pearson. 2016. "Included but Invisible? Subtle Bias, Common Identity, and the Darker Side of 'We.'" *Social Issues and Policy Review* 10(1): 6–46.

Dowling, Andrew. 2013. *Catalonia Since the Spanish Civil War: Reconstructing the Nation*. Portland: Sussex Academic Press.

Dragović-Soso, Jasna. 2002. *Saviours of the Nation?: Serbia's Intellectual Opposition and the Revival of Nationalism*. London: C. Hurst.

Dubček, Alexander. 1993. *Hope Dies Last: The Autobiography of Alexander Dubcek*. New York: Kodansha International.

Dubey, Vinod, and World Bank, eds. 1975. *Yugoslavia, Development with Decentralization: Report of a Mission Sent to Yugoslavia by the World Bank*. Baltimore: Johns Hopkins University Press.

Duch, Raymond M., and Randolph T. Stevenson. 2008. *The Economic Vote: How Political and Economic Institutions Condition Election Results*. Cambridge: Cambridge University Press.

Durham, John George Lambton. 1963. *Lord Durham's Report: An Abridgement of Report on the Affairs of British North America*. Toronto: McClelland and Stewart.

Dyson, Kenneth H.F. 1980. *The State Tradition in Western Europe: A Study of an Idea and Institution*. Oxford: Martin Robertson.

Eaton, Kent, and J. Tyler Dickovick. 2004. "The Politics of Re-Centralization in Argentina and Brazil." *Latin American Research Review* 39(1): 90–122.

Eaton, Kent, Jean-Paul Faguet, Imke Harbers, Arjan H. Schakel, Liesbet Hooghe, Gary Marks, Sara Niedzwiecki, Sandra Chapman Osterkatz, and Sarah Shair-Rosenfield. 2019. "Measuring and Theorizing Regional Governance." *Territory, Politics, Governance* 7(2): 265–83.

EFE. 2006. "Rajoy presenta en el Congreso cuatro millones de firmas por un referéndum sobre el Estatuto." *El País*, 25 April 2006. https://elpais.com/elpais/2006/04/25/actualidad/1145953019_850215.html.

Ehrlich, Charles E. 1998. "The Lliga Regionalista and the Catalan Industrial Bourgeoisie." *Journal of Contemporary History* 33(3): 399–417.

El País. 1983. "La resaca de la LOAPA." 15 August 1983. https://elpais. com/diario/1983/08/16/opinion/429832801_850215.html.

– 2005a. "Los ciudadanos piden una salida negociada para el Estatuto Catalán." *El País*, August 10, 2005. https://elpais.com/elpais/2005/10/08/ actualidad/1128759421_850215.html.

– 2005b. "El Parlamento de Cataluña aprueba el nuevo Estatuto." *El País*, 20 September 2005. https://elpais.com/elpais/2005/09/30/actualidad/ 1128068217_850215.html.

Elgenius, Gabriella. 2011. *Symbols of Nations and Nationalism: Celebrating Nationhood*. Houndmills and New York: Palgrave Macmillan.

Elkins, Zachary, and John Sides. 2007. "Can Institutions Build Unity in Multiethnic States?" *American Political Science Review* 101(4): 693–708.

Emirbayer, Mustafa. 1997. "Manifesto for a Relational Sociology." *American Journal of Sociology* 103(2): 281–317.

Ertman, Thomas. 1997. *Birth of the Leviathan: Building States and Regimes in Medieval and Early Modern Europe*. Cambridge: Cambridge University Press.

España. 1979. Ley Organica 4/1979, de 16 de Diciembre de Estatuto de Autonomía de Cataluña. *Boletín Oficial del Estado*. Vol. 306.

Etchemendy, Sebastian. 2004. "Revamping the Weak, Protecting the Strong, and Managing Privatization: Governing Globalization in the Spanish Takeoff." *Comparative Political Studies* 37(6): 623–51.

Evans, Gareth, and Mohamed Sahnoun. 2002. "The Responsibility to Protect." *Foreign Affairs* 81(6): 99–110.

Evans, Robert John Weston. 1979. *The Making of the Habsburg Monarchy, 1550–1700: An Interpretation*. Oxford: Clarendon Press.

Eyal, Gil. 2003. *The Origins of Postcommunist Elites: From Prague Spring to the Breakup of Czechoslovakia*. Minneapolis: University of Minnesota Press.

Falleti, Tulia. 2005. "A Sequential Theory of Decentralization: Latin American Cases in Comparative Perspective." *American Political Science Review* 99(3): 327–46.

– 2010. *Decentralization and Subnational Politics in Latin America*. Cambridge: Cambridge University Press.

Falleti, Tulia, and Julia Lynch. 2009. "Context and Causal Mechanisms in Political Analysis." *Comparative Political Studies* 42(9): 1143–66.

Falleti, Tulia, and James Mahoney. 2015. "The Comparative Sequential Method." In *Advances in Comparative-Historical Analysis*, edited by Kathleen Thelen and James Mahoney. Cambridge: Cambridge University Press.

Farr, James. 1985. "Situational Analysis: Explanation in Political Science." *Journal of Politics* 47(4): 1085–107.

Fazal, Tanisha M., and Ryan D. Griffiths. 2014. "Membership Has Its Privileges: The Changing Benefits of Statehood." *International Studies Review* 16(1): 79–106.

Filippov, Mikhail, Peter C. Ordeshook, and Olga Shvetsova. 2004. *Designing Federalism: A Theory of Self-Sustainable Federal Institutions.* Cambridge: Cambridge University Press.

Fioretos, Karl Orfeo, Tulia Falleti, and Sheingate, Adam D. 2016. "Historical Institutionalism in Political Science." In *The Oxford Handbook of Historical Institutionalism*, edited by Karl Orfeo Fioretos, Tulia Gabriela Falleti, and Adam D. Sheingate. Oxford: Oxford University Press.

Fiske, John. 1986. "Television: Polysemy and Popularity." *Critical Studies in Mass Communication* 3(4): 391–408.

Flaherty, Diane. 1982. "Economic Reform and Foreign Trade in Yugoslavia." *Cambridge Journal of Economics* 6(2): 105–43.

Flanagan, Tom. 2006. "Harper and the N-Word." *Maclean's*, 11 December 2006.

Fournier, Pierre. 1978. "The Parti Québécois and the Quebec Economic Situation." *Synthesis* 2(4): 15–24.

Fraser, Graham. 2001. *René Lévesque and the Parti Québécois in Power.* 2nd ed. Montreal and Kingston: McGill-Queen's University Press.

Friedland, Roger, and Robert R. Alford. 1991. "Bringing Society Back In: Symbols, Practices, and Institutional Contradictions." In *The New Institutionalism in Organizational Analysis*, edited by Walter W. Powell and Paul DiMaggio. Chicago: University of Chicago Press.

Frommer, Benjamin. 2005. *National Cleansing: Retribution against Nazi Collaborators in Postwar Czechoslovakia.* Cambridge: Cambridge University Press.

Frydenlund, Iselin. 2005. "The Sangha and Its Relation to the Peace Process in Sri Lanka." 2/2005. PRIO Report. Oslo: International Peace Research institute (PRIO).

Gagnon, Alain. 2001. "The Moral Foundations of Asymmetrical Federalism: A Normative Exploration of the Case of Quebec and Canada." In *Multinational Democracies*, edited by Alain Gagnon and James Tully. Cambridge: Cambridge University Press.

Gagnon, Alain, Geneviève Nootens, and André Lecours, eds. 2011. *Contemporary Majority Nationalism.* Montreal and Kingston: McGill-Queen's University Press.

Gagnon, Alain-G., and Arjun Tremblay, eds. 2020. *Federalism and National Diversity in the 21st Century*. Cham: Palgrave Macmillan.

Gallego, Raquel, Ricard Gomà, and Joan Subirats. 2005. "Spain: From State Welfare to Regional Welfare?" In *The Territorial Politics of Welfare*, edited by Nicola McEwen and Luis Moreno. London and New York: Routledge.

Ganguly, Sumit. 2018. "Ending the Sri Lankan Civil War." *Daedalus* 147(1): 78–89.

Geddes, Barbara. 1999. "What Do We Know about Democratization after Twenty Years?" *Annual Review of Political Science* 2: 115–44.

George, Alexander L., and Andrew Bennett. 2004. *Case Studies and Theory Development in the Social Sciences*. Cambridge, MA: MIT Press.

Germann, Micha, and Nicholas Sambanis. 2020. "Political Exclusion, Lost Autonomy, and Escalating Conflict over Self-Determination." *International Organization* [online first]: 1–26.

Gerring, John. 2005. "Causation: A Unified Framework for the Social Sciences." *Journal of Theoretical Politics* 17(2): 163–98.

Gingras, François-Pierre, and Neil Nevitte. 1984. "The Evolution of Quebec Nationalism." In *Quebec, State, and Society*, edited by Alain Gagnon. Toronto: Methuen.

Giuliano, Elise. 2011. *Constructing Grievance: Ethnic Nationalism in Russia's Republics*. Ithaca: Cornell University Press.

Globevnik, Josip. 1963. "Draft Constitution of the Socialist Republic of Slovenia." *New Yugoslav Law* 14 (issues 1–3): 27–34.

Good, David F. 1984. *The Economic Rise of the Habsburg Empire, 1750–1914*. Berkeley: University of California Press.

– 1994. "The Economic Lag of Central and Eastern Europe: Income Estimates for the Habsburg Successor States, 1870–1910." *Journal of Economic History* 54(4): 869–91.

Gordon, H. Scott. 1966. "A Twenty Year Perspective: Some Reflections on the Keynesian Revolution in Canada." In *Canadian Economic Policy Since the War*, by Canadian Trade Committee. Montreal: The Associations.

Gorski, Philip S. 2003. *The Disciplinary Revolution: Calvinism and the Rise of the State in Early Modern Europe*. Chicago: University of Chicago Press.

Government of Canada. 1975. *Federal–Provincial Fiscal Relations in Canada: An Overview*. Ottawa: Ministry of Finance.

Government of Quebec. 1985. "Draft Agreement on the Constitution: Proposals by the Government of Québec, May 1985, and the

Correspondence between Messrs. René Lévesque, Prime Minister of Québec, and Brian Mulroney, Prime Minister of Canada, Regarding These Proposals."

Granatstein, J.L. 1977. *Broken Promises: A History of Conscription in Canada*. Toronto: Oxford University Press.

– 1982. *The Ottawa Men: The Civil Service Mandarins, 1935–1957*. Toronto: Oxford University Press.

Greenhouse, Steven. 1990. "What's in a Hyphen? For the Slovaks, Plenty." *New York Times*, 28 March 1990. https://www.nytimes.com/1990/03/28/world/upheaval-in-the-east-what-s-in-a-hyphen-for-the-slovaks-plenty.html.

Greer, Allan. 1995. "1837–38, Rebellion Reconsidered." *Canadian Historical Review* 76(1): 1–18.

Greer, Scott L. 2007. *Nationalism and Self-Government: The Politics of Autonomy in Scotland and Catalonia*. Albany: SUNY Press.

Griffiths, Ryan. 2014. "Secession and the Invisible Hand of the International System." *Review of International Studies* 40(3): 559–81.

– 2016. *Age of Secession: The International and Domestic Determinants of State Birth*. Cambridge: Cambridge University Press.

Griffiths, Ryan, and Diego Muro, eds. 2020. *Strategies of Secession and Counter-Secession*. Lanham: ECPR Press.

Grinnell, David. 2007. "L & A Treasures: The Pittsburgh Agreement; Czecho-Slovak Agreement." *Western Pennsylvania History: 1918–2018*, 8–9.

Gross, Mirjana. 1979. "Croatian National-Integrational Ideologies from the End of Illyrism to the Creation of Yugoslavia." *Austrian History Yearbook* 15: 2–33.

Grzymała-Busse, Anna Maria. 2007. *Rebuilding Leviathan: Party Competition and State Exploitation in Post-Communist Democracies*. Cambridge: Cambridge University Press.

Güell, Casilda, Joaquim M. Molins, Iván Medina, and Rosa Nonell. 2010. "Business Associations Facing Regionalism." *Pôle Sud* 33(2): 83–101.

Guest, Dennis. 1980. *The Emergence of Social Security in Canada*. Vancouver: UBC Press.

Guibernau, Montserrat. 2004. *Catalan Nationalism: Francoism, Transition and Democracy*. London: Routledge.

Gunst, Péter. 1989. "Agrarian Systems of Central and Eastern Europe." In *The Origins of Backwardness in Eastern Europe: Economics and Politics from the Middle Ages until the Early Twentieth Century*, edited by Daniel Chirot. Berkeley: University of California Press.

Gupta, Akhil. 1995. "Blurred Boundaries: The Discourse of Corruption, the Culture of Politics, and the Imagined State." *American Ethnologist* 22(2): 375–402.

– 2015. "Viewing States from the Global South." In *State Theory and Andean Politics: New Approaches to the Study of Rule*, edited by Christopher Krupa, David Nugent, and Christopher Krupa. Philadelphia: University of Pennsylvania Press.

Gurr, Ted Robert. 2000. *Peoples versus States: Minorities at Risk in the New Century*. Washington, D.C.: US Institute of Peace.

Hacking, Ian. 1995. "The Looping Effects of Human Kinds." In *Causal Cognition: A Multidisciplinary Debate*, edited by Dan Sperber, David Premack, and Ann J. Premack. Oxford; New York: Clarendon Press; Oxford University Press.

Hafner, Danica Fink. 1992. "Political Modernization in Slovenia in the 1980s and the Early 1990s." *Journal of Communist Studies* 8(4): 210–26.

Haggard, Stephan. 1995. *The Political Economy of Democratic Transitions*. Princeton: Princeton University Press.

Hagy, James William. 1971. "René Lévesque and the Quebec Separatists." *Western Political Quarterly* 24(1): 55–8.

Hale, Henry E. 2004. "Divided We Stand: Institutional Sources of Ethnofederal State Survival and Collapse." *World Politics* 56(2): 165–93.

– 2008. *The Foundations of Ethnic Politics: Separatism of States and Nations in Eurasia and the World*. New York: Cambridge University Press.

Hall, Peter, ed. 1989. *The Political Power of Economic Ideas: Keynesianism across Nations*. Princeton: Princeton University Press.

– 2003. "Aligning Ontology and Methodology in Comparative Research." In *Comparative Historical Analysis in the Social Sciences*, edited by James Mahoney and Dietrich Rueschemeyer, 373–404. Cambridge: Cambridge University Press.

– 2010. "Historical Institutionalism in Rationalist and Sociological Perspective." In *Explaining Institutional Change: Ambiguity, Agency, and Power*, edited by James Mahoney and Kathleen Ann Thelen, 205–23. Cambridge: Cambridge University Press.

Hall, Peter A., and Rosemary C.R. Taylor. 1996. "Political Science and the Three New Institutionalisms." *Political Studies* 44(5): 936–57.

Hallaq, Wael B. 2013. *The Impossible State: Islam, Politics, and Modernity's Moral Predicament*. New York: Columbia University Press.

Hamann, Kerstin. 2000. "Linking Policies and Economic Voting: Explaining Reelection in the Case of the Spanish Socialist Party." *Comparative Political Studies* 33(8): 1018–48.

Hamlin, Alan, and Colin Jennings. 2011. "Expressive Political Behaviour: Foundations, Scope and Implications." *British Journal of Political Science* 41(3): 645–70.

Hansen, Lene. 1996. "Slovenian Identity: State-Building on the Balkan Border." *Alternatives: Global, Local, Political* 21(4): 473–95.

Harrison, Joseph. 1985. *The Spanish Economy in the Twentieth Century*. London: Croom Helm.

– 2009. "Early Francoism and Economic Paralysis in Catalonia, 1939–1951." *European History Quarterly* 39(2): 197–216.

Hassin, Ran R., Melissa J. Ferguson, Daniella Shidlovski, and Tamar Gross. 2007. "Subliminal Exposure to National Flags Affects Political Thought and Behavior." *Proceedings of the National Academy of Sciences* 104(50): 19757–61.

Hay, Colin. 2006. "Constructivist Institutionalism." In *The Oxford Handbook of Political Institutions*, edited by R.A.W. Rhodes, Sarah A. Binder, and Bert A. Rockman, 56–74. Oxford: Oxford University Press.

Hayden, Robert M. 1992. *The Beginning of the End of Federal Yugoslavia: The Slovenian Amendment Crisis of 1989*. The Carl Beck Papers in Russian and East European Studies, #1001. Pittsburgh: Center for Russian and East European Studies, University of Pittsburgh.

Hechter, Michael. 1992. "The Dynamics of Secession." *Acta Sociologica* 35(4): 267–83.

Hempel, Carl G. 1962. "Deductive-Nomological vs Statistical Explanation." In *Scientific Explanation, Space, and Time*, edited by Herbert Feigl. Minneapolis: University of Minnesota Press.

Hepburn, Eve. 2010. "Small Worlds in Canada and Europe: A Comparison of Regional Party Systems in Quebec, Bavaria and Scotland." *Regional and Federal Studies* 20(4–5): 527–44.

Herbst, Jeffrey Ira. 2000. *States and Power in Africa: Comparative Lessons in Authority and Control*. Princeton: Princeton University Press.

Hierro, Maria Jose, and Didac Queralt. 2020. "The Divide Over Independence: Explaining Preferences for Secession in an Advanced Open Economy." *American Journal of Political Science* [online first].

Hirschman, Albert O. 1958. *The Strategy of Economic Development*. New Haven: Yale University Press.

Hirschman, Daniel, and Isaac Ariail Reed. 2014. "Formation Stories and Causality in Sociology." *Sociological Theory* 32(4): 259–82.

Hoare, Marko Attila. 2002. "The Yugoslav Dilemma: Whose Is the Partisan Movement? Serbs, Croats, and the Legacy of a Shared Resistance." *Journal of Slavic Military Studies* 15(4): 24–41.

Hoddie, Matthew, and Caroline Hartzell. 2005. "Signals of Reconciliation: Institution-Building and the Resolution of Civil Wars." *International Studies Review* 7(1): 21–40.

Hodson, Randy, Dusko Sekulic, and Garth Massey. 1994. "National Tolerance in the Former Yugoslavia." *American Journal of Sociology* 99(6): 1534–58.

Holman, Otto. 1996. *Integrating Southern Europe: EC Expansion and the Transnationalization of Spain*. London: Routledge.

Hopf, Ted, and Bentley Allan, eds. 2016. *Making Identity Count: Building a National Identity Database*. New York: Oxford University Press.

Horowitz, Donald L. 1985. *Ethnic Groups in Conflict*. Berkeley: University of California Press.

– 1991. *A Democratic South Africa?: Constitutional Engineering in a Divided Society*. Berkeley: University of California Press.

Horvat, Branko. 1971. "Yugoslav Economic Policy in the Post-War Period: Problems, Ideas, Institutional Developments." *American Economic Review* 61(3): 71–169.

Hospodářské noviny. 1991. "Minister Hoffmann Interviewed on Reform, Slovakia." FBIS-EEU-91-091, Daily Report. East Europe, 2 May 1991.

– 1992a. "Text of Draft Czech-Slovak Constitution Treaty." FBIS-EEU-92-031, Daily Report. East Europe, 11 February 1992.

– 1992b. "ODS Chairman Senses 'Danger' From Left." FBIS-EEU-92-063, Daily Report. East Europe, 26 March 1992.

Huber, John, and Ronald Inglehart. 1995. "Expert Interpretations of Party Space and Party Locations in 42 Societies." *Party Politics* 1(1): 73–111.

Huber, Evelyne, Charles Ragin, John D. Stephens, David Brady, and Jason Beckfield. 2004. *Comparative Welfare States Data Set*. Northwestern University, University of North Carolina, Duke University, and Indiana University.

Huddy, Leonie. 2003. "Group Identity and Political Cohesion." In *Oxford Handbook of Political Psychology*, edited by David O. Sears, Leonie Huddy, and Robert Jervis. Oxford: Oxford University Press.

Huszka, Beáta. 2014. *Secessionist Movements and Ethnic Conflict: Debate-Framing and Rhetoric in Independence Campaigns*. Abingdon and New York: Routledge.

Ikegami, Eiko. 1995. *The Taming of the Samurai: Honorific Individualism and the Making of Modern Japan*. Cambridge, MA: Harvard University Press.

Innes, Abby. 1997. "The Breakup of Czechoslovakia: The Impact of Party Development on the Separation of the State." *East European Politics and Societies* 11(3): 393–435.

– 2001. *Czechoslovakia: The Short Goodbye*. New Haven: Yale University Press.

Irvine, Jill A. 1993. *The Croat Question: Partisan Politics in the Formation of the Yugoslav Socialist State*. Boulder: Westview Press.

James, Allison. 2012. "Seeking the Analytic Imagination: Reflections on the Process of Interpreting Qualitative Data:" *Qualitative Research* 13(5): 562–77.

Janssen, Jacques, and Theo Verheggen. 1997. "The Double Center of Gravity in Durkheim's Symbol Theory: Bringing the Symbolism of the Body Back In." *Sociological Theory* 15 (3): 294–306.

Jeffery, Charlie, Ailsa Henderson, Roger Scully, and Richard Wyn Jones. 2016. "England's Dissatisfactions and the Conservative Dilemma." *Political Studies Review* 14(3): 335–48.

Jenne, Erin K. 2009. "The Paradox of Ethnic Partition: Lessons from de Facto Partition in Bosnia and Kosovo." *Regional and Federal Studies* 19(2): 273–89.

Jenson, Jane, and Martin Papillon. 2000. "Challenging the Citizenship Regime: The James Bay Cree and Transnational Action." *Politics and Society* 28(2): 245–64.

Jost, John T., Alison Ledgerwood, and Curtis D. Hardin. 2008. "Shared Reality, System Justification, and the Relational Basis of Ideological Beliefs." *Social and Personality Psychology Compass* 2(1): 171–86.

Jović, Dejan. 2003. *Jugoslavija, država koja je odumrla: Uspon, kriza i pad Kardeljeve Jugoslavije, 1974-1990*. Zagreb: Prometej.

Juan, Jordi. 1998. "CiU, PNV y El Bloque Nacionalista Galego consideran caducado el modelo de estado." *La Vanguardia*, 16 July 1998.

Junquera, Natalia, and Nuria Tesón. 2006. "El PP recogerá firmas para exigir un referéndum del estatuto en toda España." *El País*, 25 January 2006. http://elpais.com/diario/2006/01/25/espana/1138143602_850215.html.

Kaldor, Nicholas. 1972. "The Irrelevance of Equilibrium Economics." *Economic Journal* 82(328): 1237–55.

Kardelj, Edvard. 1953. "New Social and Political System of the Federal People's Republic of Yugoslavia." In *Fundamental Law Pertaining to the Bases of the Social and Political Organization of the Federal People's Republic of Yugoslavia and of the Federal Organs of State Authority*. Vol. 1. Belgrade: Union of Jurists' Associations of Yugoslavia.

Katznelson, Ira. 1997. "Structure and Configuration in Comparative Politics." In *Comparative Politics: Rationality, Culture, and Structure*, edited by Mark Irving Lichbach and Alan S. Zuckerman. Cambridge: Cambridge University Press.

Kaufman, Stuart J. 2001. *Modern Hatreds: The Symbolic Politics of Ethnic War*. New York: Cornell University Press.

– 2015. *Nationalist Passions*. Ithaca: Cornell University Press.

Kaufmann, Eric P., ed. 2004. *Rethinking Ethnicity: Majority Groups and Dominant Minorities*. London: Routledge.

Kaufmann, E., and O. Haklai. 2008. "Dominant Ethnicity: From Minority to Majority." *Nations and Nationalism* 14(4): 743–67.

Keating, Michael. 2001. "Rethinking the Region: Culture, Institutions and Economic Development in Catalonia and Galicia." *European Urban and Regional Studies* 8(3): 217–34.

– 2001. *Plurinational Democracy: Stateless Nations in a Post-Sovereignty Era*. Oxford: Oxford University Press.

– 2009. *The Independence of Scotland: Self-Government and the Shifting Politics of Union*. New York: Oxford University Press.

– 2012. "Reforging the Nation: Britain, Scotland,and the Crisis of Unionism." In *Multinational Federalism: Problems and Prospects*, edited by Michel Seymour and Alain Gagnon. Houndmills and New York: Palgrave Macmillan.

– 2014. "Class, Sector, and Nation: Support for Minority Nationalism among Peak Interest Groups in Four Western European Countries." *Territory, Politics, Governance* 2(3): 322–37.

– 2015. "Plurinational State." In *The Oxford Handbook of Transformations of the State*, edited by Stephan Leibfried, Evelyne Huber, Matthew Lange, Jonah D. Levy, Frank Nullmeier, and John D. Stephens. Oxford: Oxford University Press.

Keating, Michael, and Alex Wilson. 2009. "Renegotiating the State of Autonomies: Statute Reform and Multi-Level Politics in Spain." *West European Politics* 32(3): 536–58.

Kelle, Friederike Luise. 2017. "To Claim or Not to Claim? How Territorial Value Shapes Demands for Self-Determination." *Comparative Political Studies* 50(7): 992–1020.

Kemmelmeier, Markus, and David G. Winter. 2008. "Sowing Patriotism, but Reaping Nationalism? Consequences of Exposure to the American Flag." *Political Psychology* 29(6): 859–79.

King, Desmond S., and Rogers M. Smith. 2005. "Racial Orders in American Political Development." *American Political Science Review* 99(1): 75–92.

King, Gary, Robert O. Keohane, and Sidney Verba. 1994. *Designing Social Inquiry: Scientific Inference in Qualitative Research*. Princeton Princeton University Press.

Kinnvall, Catarina. 2004. "Globalization and Religious Nationalism: Self, Identity, and the Search for Ontological Security." *Political Psychology* 25(5): 741–67.

Kirschbaum, Stanislav J. 1993. "Czechoslovakia: The Creation, Federalization and Dissolution of a Nation–state." *Regional Politics and Policy* 3(1): 69–95.

– 2005. *A History of Slovakia: The Struggle for Survival*. 2nd ed. New York: Palgrave Macmillan.

Klasić, Hrvoje. 2018. *Jugoslavija i svijet 1968*. Smederevo: Heliks.

Klatch, Rebecca E. 1988. "Of Meanings & Masters: Political Symbolism & Symbolic Action." *Polity* 21(1): 137–54.

Klaus, Václav. 1991. "Creating a Capitalist Czechoslovakia: An Interview with Vaclav Klaus." In *After the Velvet Revolution: Václav Havel and the New Leaders of Czechoslovakia Speak Out*, edited by Tim D. Whipple. New York: Freedom House.

– 1993. *The Ten Commandments of Systemic Reform*. Washington, D.C.: Group of Thirty.

Krause, George A., and Ann Om Bowman. 2005. "Adverse Selection, Political Parties, and Policy Delegation in the American Federal System." *Journal of Law, Economics, and Organization* 21(2): 359–387.

Krejčí, Jaroslav. 1996. *Czechoslovakia, 1918–92: A Laboratory for Social Change*. New York: St Martin's Press.

Krugman, Paul R. 1991. *Geography and Trade*. Cambridge, MA: MIT Press.

Kuran, Timur. 1991. "Now Out of Never: The Element of Surprise in the East European Revolution of 1989." *World Politics* 44(1): 7–48.

Kusin, Vladimir V. 1971. *The Intellectual Origins of the Prague Spring: The Development of Reformist Ideas in Czechoslovakia, 1956–1967*. Cambridge: Cambridge University Press.

Lacina, Bethany. 2020. "Opposition to Ethnic Territorial Autonomy in the Indian Parliament." *Ethnopolitics* 19(5): 459–82.

La Forest, G.V. 1981. *The Allocation of Taxing Power under the Canadian Constitution*. 2nd ed. Canadian Tax Paper no. 65. Toronto: Canadian Tax Foundation.

La Vanguardia. 1977. "Onze Setembre 1977: Manifestación decisiva en la historia de Cataluña," 13 September 1977.

– 2006. "ERC rectifica y pedirá el 'no' como opción única en el referéndum del Estatut," 5 May 2006. https://www.lavanguardia.com/politica/20060505/51262822698/erc-rectifica-y-pedira-el-no-como-opcion-unica-en-el-referendum-del-estatut.html.

– 2010. "'Nosaltres decidim, som una nació' será el lema de da marcha del 10 de Julio." *La Vanguardia*, 29 June 2010. https://www.lavanguardia. com/politica/20100629/53954278364/nosaltres-decidim-som-una-nacio-sera-el-lema-de-la-marcha-del-10-de-julio.html.

Lampe, John R. 1989. "Imperial Borderlands or Capitalist Periphery? Redefining Balkan Backwardness, 1520–1914." In *The Origins of Backwardness in Eastern Europe: Economics and Politics from the Middle Ages until the Early Twentieth Century*, edited by Daniel Chirot. Berkeley: University of California Press.

Lampe, John R., and Marvin R. Jackson. 1982. *Balkan Economic History, 1550–1950: From Imperial Borderlands to Developing Nations*. Bloomington: Indiana University Press.

Lampe, John R., Russell O. Prickett, and Ljubiša S. Adamović. 1990. *Yugoslav–American Economic Relations Since World War II*. Durham: Duke University Press.

Langford, John, and Kenneth Huffman. 1983. "The Uncharted Universe of Federal Public Corporations." In *Crown Corporations in Canada: The Calculus of Instrument Choice*, edited by Robert Prichard. Toronto: Butterworths.

Lecours, André. 2013. "The Question of Federalism in Nepal." *Publius: The Journal of Federalism*, 44(4): 609–32.

– 2020. "Nationalism and the Strength of Secessionism in Western Europe: Static and Dynamic Autonomy." *International Political Science Review* [online first].

– Forthcoming. *Nationalism, Secession, and Autonomy*. Oxford: Oxford University Press.

Lecours, André, and Geneviève Nootens, eds. 2009. *Dominant Nationalism, Dominant Ethnicity: Identity, Federalism, and Democracy*. Brussels: P.I.E. Peter Lang.

LeDuc, Lawrence, and Jon H. Pammett. 1995. "Referendum Voting: Attitudes and Behaviour in the 1992 Constitutional Referendum." *Canadian Journal of Political Science* 28(1): 3–33.

Leff, Carol Skalnik. 1988. *National Conflict in Czechoslovakia: The Making and Remaking of a State, 1918–1987*. Princeton: Princeton University Press.

Lemay-Hébert, Nicolas. 2009. "Statebuilding without Nation-Building? Legitimacy, State Failure, and the Limits of the Institutionalist Approach." *Journal of Intervention and Statebuilding* 3(1): 21–45.

Lenz, Gabriel S. 2012. *Follow the Leader?: How Voters Respond to Politicians' Policies and Performance*. Chicago: University of Chicago Press.

León, Sandra. 2015. *La financiación autonómica: Claves para comprender un "interminable" debate*. Madrid: Alianza Editorial.

Lévesque, René. 1973. *An Option for Quebec*. Toronto: McClelland and Stewart.

Levy, Michele Frucht. 2009. "'The Last Bullet for the Last Serb': The Ustaša Genocide against Serbs: 1941–1945." *Nationalities Papers* 37(6): 807–37.

Lewis-Beck, Michael S. 1988. *Economics and Elections: The Major Western Democracies*. Ann Arbor: University of Michigan Press.

Liberal Party of Canada. 1986. "Policy Resolutions Passed by the Plenary Session at the 1986 Convention."

Lijphart, Arend. 1977. *Democracy in Plural Societies: A Comparative Exploration*. New Haven: Yale University Press.

Liñeira, Robert, Ailsa Henderson, and Liam Delaney. 2017. "Voters' Response to the Campaign." In *Debating Scotland: Issues of Independence and Union in the 2014 Referendum*, edited by Michael Keating. New York: Oxford University Press.

Linteau, Paul-André, René Durocher, Jean-Claude Robert, and François Ricard. 1991. *Quebec Since 1930*. Toronto: James Lorimer.

Linz, Juan J. 1973. "Early State-Building and Late Peripheral Nationalisms against the State: The Case of Spain." In *Building States and Nations: Analyses by Region*, edited by S.N. Eisenstadt and Stein Rokkan. Beverly Hills: Sage.

Lluch, Jaime. 2014. *Visions of Sovereignty: Nationalism and Accommodation in Multinational Democracies*. Philadelphia: University of Pennsylvania Press.

Locke, Richard M., and Kathleen Thelen. 1995. "Apples and Oranges Revisited: Contextualized Comparisons and the Study of Comparative Labor Politics." *Politics and Society* 23(3): 337–67.

Loizides, Neophytos. 2015. *The Politics of Majority Nationalism: Framing Peace, Stalemates, and Crises*. Stanford: Stanford University Press.

– 2016. *Designing Peace: Cyprus and Institutional Innovations in Divided Societies*. Philadelphia: University of Pennsylvania Press.

López, César Enrique Díaz. 1981. "The State of the Autonomic Process in Spain." *Publius: The Journal of Federalism* 11(3): 193–218.

Loveman, Mara. 2005. "The Modern State and the Primitive Accumulation of Symbolic Power." *American Journal of Sociology* 110(6): 1651–83.

Lučić, Iva. 2012. "In the Service of the Nation: Intellectuals' Articulation of the Muslim National Identity." *Nationalities Papers* 40(1): 23–44.

Lustick, Ian. 2001. "Thresholds of Opportunity and Barriers to Change in the Right-Sizing of States." In *Rightsizing the State: The Politics of*

Moving Borders, edited by Brendan O'Leary, Ian Lustick, and Thomas M. Callaghy. Oxford: Oxford University Press.

Lustick, Ian, and Dan Miodownik. 2020. "When Do Institutions Suddenly Collapse? Zones of Knowledge and the Likelihood of Political Cascades." *Quality and Quantity* 54(2): 413–37.

MacDonald, Ian. 2002. *From Bourassa to Bourassa: Wilderness to Restoration*. 2nd ed. Montreal and Kingston: McGill-Queen's University Press.

– 2006. "The 'Quebec Nation' Is Symbolic – but Symbols Matter: Only a Prime Minister from the West Could Sell the Idea in Rest of Canada." *The Gazette* (Montreal), 27 November 2006.

MacIntyre, Alasdair. 1972. "Is a Science of Comparative Politics Possible?" In *Philosophy, Politics, and Society, Fourth Series: A Collection*, edited by Peter Laslett, W.G. Runciman, and Quentin Skinner. New York: Barnes and Noble Books.

Maclean's. 1995. "Taking the Pulse." 25 December 1995.

Mahoney, James. 2010. "After KKV: The New Methodology of Qualitative Research." *World Politics* 62(1): 120–47.

Mahoney, James, and Gary Goertz. 2004. "The Possibility Principle: Choosing Negative Cases in Comparative Research." *American Political Science Review* 98(4): 653–69.

Mahoney, James, and Dietrich Rueschemeyer. 2003a. "Comparative Historical Analysis: Achievements and Agendas." In *Comparative Historical Analysis in the Social Sciences*, edited by James Mahoney and Dietrich Rueschemeyer. Cambridge: Cambridge University Press.

– eds. 2003b. *Comparative Historical Analysis in the Social Sciences*. Cambridge: Cambridge University Press.

Mahoney, James, and Kathleen Thelen. 2010. "A Theory of Gradual Institutional Change." In *Explaining Institutional Change: Ambiguity, Agency, and Power*, edited by James Mahoney and Kathleen Thelen. Cambridge: Cambridge University Press.

Maiz, Ramon, Francisco Caamaño, and Miguel Azpitarte. 2010. "The Hidden Counterpoint of Spanish Federalism: Recentralization and Resymmetrization in Spain (1978–2008)." *Regional and Federal Studies* 20(1): 63–82.

Malešević, Siniša. 2019. *Grounded Nationalisms: A Sociological Analysis*. Cambridge: Cambridge University Press.

Mansell, Robert, and Ronald Schlenker. 1995. "The Provincial Distribution of Federal Fiscal Balances." *Canadian Business Economics* 3: 3–19.

Marcet, Juan, and Jordi Argelaguet. 1998. "Nationalist Parties in Catalonia: Convergència Democràtica de Catalunya and Esquerra Republicana." In *Regionalist Parties in Western Europe*, edited by Lieven de Winter and Huri Türsan. London: Routledge.

Marcos, Pilar. 2005a. "El PP presentará mociones de rechazo a la reforma Catalana en todas las comunidades y ayuntamientos." *El País*, 10 November 2005, Web edition. http://elpais.com/diario/2005/10/11/espana/1128981614_850215.html.

– 2005b. "Rajoy: 'Sólo hay una nación, la española.'" *El País*, 4 December 2005, Web edition. http://elpais.com/diario/2005/12/04/espana/1133650801_850215.html.

Marfany, Julie. 2010. "Is It Still Helpful to Talk about Proto-Industrialization? Some Suggestions from a Catalan Case Study." *Economic History Review* 63(4): 942–73.

Marks, Gary, Liesbet Hooghe, and Arjan H. Schakel. 2008. "Measuring Regional Authority." *Regional and Federal Studies* 18(2–3): 111–21.

Marshall, Alfred. 1890. *Principles of Economics*. London and New York: Macmillan and Co.

Martin, Peter. 1990. "'Scenario for Economic Reform' Adopted." *Report on Eastern Europe – Radio Free Europe* 1(42): 5–8.

Martin, Philip. 2013. "Coming Together: Power-Sharing and the Durability of Negotiated Peace Settlements." *Civil Wars* 15(3): 332–58.

Massetti, Emanuele, and Arjan H. Schakel. 2015. "From Class to Region: How Regionalist Parties Link (and Subsume) Left–Right into Centre–Periphery Politics." *Party Politics* 21(6): 866–86.

– 2016. "Between Autonomy and Secession: Decentralization and Regionalist Party Ideological Radicalism." *Party Politics* 22(1): 59–79.

McAdam, Doug., Sidney G. Tarrow, and Charles. Tilly. 2001. *Dynamics of Contention*. New York: Cambridge University Press.

McCulloch, Allison. 2014. *Power-Sharing and Political Stability in Deeply Divided Societies*. London: Routledge.

McDougall, Alex. 2009. "State Power and Its Implications for Civil War Colombia." *Studies in Conflict and Terrorism* 32(4): 322–45.

McEwen, Nicola, and André Lecours. 2008. "Voice or Recognition? Comparing Strategies for Accommodating Territorial Minorities in Multinational States." *Commonwealth and Comparative Politics* 46(2): 220–43.

McGarry, John. 2007. "Asymmetry in Federations, Federacies, and Unitary States." *Ethnopolitics* 6(1): 105–16.

– 2015. "Consociational Theory, Self-Determination Disputes, and Territorial Pluralism: The Case of Cyprus." In *Territorial Pluralism:*

Managing Difference in Multinational States, edited by Karlo Basta, John McGarry, and Richard Simeon. Vancouver: UBC Press.

McGarry, John, and Brendan O'Leary. 2005. "Federation as a Method of Ethnic Conflict Regulation." In *From Power Sharing to Democracy: Post-Conflict Institutions in Ethnically Divided Societies*, edited by Sid Noel, 263–96. Montreal and Kingston: McGill-Queen's University Press.

– 2007. "Iraq's Constitution of 2005: Liberal Consociation as Political Prescription." *International Journal of Constitutional Law* 5(4): 670–98.

McGarry, John, Brendan O'Leary, and Richard Simeon. 2008. "Integration or Accommodation? The Enduring Debate in Conflict Regulation." In *Constitutional Design for Divided Societies: Integration or Accommodation?*, edited by Sujit Choudhry. Oxford: Oxford University Press.

McLean, Iain. 2013. *Scotland's Choices: The Referendum and What Happens Afterwards*. Edinburgh: Edinburgh University Press.

McRoberts, Kenneth. 1993. *Quebec: Social Change and Political Crisis*. 3rd ed. Toronto: McClelland and Stewart.

– 1997. *Misconceiving Canada: The Struggle for National Unity*. Toronto: Oxford University Press.

Meguid, Bonnie M. 2008. *Party Competition between Unequals: Strategies and Electoral Fortunes in Western Europe*. New York: Cambridge University Press.

– 2015. "Multi-Level Elections and Party Fortunes: The Electoral Impact of Decentralization in Western Europe." *Comparative Politics* 47(4): 379–98.

Mendelsohn, Matthew. 2003. "Rational Choice and Socio-Psychological Explanation for Opinion on Quebec Sovereignty." *Canadian Journal of Political Science* 36(3): 511–37.

Mendelsohn, Matthew, and J. Scott Matthews. 2010. "The Shifting Attitudes of Ontarians toward the Federation." Mowat Centre for Policy Innovation. https://munkschool.utoronto.ca/mowatcentre/wp-content/uploads/publications/1_the_new_ontario.pdf.

Mercer, Jonathan. 1995. "Anarchy and Identity." *International Organization* 49(2): 229–52.

– 2005. "Prospect Theory and Political Science." *Annual Review of Political Science* 8(1): 1–21.

Meyer, John W., and Brian Rowan. 1977. "Institutionalized Organizations: Formal Structure as Myth and Ceremony." *American Journal of Sociology* 83(2): 340–63.

Mikesell, Marvin W. 1983. "The Myth of the Nation State." *Journal of Geography* 82(6): 257–60.

Milenkovitch, Deborah D. 1971. *Plan and Market in Yugoslav Economic Thought*. New Haven: Yale University Press.

Mitchell, Timothy. 1999. "Society, Economy, and the State Effect." In *State/Culture: State-Formation after the Cultural Turn*, edited by George Steinmetz. Ithaca: Cornell University Press.

Mitzen, Jennifer. 2006. "Ontological Security in World Politics: State Identity and the Security Dilemma." *European Journal of International Relations* 12(3): 341–70.

Mladá fronta Dnes. 1991. "Mečiar on Slovakia's 'Specific Conditions.'" FBIS-EEU-91-069, Daily Report. East Europe, 2 April 1991.

Monière, Denis. 1981. *Ideologies in Quebec: The Historical Development*. Toronto: University of Toronto Press.

Moore, Margaret. 2015. *A Political Theory of Territory*. Oxford: Oxford University Press.

Moreno, Luis. 1997. "Federalization and Ethnoterritorial Concurrence in Spain." *Publius: The Journal of Federalism* 27(4): 65–84.

– 2001. *The Federalization of Spain*. London: Frank Cass.

Moscovici, Serge. 1976. *Social Influence and Social Change*. London and New York: Academic Press.

Muñoz, Jordi, and Marc Guinjoan. 2013. "Accounting for Internal Variation in Nationalist Mobilization: Unofficial Referendums for Independence in Catalonia (2009–11)." *Nations and Nationalism* 19(1): 44–67.

Muro, Diego. 2015. "Ethnicity, Nationalism, and Social Movements." In *The Oxford Handbook of Social Movements*, edited by Donatella Della Porta and Mario Diani. Oxford: Oxford University Press.

Muro, Diego, and Martijn C. Vlaskamp. 2016. "How Do Prospects of EU Membership Influence Support for Secession? A Survey Experiment in Catalonia and Scotland." *West European Politics* 39(6): 1115–38.

Murphy, Alexander B. 1996. "The Sovereign State System as Political-Territorial Ideal: Historical and Contemporary Considerations." In *State Sovereignty as Social Construct*, edited by Thomas J. Biersteker and Cynthia Weber. Cambridge: Cambridge University Press.

Murphy, Brendan. 1999. "European Integration and Liberalization: Political Change and Economic Policy Continuity in Spain." *Mediterranean Politics* 4(1): 53–78.

Myant, M.R. 1993. *Transforming Socialist Economies: The Case of Poland and Czechoslovakia*. Aldershot: Edward Elgar.

Mylonas, Harris. 2012. *The Politics of Nation-Building: Making Co-Nationals, Refugees, and Minorities.* Cambridge: Cambridge University Press.

Myrdal, Gunnar. 1957. *Economic Theory and Under-Developed Regions.* London: G. Duckworth.

Nadeau, Richard, Pierre Martin, and Andre Blais. 1999. "Attitude towards Risk-Taking and Individual Choice in the Quebec Referendum on Sovereignty." *British Journal of Political Science* 29(3): 523–39.

Národná obroda. 1990. "Slovak Government Policy Statement Published." FBIS-EEU-90-137, Daily Report. East Europe, 30 June 1990.

Naylor, R.T. 1972. "The Rise and Fall of the Third Commercial Empire of the St. Lawrence." In *Capitalism and the National Question in Canada*, edited by Gary Teeple. Toronto: University of Toronto Press.

Nettl, J.P. 1968. "The State as a Conceptual Variable." *World Politics* 20(4): 559–92.

Newton, M.T. 1982. "Andalusia: The Long Road to Autonomy." *Journal of Area Studies* 3(6): 27–32.

Noelle-Neumann, Elisabeth. 1974. "The Spiral of Silence: A Theory of Public Opinion." *Journal of Communication* 24(2): 43–51.

Noelle-Neumann, Elisabeth, and Thomas Petersen. 2004. "The Spiral of Silence and the Social Nature of Man." In *Handbook of Political Communication Research*, edited by Lynda Lee Kaid. Mahwah: Lawrence Erlbaum Associates.

Nordlinger, Eric A. 1972. *Conflict Regulation in Divided Societies.* Cambridge: Center for International Affairs, Harvard University.

Norman, W.J. 2006. *Negotiating Nationalism: Nation-Building, Federalism, and Secession in the Multinational State.* Oxford: Oxford University Press.

Norrie, K.H., and Doug Owram. 1991. *A History of the Canadian Economy.* Toronto: Harcourt Brace Jovanovich Canada.

Norris, Pippa. 2008. *Driving Democracy: Do Power-Sharing Institutions Work?* Cambridge: Cambridge University Press.

North, Douglass C. 1990. *Institutions, Institutional Change, and Economic Performance. The Political Economy of Institutions and Decisions.* Cambridge: Cambridge University Press.

North, Douglass C., and Robert Paul Thomas. 1970. "An Economic Theory of the Growth of the Western World." *Economic History Review* 23(1): 1–17.

North, Douglass C., and Barry R. Weingast. 1989. "Constitutions and Commitment: The Evolution of Institutions Governing Public Choice in Seventeenth-Century England." *Journal of Economic History* 49(4): 803–32.

Núñez Seixas, Xosé. 2005. "De la región a la nacionalidad: Los neo-regionalismos en la España de la transición y la consolidación democrática." In *Transiciones de la dictadura a la democracia: los casos de España y América Latina*, edited by Carlos H. Waisman, Raanan Rein, and Ander Gurrutxaga Abad, 101–40. Bilbao: Universidad del País Vasco, Servicio de Publicaciones.

Oberst, Robert. 1988. "Federalism and Ethnic Conflict in Sri Lanka." *Publius* 18(3): 175–93.

OECD. 2010. OECD *Factbook: Economic, Environmental, and Social Statistics* (2010). http://www.oecd.org/site/0,3407,en_21571361_34374092_1_1_1_1_1,00.html.

Oklopcic, Zoran. 2018. *Beyond the People: Social Imaginary and Constituent Imagination*. Oxford: Oxford University Press.

O'Leary, Brendan. 2001. "An Iron Law of Nationalism and Federation?: A (Neo–Diceyian) Theory of the Necessity of a Federal Staatsvolk, and of Consociational Rescue." *Nations and Nationalism* 7(3): 273–96.

Olson, David M. 1993. "Dissolution of the State: Political Parties and the 1992 Election in Czechoslovakia." *Communist and Post-Communist Studies* 26(3): 301–14.

O'Neal, Brian. 1995. *Distinct Society: Origins, Interpretations, Implications*. Background Paper. BP-408E. Ottawa: Library of Parliament, Research Branch.

Orenstein, Mitchell A. 2001. *Out of the Red: Building Capitalism and Democracy in Postcommunist Europe*. Ann Arbor: University of Michigan Press.

Ormsby, William G. 1969. *The Emergence of the Federal Concept in Canada, 1839–1845*. Toronto: University of Toronto Press.

Ostrom, Elinor. 1986. "An Agenda for the Study of Institutions." *Public Choice* 48(1): 3–25.

Owram, Doug. 1986. *The Government Generation: Canadian Intellectuals and the State, 1900–1945*. Toronto: University of Toronto Press.

Painter, Joe. 2006. "Prosaic Geographies of Stateness." *Political Geography* 25(7): 752–74.

Palairet, M.R. 1997. *The Balkan Economies c. 1800–1914: Evolution without Development*. Cambridge: Cambridge University Press.

Parlament de Catalunya. 1987. "Resolució 106/II Del Parlament de Catalunya, Sobre l'Estatut d'Autonomia de Catalunya." *Butlletí Oficial Del Parlament de Catalunya II Legislatura* (182).

- 1993. "Resolució 115/IV Del Parlament de Catalunya, Sobre l'Orientació Política General Del Consell Executiu." Butlletí Oficial Del Parlament de Catalunya IV legislatura (161): 10343–4.
- 1996. "Resolució 5/V Del Parlament de Catalunya." Butlletí Oficial Del Parlament de Catalunya V legislatura (18).
- 2002. "Resolució 1547/VI Del Parlament de Catalunya, Sobre El Procés d'involució Autonòmica." Butlletí Oficial Del Parlament de Catalunya VI legislatura (349).
- 2005. *Propuesta de Reforma Del Estatuto de Autonomía de Cataluña.* Tram. 206-00003/07.

Partit dels Socialistes de Catalunya. 1999. "Canviar És Guanyar: Programa de Govern."

Pavlínek, Petr. 1995. "Regional Development and the Disintegration of Czechoslovakia." *Geoforum* 26(4): 351–72.

Pavlowitch, Stevan K. 2003. "Serbia, Montenegro, and Yugoslavia." In *Yugoslavism: Histories of a Failed Idea, 1918–1992*, edited by Dejan Djokić. London: C. Hurst.

Pehe, Jiri. 1990. "Power-Sharing Law Approved by Federal Assembly." *Report on Eastern Europe* 1(51): 6–9.

Pepinsky, Thomas B. 2019. "The Return of the Single-Country Study." *Annual Review of Political Science* 22(1): 187–203.

Perunović, Sreća. 2016. "Animosities in Yugoslavia before Its Demise: Revelations of an Opinion Poll Survey." *Ethnicities* 16(6): 819–41.

Pierson, Paul. 2004. *Politics in Time: History, Institutions, and Social Analysis.* Princeton: Princeton University Press.

Pinard, Maurice. 1992. "The Dramatic Reemergence of the Quebec Independence Movement." *Journal of International Affairs* 45(2): 471–97.

Pinard, Maurice, and Richard Hamilton. 1978. "The Parti Québécois Comes to Power: An Analysis of the 1976 Quebec Election." *Canadian Journal of Political Science* 11(4): 739–76.

Pleština, Dijana. 1987. "Politics and Inequality: A Study of Regional Disparities in Yugoslavia." PhD diss., University of California, Berkeley.

- 1992. *Regional Development in Communist Yugoslavia: Success, Failure, and Consequences.* Boulder: Westview Press.

Popelier, Patricia, and Maja Sahadžić, eds. 2019. *Constitutional Asymmetry in Multinational Federalism.* New York: Springer Berlin Heidelberg.

Porta, Donatella della, Francis O'Connor, and Martín Portos. 2019. "Protest Cycles and Referendums for Independence: Closed

Opportunities and the Path of Radicalization in Catalonia." *Revista Internacional de Sociología* 77(4): 1–14.

Prague čsTK. 1991a. "Differences in Slovakia's Economic Reform Conditions." FBIS-EEU-91-057, Daily Report. East Europe, 21 March 1991.

— 1991b. "Poll: 64% Support Federation." FBIS-EEU-91-212, Daily Report. East Europe, 31 October 1991.

— 1992. "Support for Confederation Up 'Slightly' in Slovakia." FBIS-EEU-92-085, Daily Report. East Europe, 29 April 1992.

Prague Domestic Service. 1990a. "Czech, Slovak Governments Joint Statement." FBIS-EEU-90-071, Daily Report. East Europe, 11 April 1990.

— 1990b. "Calfa Addresses Federal Assembly 17 Sep." FBIS-EEU-90-181, Daily Report. East Europe, 17 September 1990.

Prague Telegraf. 1992. "Klaus Views Mečiar's Post-Election Expectations." FBIS-EEU-92-092, Daily Report. East Europe, 7 May 1992.

Pryor, Zora. 1973. "Czechoslovak Economic Development in the Interwar Period." In *A History of the Czechoslovak Republic, 1918–1948*, edited by Victor S. Mamatey and Radomír Luža. Princeton: Princeton University Press.

Quebec. Royal Commission of Inquiry on Constitutional Problems. 1973. *The Tremblay Report.* Carleton Library, no. 64. Toronto: McClelland and Stewart.

Rabushka, Alvin, and Kenneth A. Shepsle. 1972. *Politics in Plural Societies: A Theory of Democratic Instability.* Columbus: Merrill.

Radan, Peter. 1997. "The Badinter Arbitration Commission and the Partition of Yugoslavia." *Nationalities Papers* 25(3): 537–57.

Raič, David. 2002. *Statehood and the Law of Self-Determination.* The Hague and New York: Kluwer Law International.

Raičević, Božidar. 1977. "The Fiscal System." *Yugoslav Survey* 18(4): 57–78.

Recio, A., and J. Roca. 1998. "The Spanish Socialists in Power: Thirteen Years of Economic Policy." *Oxford Review of Economic Policy* 14(1): 139–58.

Reform Party of Canada. 1988. "Platform and Statement of Principles."

— 1993. "Blue Sheet: Principles, Policies, and Electoral Platform."

Renaud, Marc. 1987. "Quebec's New Middle Class in Search of Social Hegemony: Causes and Political Consequences." In *Quebec Since 1945: Selected Readings*, edited by Michael D Behiels. Toronto: Copp Clark Pitman.

Requejo, Ferran. 2001. "Political Liberalism in Multinational States: The Legitimacy of Plural and Asymmetrical Federalism." In *Multinational Democracies,* edited by Alain Gagnon and James Tully. Cambridge: Cambridge University Press.

Resnick, Philip. 2012. "What Theorists of Nationalism Have to Learn from Multinational States." In *Multinational Federalism: Problems and Prospects*, edited by Michel Seymour and Alain Gagnon. Houndmills and New York: Palgrave Macmillan.

Riker, William H. 1964. *Federalism: Origin, Operation, Significance.* Boston: Little, Brown.

Robinson, Amanda Lea. 2014. "National versus Ethnic Identification in Africa: Modernization, Colonial Legacy, and the Origins of Territorial Nationalism." *World Politics* 66(4): 709–46.

Rodden, Jonathan. 2006. *Hamilton's Paradox: The Promise and Peril of Fiscal Federalism*. Cambridge: Cambridge University Press.

Rode, Martin, Hans Pitlik, Borrella Mas, and Miguel Ángel. 2018. "Does Fiscal Federalism Deter or Spur Secessionist Movements? Empirical Evidence from Europe." *Publius: The Journal of Federalism* 48(2): 161–90.

Roeder, Philip G. 2005. "Power Dividing as an Alternative to Ethnic Power Sharing." In *Sustainable Peace: Power and Democracy after Civil Wars*, edited by Philip G Roeder and Donald S Rothchild. Ithaca: Cornell University Press.

– 2007. *Where Nation-States Come From: Institutional Change in the Age of Nationalism*. Princeton: Princeton University Press.

– 2018. *National Secession: Persuasion and Violence in Independence Campaigns*. Ithaca: Cornell University Press.

Rohlfing, Ingo. 2013. "Comparative Hypothesis Testing via Process Tracing:" *Sociological Methods and Research* 43(4): 606–42.

Roller, Elisa, and Pieter Van Houten. 2003. "A National Party in a Regional Party System: The PSC-PSOE in Catalonia." *Regional and Federal Studies* 13(3): 1–22.

Rokkan, Stein. 1999. *State Formation, Nation-Building, and Mass Politics in Europe: The Theory of Stein Rokkan: Based on His Collected Works*. Oxford: Oxford University Press.

Rokkan, Stein, and Derek W. Urwin. 1983. *Economy, Territory, Identity: Politics of West European Peripheries*. London: Sage.

Rosie, Michael, Pille Petersoo, John MacInnes, Susan Condor, and James Kennedy. 2006. "Mediating Which Nation? Citizenship and National Identities in the British Press." *Social Semiotics* 16(2): 327–44.

Rothschild, Joseph. 1981. *Ethnopolitics: A Conceptual Framework.* New York: Columbia University Press.

Rovny, Jan. 2015. "Riker and Rokkan: Remarks on the Strategy and Structure of Party Competition." *Party Politics* 21(6): 912–18.

Rueschemeyer, Dietrich. 2003. "Can One or a Few Cases Yield Theoretical Gains?" In *Comparative Historical Analysis in the Social Sciences,* edited by James Mahoney and Dietrich Rueschemeyer. Cambridge: Cambridge University Press.

Rumelili, Bahar. 2015. "Identity and Desecuritisation: The Pitfalls of Conflating Ontological and Physical Security." *Journal of International Relations and Development* 18(1): 52–74.

Rusiñol, Pere, and Carlos E. Cué. 2003. "Zapatero promete apoyar la reforma del Estatuto que salga del Parlamento." *El País,* 13 November 2003. https://elpais.com/diario/2003/11/14/espana/1068764421_850215.html.

Rusinow, Dennison. 1977. *The Yugoslav Experiment 1948–1974.* Berkeley: University of California Press.

Russell, Peter H. 2004. *Constitutional Odyssey: Can Canadians Become a Sovereign People?* 3rd ed. Toronto: University of Toronto Press.

Salmon, Keith. 2001. "Privatization of State-Owned Enterprises in Spain: Redefining the Political Economy." *International Journal of Iberian Studies* 14(3): 136–47.

Sambanis, Nicholas, and Branko Milanovic. 2011. "Explaining the Demand for Sovereignty: Policy Research Working Paper 5888." Washington, D.C.: Development Research Group, World Bank.

– 2014. "Explaining Regional Autonomy Differences in Decentralized Countries." *Comparative Political Studies* 47(13): 1830–55.

Savez komunista Hrvatske. 1970. *Deseta sjednica Centralnog Komiteta Saveza Kommunista Hrvatske.* Zagreb: Vjesnik.

Savez komunista Hrvatske, ed. 1972. *Izvještaj o stanju u Savezu komunista Hrvatske u ddnosu na prodor nacionalizma u njegove redove.* Zagreb: Informativna služba Centralnog komiteta Saveza komunista Hrvatske.

Savez komunista Jugoslavije. 1965. *Program Saveza komunista Jugoslavije: prihvaćen na Sedmom kongresu Saveza komunista Jugoslavije (22-26 travnja 1958, u Ljubljani).* Politička biblioteka. Zagreb: Stvarnost.

– 1998. *Početak Kraja SFRJ: Stenogram i drugi prateći dokumenti Proširene sednice Izvršnog Komiteta CK SKJ održane 14–16. marta 1962. godine.* Belgrade: Arhiv Jugoslavije.

Saywell, John Tupper. 1977. *The Rise of the Parti Québecois, 1967–1976.*
    Toronto: University of Toronto Press.
Schedler, Andreas, and Cas Mudde. 2010. "Data Usage in Quantitative
    Comparative Politics." *Political Research Quarterly* 63(2): 417–33.
Schmidt, Vivien A. 2008. "Discursive Institutionalism: The Explanatory
    Power of Ideas and Discourse." *Annual Review of Political Science*
    11(1): 303–26.
Schmidt, Vivien Ann, and Mark Thatcher, eds. 2013. *Resilient Liberalism
    in Europe's Political Economy.* Cambridge: Cambridge University Press.
Scott, W. Richard. 1987. "The Adolescence of Institutional Theory."
    Administrative Science Quarterly 32(4): 493–511.
Sears, David O. 1993. "Symbolic Politics: A Socio-Psychological Theory."
    In *Explorations in Political Psychology*, edited by Shanto Iyengar
    and William J. McGuire. Durham: Duke University Press.
Sekulic, Dusko, Garth Massey, and Randy Hodson. 1994. "Who Were
    the Yugoslavs? Failed Sources of a Common Identity in the Former
    Yugoslavia." *American Sociological Review* 59(1): 83–97.
Sewell Jr, William H. 1996. "Three Temporalities: Toward an Eventful
    Sociology." In *The Historic Turn in the Human Sciences*, edited by
    Terrence J. McDonald. Ann Arbor: University of Michigan Press.
Shames, Israel. 1974. "French-Canadian Political Nationalism in Quebec:
    Factors Contributing to the Rise of the Parti Québecois." MA thesis,
    Carleton University.
Share, Donald. 1988. "Dilemmas of Social Democracy in the 1980s:
    The Spanish Socialist Workers Party in Comparative Perspective."
    Comparative Political Studies 21(3): 408–35.
Shoup, Paul. 1968. *Communism and the Yugoslav National Question.*
    New York: Columbia University Press.
Simeon, Richard. 1980. "Natural Resource Revenues and Canadian
    Federalism: A Survey of the Issues." *Canadian Public Policy* 6
    (supplement): 182–91.
– 2006. *Federal–Provincial Diplomacy: The Making of Recent Policy
    in Canada.* 2nd ed. Toronto: University of Toronto Press.
Simeon, Richard, and Ian Robinson. 1990. *State, Society, and the Develop-
    ment of Canadian Federalism.* Toronto: University of Toronto Press.
Simonsen, Sven Gunnar. 2005. "Addressing Ethnic Divisions in Post-
    Conflict Institution-Building: Lessons from Recent Cases." *Security
    Dialogue* 36(3): 297–318.
Sirc, Ljubo. 1979. *The Yugoslav Economy under Self-Management.*
    New York: St Martin's Press.

Siroky, David S., and John Cuffe. 2015. "Lost Autonomy, Nationalism and Separatism." *Comparative Political Studies* 48(1): 3–34.

Skey, Michael. 2009. "The National in Everyday Life: A Critical Engagement with Michael Billig's Thesis of Banal Nationalism." *Sociological Review* 57(2): 331–46.

Skey, Michael, and Marco Antonsich, eds. 2017. *Everyday Nationhood: Theorising Culture, Identity, and Belonging after Banal Nationalism.* London: Palgrave Macmillan.

Skilling, H. Gordon. 1976. *Czechoslovakia's Interrupted Revolution.* Princeton: Princeton University Press.

Skocpol, Theda. 1985. "Bringing the State Back In: Strategies of Analysis in Current Research." In *Bringing the State Back In*, edited by Peter B. Evans, Dietrich Rueschemeyer, and Theda Skocpol. Cambridge: Cambridge University Press.

Slater, Dan. 2010. *Ordering Power: Contentious Politics and Authoritarian Leviathans in Southeast Asia.* New York: Cambridge University Press.

Slater, Dan, and Daniel Ziblatt. 2013. "The Enduring Indispensability of the Controlled Comparison." *Comparative Political Studies* 46 (10): 1301–27.

Smith, Angel. 2014. *The Origins of Catalan Nationalism, 1770–1898.* Houndmills: Palgrave Macmillan.

Smith, Anthony D. 1986. *The Ethnic Origins of Nations.* Oxford: Basil Blackwell.

– 2009. *Ethno-Symbolism and Nationalism: A Cultural Approach.* London: Routledge.

Snyder, Jack L. 2000. *From Voting to Violence: Democratization and Nationalist Conflict.* New York: W.W. Norton.

Solbés Mirá, Pedro. 2013. *Recuerdos: 40 Años de Servicio Público.* Barcelona: Ediciones Deusto.

Sorens, Jason. 2005. "The Cross-Sectional Determinants of Secessionism in Advanced Democracies." *Comparative Political Studies* 38(3): 304–26.

– 2012. *Secessionism: Identity, Interest, and Strategy.* Montreal and Kingston: McGill-Queen's University Press.

Spruyt, Hendrik. 1996. *The Sovereign State and Its Competitors: An Analysis of Systems Change.* Princeton: Princeton University Press.

Srpska akademija nauka i umetnosti. 1995. "*Memorandum SANU*": *Odgovori na kritike.* Beograd: Srpska akademija nauka i umetnosti.

Staerklé, Christian, Jim Sidanius, Eva G.T. Green, and Ludwin E. Molina. 2010. "Ethnic Minority–Majority Asymmetry in National Attitudes around the World: A Multilevel Analysis." *Political Psychology* 31(4): 491–519.

Štatistický úrad Slovenskej republiky. 1995. *Štatistická Ročenka Slovenskej Republiky = Statistical Yearbook of the Slovak Republic*. Bratislava: Štatistický úrad Slovenskej republiky.

Stein, Eric. 1997. *Czecho/Slovakia: Ethnic Conflict, Constitutional Fissure, Negotiated Breakup*. Ann Arbor: University of Michigan Press.

Steinmetz, George. 2004. "Odious Comparisons: Incommensurability, the Case Study, and 'Small N's' in Sociology." *Sociological Theory* 22(3): 371–400.

Stepan, Alfred C. 1999. "Federalism and Democracy: Beyond the U.S. Model." *Journal of Democracy* 10(4): 19–34.

Stepan, Alfred C., Juan J. Linz, and Yogendra Yadav. 2011. *Crafting State-Nations: India and Other Multinational Democracies*. Baltimore: Johns Hopkins University Press.

Stojanović, Nenad. 2011. "When Is a Country Multinational? Problems with Statistical and Subjective Approaches." *Ratio Juris* 24(3): 267–83.

Swenden, Wilfried. 2013. "Territorial Strategies for Managing Plurinational States." In *Routledge Handbook of Regionalism and Federalism*, edited by John Loughlin, John Kincaid, and Wilfried Swenden. New York: Routledge.

Swenden, Wilfried, and Simon Toubeau. 2013. "Mainstream Parties and Territorial Dynamics in the UK, Spain, and India." In *Federal Dynamics: Continuity, Change, and the Varieties of Federalism*, edited by Arthur Benz and Jörg Broschek. Oxford: Oxford University Press.

Taylor, A.J.P. 1976. *The Habsburg Monarchy, 1809–1918: A History of the Austrian Empire and Austria-Hungary*. Chicago: University of Chicago Press.

Taylor, Charles. 1994. "The Politics of Recognition." In *Multiculturalism: Examining the Politics of Recognition*, edited by Amy Gutmann, 25–73. Princeton: Princeton University Press.

Telford, Hamish. 2003. "The Federal Spending Power in Canada: Nation-Building or Nation-Destroying?" *Publius: The Journal of Federalism* 33(1): 23–44.

Thelen, Kathleen, and James Mahoney, eds. 2015. *Advances in Comparative-Historical Analysis*. New York: Cambridge University Press.

Thelen, Kathleen, and Sven Steinmo. 1992. "Historical Institutionalism in Comparative Politics." In *Structuring Politics: Historical Institutionalism in Comparative Analysis*, edited by Sven Steinmo,

Kathleen Thelen, and Frank Longstreth. Cambridge: Cambridge University Press.

Thomson, Dale C. 1984. *Jean Lesage and the Quiet Revolution*. Toronto: MacMillan of Canada.

Thomson, J.K.J. 2003. *A Distinctive Industrialization: Cotton in Barcelona 1728–1832*. Cambridge: Cambridge University Press.

– 2005. "Explaining the 'Take-off' of the Catalan Cotton Industry." *Economic History Review* 58(4): 701–35.

Tierney, Stephen. 2004. *Constitutional Law and National Pluralism*. Oxford: Oxford University Press.

Tillin, Louise. 2013. *Remapping India*. London: C. Hurst.

Tilly, Charles, ed. 1975. *The Formation of National States in Western Europe*. Princeton: Princeton University Press.

– 1992. *Coercion, Capital, and European States: AD 990–1992*. Cambridge, MA: Wiley-Blackwell.

Tirado, Daniel A., Elisenda Paluzie, and Jordi Pons. 2002. "Economic Integration and Industrial Location: The Case of Spain before World War I." *Journal of Economic Geography* 2(3): 343–63.

Tomasevich, Jozo. 1955. *Peasants, Politics, and Economic Change in Yugoslavia*. Stanford: Stanford University Press.

– 2001. *War and Revolution in Yugoslavia, 1941–1945: Occupation and Collaboration*. Stanford: Stanford University Press.

Toubeau, Simon, and Emanuele Massetti. 2013. "The Party Politics of Territorial Reforms in Europe." *West European Politics* 36(2): 297–316.

Toubeau, Simon, and Markus Wagner. 2016. "Party Competition over Decentralisation: The Influence of Ideology and Electoral Incentives on Issue Emphasis." *European Journal of Political Research* 55(2): 340–57.

Trudeau, Pierre Elliott. 1987. "P.E. Trudeau: 'Say Goodbye to the Dream' of One Canada." *Toronto Star*, 27 May 1987.

Tuković, Ana Holjevac. 2003. "Društveno-gospodarske reforme 1950-1952. i njihov odraz na upravu Narodne republike Hrvatske." *Arhivski Vjesnik* 46: 131–46.

Verge, Tània. 2013. "Party Strategies on Territorial Reform: State-Wide Parties and the State of Autonomies in Spain." *West European Politics* 36(2): 317–37.

Vertovec, Steven. 2007. "Super-Diversity and Its Implications." *Ethnic and Racial Studies* 30(6): 1024–54.

Vineberg, R.A. 1987. "Federal–Provincial Relations in Canadian Immigration." *Canadian Public Administration* 30(2): 299–317.

Viver Pi-Sunyer, Carles, and Mireia Grau Creus. 2016. "The Catalan Parliament's Contribution to the Consolidation and Development of Self-Government and the Defence of Catalonia's National Identity." In *The Parliaments of Autonomous Nations*, edited by Guy Laforest and André Lecours. Montreal and Kingston: McGill-Queen's University Press.

Vladisavljević, Nebojša. 2008. *Serbia's Antibureaucratic Revolution: Milošević, the Fall of Communism, and Nationalist Mobilization.* Basingstoke and New York: Palgrave Macmillan.

Vojnović, Branislava, Tatjana Šarić, and Marijana Jukić, eds. 2008. *Zapisnici Izvršnoga komiteta Centralnoga komiteta Saveza komunista Hrvatske, 1959-1963.* Zagreb: Hrvatski državni arhiv.

Vu, Tuong. 2010. "Studying the State through State Formation." *World Politics* 62(1): 148–75.

Vujačić, Veljko. 1996. "Historical Legacies, Nationalist Mobilization, and Political Outcomes in Russia and Serbia: A Weberian View." *Theory and Society* 25(6): 763–802.

– 2004. "Perceptions of the State in Russia and Serbia: The Role of Ideas in the Soviet and Yugoslav Collapse." *Post-Soviet Affairs* 20 (2): 164–94.

– 2015. *Nationalism, Myth, and the State in Russia and Serbia: Antecedents of the Dissolution of the Soviet Union and Yugoslavia.* Cambridge: Cambridge University Press.

Vušković, Boris. 1982. "Tko su Jugoslaveni? Temeljna demografska i socijalna obilježja populacije." *Naše Teme* 26(10): 1703–12.

Wade, R.H. 2002. "US Hegemony and the World Bank: The Fight over People and Ideas." *Review of International Political Economy* 9(2): 215–43.

Wagner, Helmut R. 1974. "Signs, Symbols, and Interaction Theory." *Sociological Focus* 7(2): 101–11.

Walter, Barbara F. 2006. "Building Reputation: Why Governments Fight Some Separatists but Not Others." *American Journal of Political Science* 50(2): 313–330.

Walzer, Michael. 1967. "On the Role of Symbolism in Political Thought." *Political Science Quarterly* 82(2): 191–204.

Ward, Benjamin. 1957. "Workers' Management in Yugoslavia." *Journal of Political Economy* 65(5): 373–86.

Wibbels, Erik. 2005. "Decentralized Governance, Constitution Formation, and Redistribution." *Constitutional Political Economy* 16(2): 161–88.

Williams, Kieran. 1997. *The Prague Spring and Its Aftermath: Czechoslovak Politics, 1968–1970.* Cambridge: Cambridge University Press.

Wimmer, Andreas. 2011. "A Swiss Anomaly? A Relational Account of National Boundary–Making." *Nations and Nationalism* 17(4): 718–737.

– 2013. *Waves of War: Nationalism, State Formation, and Ethnic Exclusion in the Modern World*. Cambridge: Cambridge University Press.

– 2018. *Nation Building: Why Some Countries Come Together While Others Fall Apart*. Princeton Studies in Global and Comparative Sociology. Princeton: Princeton University Press.

Wimmer, Andreas, Lars-Erik Cederman, and Brian Min. 2009. "Ethnic Politics and Armed Conflict: A Configurational Analysis of a New Global Data Set." *American Sociological Review* 74(2): 316–37.

Wlezien, Christopher, and Stuart N. Soroka. 2011. "Federalism and Public Responsiveness to Policy." *Publius: The Journal of Federalism* 41(1): 31–52.

Wolchik, Sharon L. 1994. "The Politics of Ethnicity in Post-Communist Czechoslovakia." *East European Politics and Societies* 8 (1994): 153–88.

Wolin, Sheldon S. 1969. "Political Theory as a Vocation." *American Political Science Review* 63(4): 1062–82.

Wolff, Stefan. 2009. "Complex Power-Sharing and the Centrality of Territorial Self-Governance in Contemporary Conflict Settlements." *Ethnopolitics: Formerly Global Review of Ethnopolitics* 8(1): 27–45.

Woodward, Susan L. 1995. *Socialist Unemployment: The Political Economy of Yugoslavia, 1945–1990*. Princeton: Princeton University Press.

Young, Crawford. 1997. *The African Colonial State in Comparative Perspective*. New Haven: Yale University Press.

Young, R.A., Philippe Faucher, and André Blais. 1984. "The Concept of Province-Building: A Critique." *Canadian Journal of Political Science* 17(4): 783–818.

Yugoslavia. 1953. "Fundamental Law Pertaining to the Bases of the Social and Political Organization of the Federal People's Republic of Yugoslavia and of the Federal Organs of State Authority: Chapter I." In *New Fundamental Law of Yugoslavia*, 53–9. Belgrade: Union of Jurists' Associations of Yugoslavia.

– 1963. *Constitution of the Socialist Federal Republic of Yugoslavia*. Collection of Yugoslav Laws, vol. 7. Beograd: Sekretarijat saveznog izvršnog veća za informacije.

– 1974. *The Constitution of the Socialist Federal Republic of Yugoslavia*. Ljubljana: Dopisna Delavska Univerza.

Zahra, Tara. 2010. "Imagined Noncommunities: National Indifference as a Category of Analysis." *Slavic Review* 69(1): 93–119.

Ziblatt, Daniel. 2006. *Structuring the State: The Formation of Italy and Germany and the Puzzle of Federalism*. Princeton: Princeton University Press.

Index